Explorations in Nonfiction

VOLUME 9   NUMBER 1   SPRING 2007

Published by Michigan State University Press, *Fourth
Genre* is supported by Michigan State University's
College of Arts and Letters and the Department of
Writing, Rhetoric, and American Cultures.

MICHIGAN STATE
UNIVERSITY PRESS
1947· CELEBRATING 60 YEARS of
SCHOLARLY PUBLISHING ·2007

Fourth Genre: Explorations in Nonfiction (ISSN 1522-3868) is published twice a year (Spring, Fall) by Michigan State University Press with contributions from the College of Arts and Letters; the Department of Writing, Rhetoric, and American Cultures; the Office of the Vice President for Research and Graduate Studies; and the Office of the Provost.

Editorial Office
(Manuscript submission: For guidelines, see back inside cover or visit www.msupress.msu.edu/journals/fg)
Address all editorial inquiries and manuscript submissions to:
David Cooper and Michael Steinberg; Editors; *Fourth Genre*
Department of Writing, Rhetoric, and American Cultures
Michigan State University
285 Bessey Hall
East Lansing, MI 48824-1033
Direct all submission-related queries to the editor at *genre4@msu.edu*.
Send manuscripts to editorial office only; do *not* send manuscripts to MSU Press.

Business Office
(Subscriptions, change of address, claims for missing issues, advertising inquiries, reprint requests, etc.)
Michigan State University Press, Journals Division
1405 S. Harrison Rd., Ste. 25; East Lansing, MI 48823-5245
Tel: 517-355-9543 x 130; Fax: 517-432-2611; Email: journals@msu.edu

ANNUAL SUBSCRIPTION RATE (2 ISSUES)

[2006-2007]	1 Year	2 Years Save 5%	3 Years Save 20%
U.S. Individual	$35	$67	$84
U.S. Institution	$50	$95	$120
International Individual	$47	$90	$113
International Institution	$68	$128	$162
Student Rate	$26	$50	$63

Single copy: $20
Airmail: Add $16 per year to above rate

For more information, visit the *Fourth Genre* website at *www.msupress.msu.edu/journals/fg.*

Prepayment required: check, money order, Visa, MasterCard accepted. Payment must be in U.S. currency drawn from a U.S. bank.

Returns are not accepted. MSU Press Journals Division can provide full or partial credit only for subscription orders. Credits issued for cancellations will be pro-rated. Credit can be transferred only to other MSU Press journals, not to MSU Press book products. Pending subscriptions can be refunded in full. Allow 8-12 weeks for processing. Domestic claims must be received within 6 months of publication date. International claims must be received within 12 months of publication date.

Fourth Genre participates in Project MUSE®, a Johns Hopkins University initiative that provides online institutional access to leading scholarly publications in the arts, humanities, and social sciences at *http://muse.jhu.edu.*

green press INITIATIVE Michigan State University Press is a member of the Green Press Initiative and is committed to developing and encouraging ecologically responsible publishing practices. For more information about the Green Press Initiative and the use of recycled paper in book publishing, please visit *www.greenpressinitiative.org.*

Fourth Genre

You Are Cordially Invited to Join
the Friends of Fourth Genre

Please consider becoming a special friend of *Fourth Genre* by contributing a gift to our **Patrons Program** or by becoming a **Sponsor** for an issue of *Fourth Genre.* Your generous support will help us continue our dual mission to publish the best and most innovative contemporary literary nonfiction while conducting an open and critical conversation about the "fourth genre." Your tax-deductible contribution can be made by check or credit card. We will gratefully acknowledge your gift in the journal (unless you wish to remain anonymous) and in a personal letter of receipt.

Patron Program

_____	Individual:	$75 (includes a one-year subscription)
_____	Family:	$150 (includes a one-year subscription)
_____	Friend:	$250 (includes a one-year subscription + 1 guest subscription)
_____	Patron:	$500 (includes a one-year subscription + 2 guest subscriptions)
_____	Benefactor:	$1,000 (includes a one-year subscription + 3 guest subscriptions)
_____	Founder:	$5,000 (includes 5 lifetime subscriptions)
_____	Other:	_____

Sponsor Program

_____	Essay and Memoir Section Sponsor:	$500 (includes a one-year subscription)
_____	Interview Sponsor:	$1,000 (includes a one-year subscription)
_____	Roundtable Sponsor:	$1,000 (includes a one-year subscription)
_____	Issue Sponsor (Spring *or* Fall issue):	$2,500 (includes a one-year subscription and 2 guest subscriptions)
_____	Volume Sponsor (Spring *and* Fall issues):	$5,000 (includes a one-year subscription and 4 guest subscriptions)

Gifts

Please complete this form, make credit card gifts and checks payable to **Michigan State University**, and specify *Fourth Genre* on the memo line. Send to: Michigan State University Press, Journals Division; 1405 S. Harrison Rd., Ste. 25; East Lansing, MI 48823-5245.

Name _____

Signature _____

Address _____

☐ Visa   ☐ MasterCard

City _____

Credit Card # _____

State/Zip _____

Exp. Date _____

☐ I wish to remain anonymous

Email _____

*Tax Deduction Information: Contributions to Michigan State University Press are tax-deductible. However, according to IRS guidelines, the value of any goods/services (subscriptions) received in connection with your gift must be deducted from the gross amount of your contribution to determine the amount eligible for tax advantages and employer matching gift programs.

This form is available for download at *www.msupress.msu.edu/journals/fg.*

Thank you for your generous support of this exceptional publication!

Fourth Genre

Explorations in Nonfiction

VOLUME 9   NUMBER 1   SPRING 2007

Contents

Editor's Notes

This issue of *Fourth Genre* features an extended conversation among four authors about the role of research in literary nonfiction, a historical cover photograph (a first for us) by Luke Swank accompanied by a photo essay by Howard Bossen tracking the photograph's serendipitous origins, and, in addition to a line up of personal essays and our usual spread of book reviews, the winning entries in *Fourth Genre*'s Third Annual Editors' Prize contest judged this year by Maureen Stanton.

The roundtable on "Research in Nonfiction" and Howard Bossen's fascinating story about discovering the long-lost photographs of Luke Swank take us to the ground floor, if not the very foundations, of nonfiction into those domains where writers spend vast amounts of time and expend enormous energy, often largely invisible to readers: research, source work, rigorous documentation. As moderator Robert Root notes in his introduction to the roundtable, new forms of literary or creative nonfiction may have blurred or relocated the boundaries of the genre, but that does not weaken or compromise a writer's responsibility—indeed, the *need*—to incorporate sound source work and documentation into their writing practices. That responsibility, as much of the work in this issue reflects, is hardly ever an onerous chore or a clinical matter of fact checking alone. On the contrary, rigorous research grounded in a writer's personal commitment to a subject brings its own rewards and satisfactions that complement—indeed, "intimately link" according to roundtable participant Kristen Iversen—the daily challenges of organizing, composing, revising, and struggling with words.

The roundtable and Bossen's photo essay gave us a new sight line for re-reading the contents of the Essays and Memoirs section—our usual practice in drafting these notes before going to press. There we found other writers braiding together memoir and exposition, exploring the way that a personal journey through a subject can profoundly impact, as John Calderazzo points out in the roundtable, a writer's inner life—and, we might add, a reader's *insight* into a subject.

Nedra Rogers, our Editors' Prize winner, for example, painstakingly researches a single lesson in an elementary school science class that forever alters her understanding of history, the quotidian world, and her place in the biological scheme of things. Her "sources" include Mark Twain, Rock Hudson, the etymology of Latin words, even the shade of her science teacher's glazed nail polish. Similarly, runner-up Casey Fleming meticulously investigates a deep wound she's carried since her high school Drill Team initiation. While the result of her investigation is layered and complex, Fleming uses the rigors of sorting through her library of memories—often turning a memory to different angles of view—to find some acceptance, perspective, clarity, even forgiveness.

Throughout our Essays and Memoirs section other writers work at the crossroads of memoir and exposition. Their subjects of inquiry range from a 17th century painting by a Dutch master, a woodpecker, garlic, and the assassination of John Lennon, to a clothes closet, an autopsy, the Glen Canyon Dam, and the awful hard luck of a friend. Like the writers joined together in our roundtable and Howard Bossen's adventure into the work and legacy of Luke Swank, each of these writers is a player and a presence in the subjects they explore.

We find this balance of personal reflection and solid source work reassuring. At a time when some critics of the contemporary essay and memoir question the credibility of first person narration, these essays remind us that a deeply personal story, objectivity, and scrupulous documentation need not be mutually exclusive. In fact, merging memoir and exposition often brings a higher burden of integrity to bear on an essay, compelling a writer to greater diligence and thoroughness in research.

On a sad note: we learned recently that Deborah Tall passed away in early November, 2006. Poet, essayist, editor of the *Seneca Review* for twenty-four years, Tall is the author of *Summons*, *From Where We Stand: Recovering a Sense of Place*, and most recently, *A Family of Strangers* from which we featured an excerpt in the Fall 2006 number of *Fourth Genre*. Her last gift to us.

—DDC

Mammalian

Nedra Rogers

Man is the only animal that goes out of this world as he came in—on milk.

William Osler

I've noticed lately, that my separate selves are growing more and more autonomous. Last evening, for example, as I tied my walking shoes, my feet grew tired of waiting for the second double knot. Without warning, they jumped up, ran out the door, and headed down the graveled Kaw River levee without me. I caught up with myself, of course. My mind, the tireless governor, persuaded my feet to jog in place until I joined them near the levee entrance off Sunset Avenue.

I understand my body's recent desire to act independently. Who could blame her? After more than half a century of working for the governor, Body has grown tired—tired of hauling the boss to and from the office, tired of being immobilized in cubicles and meeting rooms for hours on end. She's sick to death of being curbed by good manners, of being hidden beneath fabric, hampered by underwear and outrageous shoes. Body is tired of the straitjacket, tired of restrictions, tired of the contradiction of being a holy temple rated X.

I'm not alarmed much anymore when I sense a part of me has gone off on its own. With each passing year, I become more conscious of a separation process gearing up internally. I can only guess that I'm preparing in some obscure way for the final curtain's fall, when Body will exit stage left, and I will exit stage right.

When does it begin, this awareness of having more than a physical existence? As far as I can remember, I began to ponder the nature of my being back in elementary school soon after discovering my status as a mammal. It was my fourth grade teacher, Miss Butterfield, who introduced me to the bewildering and somewhat appalling notion. I still remember the afternoon she fastened an oversized poster with the curious heading *Homo sapiens* to the blackboard, lifted her wooden pointer, and tapped it three times against her desk. Three taps meant that Miss Butterfield was broaching a serious subject and that we must sit up straight and give her our undivided attention. She began the lesson on scientific classification by explaining to the class that we all belong to a kingdom. My restless classmate Richard, who had a talent for answering questions that hadn't been asked, shot up his hand and blurted out, "I know. I know—it's the kingdom of God!"

Miss Butterfield studied the floor for a moment before facing Richard squarely. "I am talking about a scientific kingdom, Richard. I am talking about the kingdom Animalia." Raising her voice, she pronounced the word carefully, pausing briefly between syllables, "An-i-mal-i-a."

I was glad for the Latin word. There was something about the serious, exacting nature of science that called out for song, for the melodious, lilting tone of Latin. I was delighted to know I belonged to a kingdom. Perhaps a king and queen would be involved, perhaps a charming prince, a golden-haired princess in a billowing gown.

Miss Butterfield rapped the pointer against the blackboard, directing us in rhythmic unison as we repeated, *animalia, animalia, animalia,* followed by *mammalia, mammalia, mammalia.*

It was not until she displayed the second poster that the implication of our science lesson began to dawn on me. Under the heading *What is a Mammal?* were sketches of an assortment of animals assembled in some sanctuary that closely resembled the paintings of Eden on my Sunday school room wall. There were zebras, coyotes, gophers, giraffes, monkeys, panda bears—a virtual Who's Who of Noah's Ark. To my alarm, a man and woman were included in this bizarre group portrait. What was this couple, this modern version of Adam and Eve (they'd apparently traded in their fig leaves for polyester attire) doing in a chart headed *What is a Mammal?* Mammals were animals. Miss Butterfield had made that perfectly clear. Surely she was not suggesting that humans were animals.

Baffled, I fixed my eyes on the poster and concentrated on the tapping of the pointer as Miss Butterfield's distant, hypnotic voice guided the class through the six characteristics of a mammal.

Character One: A mammal suckles its young. I didn't know what *suckle* meant, but the word had a decidedly ridiculous sound. The accompanying sketch of a dog nursing a litter of puppies only confused the issue. I understood how puppies were fed, but I had three younger siblings and knew perfectly well that human babies were fed homogenized cow's milk from sterilized glass bottles.

Character Two: A mammal has hair. I had to admit that humans have hair, but animals had fur, not hair, didn't they? And they certainly didn't brush or shampoo it, or give themselves perms. Shouldn't that distinction count for something?

Characters three through six involved jawbones, middle ears, aortic arches, and diaphragms. I had no use for these details. The entire proposition was absurd.

I scanned the faces of my classmates. They appeared unfazed by the alarming disclosure. Was I making too much of this disagreeable revelation? But how could Miss Butterfield, with her glazed nail polish, her wooden pointer, and her high-heeled shoes, possibly be a mammal? And what about my own parents, who ate their meals with forks and spoons and drove a Chevrolet? What about Dwight D. Eisenhower? Wasn't it something akin to blasphemy to call the president of the United States of America an animal?

But while I had my doubts, I knew that Miss Butterfield had never been mistaken and that she would never lie to us. Eventually, I knew, I would have to accept my mammal status. I was, no doubt, an animal. But while sitting at my desk, struggling to comprehend the six characteristics that made me a mammal, I couldn't help but notice that outside the classroom window squirrels chased each other up and down the blackjack oaks, and a stray dog barked and ran about the schoolyard in circles, chasing its tail. Something seemed terribly wrong with this picture.

The closest thing to a sex education manual available to students in the late '50s was *National Geographic,* and at Bison Elementary, it was nearly impossible to get a copy from the school library that had not been tampered with. Our ever-vigilant school librarian, Miss Banks, made sure that all unwholesome photographs were snipped from its contents before it was shelved. And if that were not enough, she interrogated any student showing an interest in the magazine. "You're giving *another* geography report, Meredith? Are you *sure* Mr. Woodward assigned a paper on the Mayan ruins? I'll be checking with him."

My friends and I never dared reach a hand toward the top shelf of the magazine section. Perhaps we were unrealistically apprehensive, but more than one parent had received a phone call involving a *National Geographic* incident, and we weren't willing to take that risk. Stanley Feldman, however, would do just about anything for a quarter. He was a frail asthmatic, and even Miss Banks was wary of upsetting him.

So, despite the librarian's watchful eye, during every school term, several *National Geographic* naked pictures managed to slip past security and make the coat-closet rounds. Amid woolen scarves and snow boots, they were passed cautiously from hand to hand by whispering preadolescents desperate to know what their changing bodies would someday become. It was in the coat closet of my sixth-grade classroom that I finally discovered what Miss Butterfield had meant by *Character One*. Humans did, after all, suckle their young—at least in Zimbabwe and Guadalajara.

Years later, when I was 20 and suckling my own young, I became acutely aware of my mammalian condition. The word *mammal* itself alludes to the breast. When zoologists of the eighteenth century decided that humans were a type of animal and in need of a name that would link them to other species with like traits, Swedish taxonomist Carolus Linnaeus came up with the term *mammalia*, meaning "of the breast." (He also gave humans the name *Homo sapiens*, which means "man of wisdom.")

Before my own lactating experience, I had no sense of the functional design of the human breast. In our culture, breasts are profitable as bait, as visual attractions capable of selling Bud Light, Coca-Cola, and Levi jeans. They are valuable calling cards, important enough that fortunes are spent on their enhanced presentation. We squish them together and hoist them up. We amplify, magnify, push, prop, and pad. We cup, cap and condense them. We inflate, deflate, elevate, decorate, revise, restore, and escalate them.

Whole societies can be misled, and generation after generation of Coca-Cola drinkers can be bamboozled, but every nursing mother quickly discovers the truth about the breast. It is fundamentally a mammary gland with an agenda. All it really wants to do is suckle the young.

This fact was recently brought home to my daughter Maria, who gave birth to twins last March. The babies had to be nursed every 3 hours, which meant 8 breast-feeding sessions every 24 hours. She nursed each twin for 30 minutes during every feeding, which added up to a total of 8 hours a day spent breast-feeding.

It wasn't exactly the joyful, fulfilling experience advertised by La Leche League. She frequently experienced nipple soreness and painful breast infections accompanied by chills and fever, and because her breast had increased in size to a double E, she suffered almost constant backaches and couldn't find a comfortable sleeping position at night. One day she confided that her nursing experience had been a crucial revelation and somewhat of a shock. She had suddenly become aware of her tie to the animal world and had discovered what the female breast was really designed for. "Welcome to the Kingdom of Animalia," I told her in so many words, "and to the class Mammalia, under whose banner the lactating stand."

One of Maria's biggest disappointments as a nursing mother was that she was no longer able to be physically active. Before her pregnancy, she'd been an avid bicyclist and a jogger, and was training for a half-marathon. She'd been looking forward to summer, hoping to rejoin her Ultimate Frisbee team, but she was having trouble finding a double E bra with enough support to allow her to run. When she finally encountered a bra with the name The Last Resort Bra, she had a hunch it was the one for her. The 60-dollar navy-blue apparatus was downright humongous. The shoulder straps were three inches wide. The bra, which extended a few inches above the waist and fastened down the front with 12 tiny hooks, was a bit ungainly, but it worked. Maria, able to run at last, bounded through the grass chasing a Frisbee in that marvelous spandex contraption— living proof that lactating mammals *can* participate in Ultimate Frisbee, *if* they are tremendously determined, and *if* they are sporting The Last Resort Bra.

Man is a smart animal. He not only possesses the ingenuity to produce a plastic orb and the imagination to invent a sport for its use, but he also has the insight to fashion a utilitarian brassiere that enables the lactating *Homo sapien* to pursue that orb.

Maybe it is because we are such clever organisms that our scientific classification as mammals seems like an uncomfortable fit. Humans are always looking for qualities that separate them from the animal kingdom, and they've come up with some interesting observations:

> Man is the only animal that laughs and weeps; for he is the only animal that is struck with the difference between what things are and what they ought to be.
>
> William Hazlitt

> Man is the only animal that blushes, or needs to.
>
> Mark Twain

> Man is the only animal that goes to sleep when it is not sleepy and gets up when it is.
>
> Anon.

Man is the only animal clever enough to build the Empire State Building and stupid enough to jump off it.

Rock Hudson

Man is the only animal for whom his own existence is a problem which he has to solve.

Erich Fromm

Man is the only animal that contemplates death, and the only animal that shows any signs of the doubt of its finality.

William E. Hocking

Regardless of the distinctions we make between animal and man, there remains one experience we have in common; that is the experience of life itself. Man realizes that whatever lives must also die—he knows he will terminate like all other species, but unlike other species, he has the blessing and the curse to be able to think about it. The tendency of man is to wonder what it's all about, to ask questions: "Is nonexistence conceivable? What, if anything, survives physical death?"

> *There is part of us that believes*
> *we will never die—otherwise*
> *how could we watch so much television?*

Billy Collins, "The Teacher"

Body must sense that her days are numbered, for she refuses to sit for long watching television. She's had her fill of television, of repression, of the entire civilizing process. She's been insisting lately on side trips. She wants to breaststroke naked in the sun, dance unbridled through the forest, kick up leaves while she may. She wants to eat chocolate and sit on the creek bank at sunset. Now and again she catches the governor off guard and goes her own way. I find myself, lately, cheering her on.

Evenings when we take our walks, the governor, who has concluded that life is eternal, engages me in weighty conversation. I discuss with him the subjects of what was, and is, and is to be, as I try to catch up with my animal out on the Kaw River levee. ◼

Take Me with You

Casey Fleming

If I could tell this story as my former self I would. If I could tell it in your words. But I can't. I hardly know you anymore. I hardly know the place you come from, the place you live, the place I loved once. If I could tell the truth, I would do that too. This is my truth—not yours. You would have kicked and screamed at some of the things I will say about you and your native home, about your parents. No, you were not a screamer. You would have grieved quietly, and alone, as usual. You might have—maybe—written an enigmatic sentence or two in your journal and then laid your head down for a restless sleep.

What haunt me are the things you will never know. You will never know that the woman I am now wants to tell you, it's okay, you're okay. I need you to believe me.

Houston. September, 1992. The football boys were already lined up around the edge of the pool, their feet dangling in the water, splashes shattering into the air like fireworks. They were a happy bunch. Rachel hissed into your ear, *Oh, GOD, this is going to be embarrassing. Look, look. Mike is right in front of the diving board!* Rachel let out a squeal that annoyed you. It seemed childish, and on this day you wanted to be anything but a child.

Your new bathing suit had padded lining, so your boobs, at least at first glance, appeared to stick out further than your rib cage. You tugged at the elastic edges, already self-conscious about having a significantly larger backside than other 15-year-old girls. Only three weeks earlier Joe Kleinfelder told you that you looked like a pear—little on top and big on the bottom. You wanted to be mad, but deep down knew he was right. *It's okay,* he said, *the black guys will like you.* Your biggest fear that day, besides being a child, was being too much of a woman. You couldn't imagine anything much

7

worse than your ass hanging out the back of your bikini for the whole free world to see.

You and her friends had planned for this day—you all knew it was coming. Drill team initiation. No one could dance during football season, unless they went through this process. The current members of the team prepared you: you learned a special dance, a song to sing, and a certain way to swing your hips, the perfect form to use when jumping, in full straddle, from the high diving board. Each girl was to dance, by herself, around the deep end of the pool where the players eagerly anticipated the show, climb up the ladder to the high dive, and sing the required song before jumping. The players formed a fence around the deep end and stared toward the diving board, awaiting this performance; the sweat of their muscled shoulders gleamed; their lower legs disappeared into the water. *We all went through it,* the elder girls assured the freshman, *it's supposed to be embarrassing. You'll survive,* said Allison Cauldwell. Allison was your "big sister," a sophomore, so she had already been initiated last year. Like you, Allison had a crush on Mike McCormick, but she also put hand-decorated picture frames and a gold-and-black teddy bear in your welcome basket that morning, so you didn't confide in her that Mike walked you to your locker every day after sixth period, and that sometimes his hand slid across your lower back when he left you.

When you first arrived Coach Ryan greeted you. *Howdy, little one. Where's your mama?* You told him she was at a swim meet with your brother. Coach Ryan was friends with your mother, who taught down the hall from him in the science wing of your high school.

Rachel giggled again. Amy Howard complained to her mother, a chaperone, that she didn't want to do it. That she couldn't do it. Her voice cracked, but her mother pushed her into line behind Rachel and said, *Oh, Amy.* You felt sorry for her—Amy never wore shirts that didn't cover her stomach, or shorts that ended above her knees, and she limited her makeup to mascara. Today she was the only girl wearing a one-piece swimsuit.

You scanned the crowd of players for a familiar face. Mike McCormick caught your eye briefly and smiled—a gentle smile and then a quick wave. For a second, you felt safe because you remembered what Mike's hand felt like on your thigh the other day in Spanish class, when he asked you for a pen. It felt warm, and strong, and seeped through your jeans like hot water.

Hallie Spencer was the first girl to go. The rest of you coerced her into being the guinea pig because you knew she'd get more applause than anyone else. She had a killer body. Her voice was unnaturally soft, almost broken, when she stood at the edge of the board and sang: *I'm a gopher girl and I always gopher guys, and when they don't gopher me, I always wonder why.* Then she crossed her hands over her chest when she jumped, and so couldn't touch her toes on the straddle jump like she was supposed to. The football players booed and cracked up. Hallie slowly emerged and broke the surface of the water, her painstakingly hair-sprayed bangs slapped tight to her forehead.

⌐

I ran into one of those football players not too long ago. I saw him at some shady night club I was coerced into visiting by some of my old high school friends. Marcus— a black football player, also voted Best Looking Male of your graduating class.

I expected him to be as you described him to me: arrogant, dismissive, cocky. But instead he too seemed uninterested in the club patrons, the neon disco globes, the bad DJ. He pulled me into a corner booth and asked a lot about my life. He remembered you fondly. I told him about the East Coast, and he filled me in on the West Coast. He'd been living in L.A. the past three or four years.

You'll see me, *he said,* on the next season of *The Bachelorette*.

Get out! *I said.* So, it's already been filmed. Can't you tell me what happens?

No. I'm under contract.

I bet you make it to the final round. Obviously, you don't win, because you're not married, *I said.*

He winked.

A few months later I sat all my closest friends down in my apartment living room to watch The Bachelorette, *a silly show about a young woman who picks a husband from a group of bachelors the TV station has chosen for her. Marcus only made it to round two. I was surprised, but Avé, my most honest friend, said,*

"Yeah, right. They always get rid of the black guy on the second episode. They don't want to appear racist by cutting him the first round, so they wait until the second. But they sure as hell don't want to bring a black guy home to mama, let alone the national viewing public."

⌐

You can't remember much of your turn, except for the bile threatening its way up your throat and the heart's endless hammering. You were, however, keenly aware of the way your bathing suit rode up in the back as your hips popped from side to side. You climbed the diving board. You had to go slowly because your legs shook. You walked to the end and sang your song. You sent up a quick prayer that when you straddled the air your pubic hair didn't hang out. Somehow you hadn't anticipated anything after the jump—that blessed freefall. Under water, all you could see were the players' swollen calves and feet in all directions, so you swam toward the shallow end of the pool to avoid them, and watched from there while Rachel, and Maria, and poor Amy Howard, and Gabriela, and Latisha, and everyone else took their turn. Each of their tender bodies glowed briefly against the blank, hot sky and you wanted to remember them that way: frozen in time above the diving board.

⊔

When I went North for college, I entered the first-year class of Smith College the same year that fellow Texan Ruth Simmons took office there as the first black president of an Ivy League school. The Houston Chronicle *headline read:* Making History. *The newspaper explained:*

> When she is installed as president of Smith College on September 30, Ruth Simmons, the great-great-granddaughter of slaves and the daughter of Texas sharecroppers, will become the first black woman to head a top-ranked college in the United States.

I told some women there your story. I joined a group called Rape Awareness and was promptly assured that your story did not qualify, and more importantly, that everyone knows what kind of girls become cheerleaders. A young woman with a shaved head and thrift store clothing and a house on Martha's Vineyard told me I could support survivors but not be one, as though I was trying to join a sorority. I tried to explain the difference between a cheerleader and a drill team colonel, but at the end of the day, they both have pompoms.

Ruth Simmons and I went North together, experienced the heaviest snowfall of the century that first fall semester. I did not even own a scarf.

My senior year, after someone had drawn a stick figure hanging from a noose on the marker board outside a black student's dorm room, the Black Students Alliance organized a rally. I attended. So did Ruth. None of us expected her. If I could explain to you the composure and grace and quiet strength this woman exuded every day, you might understand why we all adored her so much. How many student bodies do you know that erupt into applause every time their college president enters a room? If I could explain to you the example of success and refinement she offered us, you might understand the vast silence, and the quickening pulse of the crowd when she began, unabashedly, to cry, as she said into the microphone: I moved away from Houston a long time ago, and I had hoped that I would never see anything like this outside of the South. I believed this place was different.

After everyone took their turn jumping off the diving board, the players and elder drill team members joined you all to play in the shallow end of the pool. All you recall is a number of baritone voices and tanned bodies all around, and being pushed toward the center of the group. *They'll throw you in the air*, someone yelled to you—you think maybe Hallie. *It's fun.* Then you were there with all their big hands everywhere, sliding across your skin, slithering, preparing you to be launched. You balled yourself up to be shot into the air like a cannonball. It was only a split second, but your skin crawled and you realized your bikini bottom was creeping up and you felt something like a tampon, but harder, alive, moving—a finger, then several fingers, then somebody else's fingers—and then a moment of nothing but bright blue before you hit the water again. For a brief second, you expected to see a brownish cloud appear in the water between your legs, and then you thanked God you weren't hurt bad enough to bleed.

At the other end of the pool you coughed up water and then told Rachel. *Someone stuck their fingers*, you whispered. She threw you a wild-eyed look, but she also touched your arm. *Someone stuck their fingers inside me. And moved them around.* Thighs clamped shut—hers and yours—and then there was the commotion.

Allison Cauldwell was crying on the side of the pool, her wet blonde hair turned a slimy shade of green, and directors' and coaches' mouths moved in a mad frenzy. The football players shook their heads and threw their hands up like *we don't know what you're talking about.*

Please stop crying Allison, you thought, *you're making a scene.* Rachel whispered, *do you think they did it to her too?* And then it did became a scene: mothers hastily plucking their daughters out of the water, Ms. Bates—the drill team director—screaming at Coach Ryan about protecting her "girls," a few angry football players pointing fingers or standing quietly in the background with their eyes nailed to their feet.

In college I took a class that reminded me of you. Gender in the African American Community. To this day, I swear that it was my best college course, even though it wasn't at Smith College—it was during the fall semester of my year at the University of Texas. I also swear that Professor Anderson, with his brown skin and sea-green eyes, was the best teacher I ever knew and the first in a long string of professor-crushes I would have in my adulthood. He drew a triangle on the blackboard, and at each of three points wrote the words in scrawling letters: race, class, gender. *Then he asked the men in the class, mostly athletes and black, if they thought racism or sexism a worse crime. They laughed.*

One Tuesday I raised my hand to point out that the Black Panthers treated their female members like slaves. I felt mean when I said it, but my voice did not quiver. I actually used the word slaves. *When the men began to argue with me—vehemently—Professor Anderson raised his right hand high into the air to silence them.* I think she has a good point, *he said in his calm, velveteen voice.*

I thought of you then. I couldn't help it. That tiny scar I have somewhere inside me pulsed and grew pink—it ached as though it could sense a heavy storm on the horizon.

Monday morning at school gossip whirled through the halls in hurricane fashion, turning heads, slamming lockers, and raising voices. *Allison is leaving school, she's switching schools,* someone told you. Rachel passed you a note in biology: *Allison's parents came into the building this morning, all hell is about to break loose.* Her face barely contained her excitement when she slid the note over your desk. And then Corey Locklin, a cheerleader, told several girls at your lunch table that DeAndre Lewis did it, and Allison's parents wanted him expelled and maybe charged.

DeAndre Lewis. His name did not ring a bell. But you envied Allison her memory. In your mind, those fingers inside you had many faces—all those hands, how could you have connected them to one specific face? Your perpetrator looked like a team, not a person.

During sixth period you wondered if Mike would meet you outside class, whether he would pretend to have passed by with friends as usual, and whether he might hold your hand this time. Sometime between *Great Expectations* and semicolons, a student aide popped her head into your English classroom—*excuse me,* she said, *Ms. Jackson wants to see Casey Fleming in her office.*

The walk to Ms. Jackson's office was long, and abnormally quiet, so quiet you could hear each footstep as it rattled the lockers and echoed. Ms. Jackson was an assistant principal and in all your years of schooling you had never been called to a principal's office for any reason. And she was not just any assistant principal—other students warned of her potential for meanness. She had pale skin and her hair was huge and curly; most people referred to her by her student-given nickname: the Fro Ho. Although it seemed unlikely, you couldn't help but feel as though you were in trouble, so you pulled hard on your lower lip and your bladder tightened.

Four people stood in Ms. Jackson's office when you arrived: Coach Ryan, an assistant football coach whose name you never knew but who had deep acne scars pocked into his cheeks and forehead, Ms. Jackson, and Corey Locklin.

Casey, come on in and sit down. This is about the Drill Team Initiation this past Saturday.

Ms. Jackson looked up briefly at Coach Ryan as if they shared some secret. Her enormous hair cast shadows on the wall behind her. Coach Ryan nodded.

Something unfortunate happened, I understand, and I don't want to pressure you, but Corey here informed us that you may have been involved as well?

The only thing you knew about Corey Locklin was that she had a huge forehead, went to fake tanning beds, and had an alcoholic mother who wore gaudy, jewel-heavy rings on her fingers. She was not your friend.

Corey, Coach Ryan interjected, *thank you for being so honest with us and concerned about your friend. You can go now. Go on. Git.*

Corey left and as she closed the door her hair swung over her shoulder—it reminded you of a hand-painted fan your grandmother brought back from China, black and very thick.

Casey. We need you to tell us exactly what happened to you. Allison's parents are very upset.

You told them what you could.

Thank you. I understand this is hard, but we need you to tell us exactly where he touched you. Don't be embarrassed to use the word.

The voice you used then—*vagina?*—sounded like a stranger's voice and your insides cringed to hear it.

Okay, now. Coach Ryan here is prepared to kick DeAndre off the team and speak to his parents. Does that sound okay to you?

I don't know. Coach Ryan's smile scared you. *I don't—I can't be sure it was him. Just him, I mean. I couldn't tell. There were so many people.*

But was it a black boy? With a gold tooth?

I don't—probably.

DeAndre? We need at least two witnesses to take any action.

I don't know.

The air-conditioner's whirring rubbed up against the silence. The leather chair squeaked against your jeans. Everyone waited for you to say something more, but you didn't.

⌐┐

The things you confessed to me years later: There were more black players than white on the football team. You never knew many of their names. There were only 3 black girls on the entire 70-member drill team, and no black cheerleaders. After that day, you never dated Mike McCormick. You wanted it to be DeAndre. You wanted to blame him too. It would have made everything easier. You had a nightmare that night that would reoccur throughout your adulthood. In it, you drive a car up the Sam Houston Tollway, where it climbs up and up before splitting off into I-10 East and I-10 West. Your brakes give out, you can't turn right or left. You crash through the barrier and go flying off the end of the highway into a sheet of clouds.

⌐

After you returned to class, and the bell rang, you saw Mike standing against the wall, alone, staring right at you. He did not even pretend to be passing by with friends. The two of you walked in silence. You walked all the way down the stairs and out the front entrance of the building together. In contrast to the cold inside of the school, the daylight shimmered, the warm wind raced, and you could hear the flags—Texas and the U.S.—clap in counterpoint against the flag pole. This sound comforted you until Mike finally whispered, *Corey Locklin says that you told everyone it happened to you too, but that you just wanted attention.* Casey, *tell me the truth*—his blue eyes burned red, which made your stomach ache and you wanted so badly to kiss him then—*did that nigger hurt you too?*

⌐

That same year I had my crush on Professor Anderson, I started to date Al Johnson, an old friend from middle school, from before drill team. He was beautiful, a baseball player, and had loved me since we were ten years old. His skin was so black, so very black, that the tiny wrinkles around his eyes shimmered and moved, spider webs or rivers. If I were a fish, or a dragonfly, I could have crawled right inside them and disappeared.

I want to tell you this. Sometimes it makes me angry with you. A bottomless, raging angry. When Al held my hand, or touched my body, the skin on his palms felt rough, foreign, like sandpaper. He never knew but it scared me, his skin. If he woke me in the night, when I least expected it, and pressed a coarse hand to my back, my body trembled and, I swear to you, I could not tell if it was love or fear.

My friend would tell me years later that I exoticized Al, and maybe she's right, and maybe that's the real source of my anger. Because when I was 12 he was Al who passed me notes in Spanish, and Al who sat with me on the school bus, and Al who laughed way down deep in his throat, and I have no memory at all of what his skin felt like next to mine. I only remember that it made me happy.

⌐

You went home that night shaken. When you arrived you walked down the skinny front hallway lined with family photos and then took your shoes off and placed them toe to toe next to your father's, mother's, and brother's shoes, already abandoned there by the side table. Yours were by far the smallest. Your father sat in his usual spot, on the right side of the couch, TV remote control in hand, glasses perfectly perched on his nose.

How was school, Sister Girl? your father asked. He meant it. He was that kind of parent, not the kind who asked because they were supposed to. He really wanted to know.

Fine, you said in a small voice.

This is the important part of your story. Because you told him then, about the pool, about the principal's office. And your mother appeared from behind the kitchen counter to listen. But you must not have said it clearly, or loudly enough, because neither of them got sad. Neither of them got angry. Neither of them pulled you to them in a rush of parental empathy. You got no ice cream, no chicken fingers and French fries (your favorite meal), no nothing. Your father looked at you perhaps a little longer than usual—in that way he did when he was studying something. But that was it.

You didn't cry. Maybe that's why they didn't know to react, since you were the kind of girl who cried easily and often. Maybe if you had shed a tear an alarm would have gone off—a high-pitched, steely one and your father would have asked you to sit next to him on the couch and your mother would have ripped someone at the school a new asshole for not bringing her into the principal's office from her classroom down the hall, for daring to interview her daughter without her mother there to protect her.

But you didn't cry. You thought maybe what happened wasn't so bad. Maybe what happened was part of growing up and you, a perfect A student, couldn't bear to fail at that. You thought maybe you did something wrong too.

Your parents laughed out loud together at a sitcom on television, and everything fit neatly into its place. The fan above your heads hummed at its usual rhythm and the sun fell in squares from the French doors onto the carpet. So you went to your bedroom, closed the door, and fell into the bed.

Lying there, you remembered all their faces—Corey Locklin's proud eyes and black, black hair, Coach Ryan's patient and encouraging but stiff smile, and Ms. Jackson's expectant, hopeful prodding. And you remembered walking out of the office and the heavy door taking its time to close behind you, and the way you stood outside it looking down the tunnel of endless orange lockers, and how you felt then such a darkness.

⌐⌐

At one of Al's baseball games in college I tried to tell your mother again what happened to you. This time she did cry; so did I. She didn't believe that you ever told her—she swore she would remember that. I ended up consoling her, because her response to sadness is always anger first and she yelled at me. She accused you of having an exaggerated adolescent sense of drama; she doubted your recount of events. Luckily, we were separated from the other spectators, sitting on our own splintery wooden bleachers along the first base line. Al stood in the outfield, his dark skin shiny in the humid, thick-as-syrup mid-evening heat. From his vantage point, we were nothing more than pale outlines that stood every once in a while to cheer for a great throw or catch, then sat, then stood and sat again. We could sense when we were supposed to do this without paying any attention at all.

He could not have seen our blotchy faces, all shades of red and pink, mine lined in mascara, my mother's streaked only with salt. You would have felt betrayed by her outbursts and denials, but I understood her heart was breaking. I could see by the way she gripped the bleacher, her knuckles impossibly white.

I believed her when she said that she would have done something had she heard you the first time. She is the kind of mother that acts, and reacts, relentlessly, and pushes her children to be as relentless. Like that time you got stung by a bee while waiting on deck for your swimming relay when you were eight years old. Your mother, who also happened to be the swim team coach, said, "You're okay," *quickly made you the first swimmer of the relay instead of the fourth, threw you onto the block, swatted your butt when the start gun went off (your bee sting pinched and ached, still unattended to), and said,* Go, Casey. Swim. Fast. *And you did, your right leg full of sting the whole lap. And your relay won first place, and she was there at the other end of the pool to pull you out, all slippery and wet as a seal, and she tenderly pressed tobacco into your sting, which made it sting less, and then she brought you ice for the swelling. See, she said.* You're okay.

And she acted then too, at the baseball game. When Al trotted in from the field and filed with the other players out of the dugout, and said, Hi, Mrs. Fleming. Thanks for coming, *she kissed him hard on the cheek, took his hand and then took mine and said with utmost cheer,* Let's get some Frito Pie.

⌐⌐

At the pep rally the next day at school, the gymnasium roared with students. From down the hall you heard the approaching thump of a giant
drum as the band marched into the gym. Because you passed initiation
with flying colors, you sat for the first time in full uniform: the bodice
newly dry-cleaned so the sleeves popped out of the black and gold cum-
merbund a bright, pure white, your hair pulled back and held in place by
a bright gold bow, your black skirt barely covering your ass and from
beneath it your panty-hosed legs locked together in perfect position.
Lipstick gathered in the corners of your mouth.

The first game of the season was that night. You could feel the anticipation slide off the football players' and cheerleaders' backs and into the
sweaty air, filling your lungs too. Banners and streamers in all shades of gold
and black swung from the rafters, and a podium stood center court, awaiting Coach Ryan's address to the student population.

After he spoke, you would dance the first dance of your drill team career
before the entire student body. Your stomach hollowed at the thought of it.
You tried to ignore what felt like a giant bruise between your legs that stung
each time you peed since last weekend's initiation pool party.

Coach Ryan stepped up to the podium then and the crowd hushed. The
cheerleaders' pompoms shivered against the basketball court floor. You
noticed that Coach Ryan's gut kept him from standing too close to the
microphone.

I'll tell you what, he said. *These young men behind me are ready for a great
season.*

The students cheered.

Yes, sirree. These boys are strong as iron ore.

Rachel giggled next to you, and poked you in the ribs. When Coach
Ryan talked in his thick Texas accent "iron ore" came out sounding like
"aaarn ore," at least four syllables long, and it struck you both as hilarious.

*This team is like aaarn ore, I swear to you. Ya'll are gonna get quite a show
tonight. These boys have a lot of Po-tential. I'm proud to work with 'em every day
and ya'll should be proud to watch 'em. Aaarn ore, I tell you. Aaarn ore.*

⌐⌐

*Today I look through your memory box, your scrapbooks from high school. I find
three letters from your father. He started leaving them for you the summer after
you were hurt in the pool. Maybe a famous quote, or passage from a book, some-*

times just his own thoughts. He'd fold the piece of paper in two and hang it over your steering wheel so that you'd sit in the platinum heat of the driver's seat and read them before heading for school each morning. It was his way of saying things fathers have a hard time saying to daughters, his way of educating you. The notes I found:

A message to Casey Fleming from her father—
The soliloquy of the Cowardly Lion from *The Wizard of Oz:*
What makes a king out of slave? Courage!
What makes the flag on the mast to wave? Courage!
What makes the elephant charge his tusk
In the misty mist or the dusky dusk?
What makes the muskrat guard his musk? Courage!
What makes the Sphinx the Seventh Wonder? Courage!
What makes the dawn come up like thunder? Courage!
What makes the Hottentot so hot?
What puts the ape in apricot?
What have they got that I ain't got? Courage!

Courage!
Dad

And then another:

A message to Casey Fleming from her father—
"I know moon-rise, I know star-rise,
I lay this body down.
I walk in the moon-light; I walk in the star-light
To lay this body down.
I walk in the graveyard, I walk through the graveyard
To lay this body down.
I lie in the grave and stretch out my arms,
To lay this body down."

—One of the 10 Master Spiritual Songs of the African slaves in America

Love,
Dad

And then another:

A message to Casey Fleming from her father—
You're way cool and doing as good as you can when you're only 16.

⊓

When Coach Ryan finished his speech, Corey Locklin led the cheerlead-ers out onto the court, and they made fists with their hands and jumped in the air, curls bouncing everywhere. Players and students whistled. The cheerleaders chanted: *We got spirit, yes we do, we got spirit, how 'bout you.*

Then it came time for the drill team to dance. You stood. You all marched, hands on hips, head high, in single file onto the gymnasium floor and waited for the music to start.

When song finally filled the gym, you danced with all your might that day, and smiled so hard your cheeks throbbed and your jaw ached. The stands became a giant smudge of faces. You hit every pose, every beat, exactly right. When the song ended, and applause broke out, your heart banged loudly against its cage and your lungs heaved in and out the dense, spectacular air of perfection. Then you watched Mike McCormick stand up from the hordes of players in front of you. He looked right at you, through you, then turned his head away and blew Allison Cauldwell a kiss, and you heard her delighted squeal in your ears for a long time afterwards.

⊓

I find something else tucked away between ribbons and senior photos, messages hastily scrawled from friends that say things like "Stay sweet!" or "It was fun know-ing you." I find a photo of you on the football field.

You must have just finished a performance, because you are marching off the field in a line of girls and all of you head back into the stands. Behind you, football play-ers and band members and cheerleaders (there is the briefest side angle of Corey Locklin's enormous forehead in the crowded background) file out of the stadium too; one injured player receives help from an assistant coach. A ripe green turf stretches beneath your feet. You are smiling into the stands—a wide, effervescent smile that rises between your clownishly rouged cheeks—most likely at your mother's camera. This photo was taken only weeks after the incident, and what strikes me most is that you are happy, blissfully so. It takes my breath away.

I look at you smiling up at your parents and know that you stored up that smile especially for them. Because they prepared you to be the kind of person who dares

*to stand on a dangerous strip of land and dance. They prepared you to do that even
without them.*

*I look at the players behind you, and I cannot tell the color of their faces, which
of them will be a good man and which will not. I look at this photo and realize it
was never their faces that scared you, but their masks.*

*I look at you smiling and I remember the wind rushing into my face, the exhil-
aration of a 100-yard stage, a stadium full of rapt observers, my nimble body, the rat-
tat-tat of a drum roll. I remember kicking my leg high into the night sky, my toes
disappearing into the stars, the persistent feeling of hope, hope, hope in each choreo-
graphed step.*

*I pretend it is me in the stands, and your smile is telling me something too. That
smile says, like my mother and father before it,* you're okay. I'm okay. *And I
believe you.* ▇

Alone in Amsterdam

P. M. Marxsen

Even the shopkeepers looked like professors, the street sweepers like jazz musicians. There was never a city more rationally ordered.

Ian McEwan, *Amsterdam*

The Syndics of the Draper's Guild, oil on canvas, 1662, by Rembrandt van Rijn, Rijksmuseum, Amsterdam, Netherlands

On a quiet morning in late November, the eyes of five men lock with mine as I approach the canvas of *The Syndics of the Drapers' Guild*, one of Rembrandt van Rijn's most successful group portraits. As an undisputed masterpiece from an undisputed genius of the Golden Age of Dutch art, the super-sized painting occupies most of a wall in Amsterdam's Rijksmuseum. These are the "Dutch Masters" often associated with cigar boxes. In 1662, they were the well-heeled businessmen of Holland's flourishing economy, a corporate board of directors huddled over a ledger whose job it was to monitor the quality of dyed cloth in the Netherlands. Surely they kept track of volumes of data. Surely they knew of each shipment of indigo delivered from the Far East by the Vereenigde Oost-Indische Compagnie (VOC), or the Dutch East-India Company. Ships owned by this unique corporation, which was chartered in 1602 by the Dutch government, sailed in and out of Amsterdam's harbor like clockwork, unloading their cargo of spices, indigo, coffee, and textiles. Perhaps a shipment had just arrived from Java or Sri Lanka. Perhaps there was a problem to solve, a deal to be made on this very day. We will never know.

As I walk toward these men in their crisp collars and dark suits, I have the sensation that my presence here, nearly 350 years later, has interrupted a conversation. All but the man at the center, whose eyes shift slightly to his right, stare at me with polite disdain. I am an unwelcome intrusion for him as well, but he is momentarily distracted by the man with goatee rising slowly from his chair, the one who seems to be whispering under his breath as he lifts himself up, eyes fixed on the intruder in the room.

"Wait a minute," he seems to say in hushed tones. Then, "Who's there?"

"A woman from America, come to see your Golden Age, come to pay homage to your improbable city, your flows of global culture, your flowers and swans, your watery world that never seems to rest," I reply.

"You come here alone?"

"Yes. Women travel alone now," I say, standing my ground.

I consider asking a question about their beloved Rembrandt for whom each of them must have sat long hours in order to achieve what art historian Helen Gardner described as a "harmonizing of the instantaneous action with the permanent likeness" of each man. In the same room, I see Rembrandt's shadowy self-portrait at 22 and self-depicted many years later as St. Paul, naked with human isolation.

"Alone in Amsterdam?" The man poised to turn a page joins the conversation. I can see that he is half-amused, imagining me squeezing in and out of taverns in my peculiar clothes, sidling past overloaded wagons in the street. The others, even the servant, the one in the back without a hat, wear masks of suspicious resistance. Do I see fingers tightening around a sack of money on the far right? Does that one imagine me a thief?

"Yes. Alone in Amsterdam," I reply. "So sorry to disturb you."

And so I leave them there, frozen forever in speechless disapproval.

Out in the street, a damp day huddles beneath a canopy of low-lying clouds. A flat gray light falls over the canals, turning ripples of dark water into heavy steel. When sun appears, these waterways reflect the tall, shimmering façades of narrow brick houses. But in this light, all is gray.

I walk along the Museumplein past the Van Gogh Museum toward the Van Baerlestrasse where I spot a café on the corner. Interludes spent in cafés and pubs have always been as much a part of my travels as museums and monuments. This seems especially true in Amsterdam where cafés like this one beckon with paneled walls and upholstered chairs. I feel a mixture of comfort and relief as I settle into a corner table and order "brunch," though I have no clear idea of what time it is inside my body. Nostalgia overcomes fatigue as I catch a whiff of Europe in the 1950s where I spent my early childhood. This feeling has something to do with the vowel-heavy sound of German and Dutch voices, the ubiquitous presence of trams, and the faint odor of smoke. People smoke in public here, and without apology. They light each other's cigarettes, gesticulate with flickering light, exhale their smoke like sighs from the inner core of contemplation. So what if we all die of secondhand smoke? For now, we're snug in a café with good coffee and sensible people whose ancestors were clever enough to fashion this place out of a marsh submerged below sea level.

As Simon Schama explains in *The Embarrassment of Riches: An Interpretation of Dutch Culture in the Golden Age*, the "moral geography" of the Dutch psyche encompasses a deeply embedded sense of being a chosen people. After all, was it not God who endowed them with the power to push back the force of Nature through the invention of the water-pumping windmill and an ingenious system of dykes and canals? Without these blessed inventions, could they have overcome the threat of inundation? Furthermore, would the national identity that came with global commerce, exploration, and urban capitalism have taken shape without cultivatable land?

Amsterdam is Old-World and fast-paced, grounded in tradition yet overflowing with youth. There are over 600,000 bicycles in Amsterdam and 2,500 houseboats floating along the edges of the canals. The taverns are full, the restaurants and cafés alive with laughter. I exchange a few words with a couple seated nearby, trying to enter into this communitarian spirit, but the eyes of *The Syndics of the Drapers' Guild* continue to bore holes in my mind.

"Traveling alone?" the gentleman asks, with a slight German accent.

"Yes," I say with a smile. It seems I have said this a dozen times in the past week or two as I announced my travel plans to friends.

"You're going *alone?*"

"Yes. Why not?"

"But what will you do? Won't you feel . . . lonely?"

"No." After all, if I get along solo in Boston, why wouldn't I be able to do it here, in a city of museums, parks, shops, and gardens where whole worlds of culture—past and present—are laid out at my feet like a carpet of flowers?

Ah, flowers. It was the room before the *Drapers' Guild* at the Rijksmuseum where I saw them, those concoctions of flowers, bees, and leaves gathered into colorful zeniths of form. I should go back and have another look, I tell myself. After all, these are more than mere bouquets. In *Gardner's Art Through the Ages*, we're reminded that "[t]he globule of dew on a leaf in a Dutch flower painting becomes the aqueous globe of Earth itself." Indeed, with its symbolic lexicon of blossoms and overloaded vases, Dutch flower painting constitutes a kind of code language, as do the opulent still lifes of Willem Kalf, Willem Claesz Heda, and Pieter Claesz. Their canvases are laden with shimmering goblets, half-peeled lemons, shells, fish, and loaves of bread cut open to reveal the inner substance. Some of these canvases are simple and soothing, others—called *banketgen*—capture overabundant platters of food intended to reassure the prosperous of their prosperity, as if good fortune might be a fragile and indiscriminate state.

It was Paul Claudel writing in his 1946 classic *L'oeil écoute*, or *The Eye Listens*, who cracked the code, so to speak, when he observed that "[t]he still life in Dutch painting is an arrangement in the process of disintegration." Claudel's *désagrégation* is felt through the counterbalance of stillness and decomposition. The calm surface of liquid in a glass is juxtaposed with the lemon peel curling away from the fruit. The surface of the glass reflects the spiraling lemon peel. It is all one, held together by insubstantial threads of light. Thus the French phrase for "still life," *nature morte* or "dead Nature," is ironically off the mark. Nothing is dead but everything is dying, balanced precariously on the edge, unraveling before our eyes. The stuff of everyday life takes on a sacred portent in these works as each still life becomes a kind of altar to the "domestic paradise," to quote Claudel. The fruit and flowers have been gathered, the silver polished, the wine ready to pour, as if for Communion. But soon the decomposition will begin. The fruit will rot, the wine evaporate. Even the silver will change color as the light wanes, as time passes.

The same principle is at work in glossy bouquets at the height of their opulence, or in the syndics of the Draper's Guild clothed in their aura of well-being as their meeting disintegrates, or in Rembrandt's monumental *Night Watch* where the group sets off like a knot suddenly untied. Claudel's insight reminds us that even as we observe perfection, we enter into a torrent of time. The clock is always ticking in Dutch art; the moment the painting is done becomes the moment of its undoing.

This idea of *désagrégation* stays with me as I finish my eggs, bacon, and coffee and walk back into the center of the city. I'm still not ready for Van Gogh, still immersed in a deeper past. I cross the Prinsengracht along the Nieuwe Spiegelstrasse, peering into antique shops filled with timeless objects. Shards of the past live comfortably in this place; they are the true "still life" of Amsterdam. Among them I find carved boxes, leatherbound books, Delft tiles decorated with frozen images of childhood, animals, flowers. Tulips, in particular, hold a place in the Dutch consciousness, as objects of beauty, Nature, and commerce. In the early seventeenth century fortunes were made and lost within hours when "tulipmania" led to wild speculation on shipments of exotic bulbs that became little more than promises on paper. All is calm now. Tulips, like so many commonplace things here, have been transformed into symbols.

Dutch art dazzles the eye. It is carefully composed and consciously created for optical effect. And yet the subject is not what you see. The factual objects that most anyone could reach for within the confines of a middle-class kitchen are like rafts floating on water. Even the portrait of a *Girl with a Pearl Earring*, whose face hovers over this city, is not what she appears to be. In fact, rather than mere likeness this is a portrait of a moment in time, a moment signified by a turned head and the gravitas of that luminous pearl hanging in the center of the picture, reflecting everything in a flash of pure feeling. The substance of her gaze, like the substance of Dutch art itself, is the undercurrent, the relentlessly fleeting, flowing nature of time itself, what Claudel refers to as a "liquification of reality" achieved through the added ingredient of "silence, this silence that allows one to hear the soul, or at least to listen to it."

Turning back onto the Keizersgracht, I glance down into the first-floor rooms of the houses I pass. The rooms closest to the street are kitchens and further back, receding in serene shadows, I catch glimpses of dining rooms and book-lined studies. Here is a man loading a dishwasher; there, a woman talking on the telephone. Like Vermeer's interiors, these neat spaces are carved into elegant squares and rectangles. From their safely sunken rooms, Amsterdammers must feel the shadows of people walking past, just as they feel the perpetual motion of water. There is a double reality here—exterior and interior, surface and subterranean. Perhaps this accounts for the strange sense of illusion I've had all morning.

⌐

When the German occupation began on May 15, 1940, Amsterdam's population included approximately 100,000 Jews. Never before, or since, have so many been so alone in this city. So alone, in fact, that by the end of the war, 80 percent of Amsterdam's Jews had been murdered in concentration camps. With the firing of all Jewish government employees in the fall of 1940 and the 1941 prohibition against Jewish children attending public schools, the Nazis tightened the noose with characteristic cruelty. The Dutch population was appalled. Ordinary people, from tram operators to garbage men, risked their lives in a general protest strike that brought the city to a halt in February 1941. Indeed, many of the strikers were arrested and shot within days of the event. Even so, this strike remains a point of pride as it represents the only such collective protest in occupied Europe at the time.

Otto Frank and Edith Frank-Hollander had come to Amsterdam in 1933 with their two young daughters to escape the threat of Adolf Hitler. By the eve of the German Occupation, Frank was the managing director of the Dutch Opekta Company, a firm that made pectin for use in jams and jellies. The Opekta warehouse and offices were located in a typical canal-side building on the Prinsengracht near the Westerkerk, or Western Church, not far from the center of town. As more and more Jews were called to report to "work camps," including their older daughter Margot, Otto and Edith decided in July 1942 to go into hiding. They were joined by friends, Hermann and Auguste van Pels and their teenage son Peter. A few months later, another friend, Fritz Pfeffer, moved in with them in the rooms above and behind the offices where Miep Gies, Bep Voskuijl, Victor Kugler, and Johannes Kleiman worked. These four Opekta employees would support the eight people who lived in the "secret annex" for nearly two years. In a very real sense, they remain the true heroes and heroines of Anne Frank's diary:

Our own helpers have managed to pull us through so far. Never have they uttered a single word about the burden we must be.

January 28, 1944

Stirring quotes like this comprise the most powerful aspect of a visit to the Anne Frank House at 263 Prinsengracht, for the story this house has to tell lives through the words of a young girl's diary. It is through her words that I enter into these rooms, step through the membrane of time, and imagine the prospect of coming of age in this hopeless place. As I read her quotes and encounter her face, along with images of the others who hid here with her, I am troubled by my knowledge of their fate. It seems indecent, somehow, to know when and where and how she died.

As I enter these hollow rooms, I'm confronted with a knot of feelings for which I am not at all prepared. Instead of Rembrandt's eyes shining with humanity, it is the absence of humanity that follows me from room to room. This is a sad place, a heroic place. As I move through simple exhibits toward the annex, I experience a sense of foreboding, then anger, then grief. Perhaps the impact of the Anne Frank House rests on the great simplicity with which the curators have presented the story. There is no "big picture," no images of Hitler's army or a wall-size chronology of World War II. Instead I find quotes from the diary etched in Plexiglas, black-and-white pictures of the eight who hid here, and photos, videos, and tributes to the four who made this hiding place work.

The stairs are steep, as they are in all of Amsterdam's narrow houses, and the bookcase concealing the door to the annex is frozen in space, half-opened. Inside, there are more stairs to unfurnished rooms lit with bare bulbs. Rather than life, there is only evidence of life in this stark atmosphere. Here is a board game Peter received as a 16th birthday present. Here are images of movie stars cut from magazines in the room Anne shared with Fritz. And here, oh god, is a map of Normandy, yellow with age, where Otto Frank plotted the progress of the Allied invasion in 1944 with colored pins. This tiny monument to hope screams at me as I stand alone in the room that was their kitchen and living space. Normandy. There was death there too: blood, fear, action. But here, in this room, there was just this map, this tiny square representing what so many were counting on, praying for, tracking day by day. I touch the wall next to it, as those who lived here must have done.

On the other side of the room there are windows covered with gray cloth. Through this shadowy surface, the world outside looks translucent, dreamlike. Peeking past the curtain, I feel the suspense of Anne's presence. I hear the church bells that she heard, probably from the Westerkerk. There, just beyond the window, is a tree that will blossom in the spring. Such sights and sounds marked time for them: birds flying overhead, barking dogs, doors and windows opening and closing, voices in the street. What is it like to sense normal life going on around you when your life has been reduced to a shameful secret?

> *Our thoughts are subject to as little change as we are. They're like a merry-go-round, turning from the Jews to food, from food to politics. By the way, speaking of Jews, I saw two yesterday when I was peeking through the curtains. I felt as though I were gazing at one of the Seven Wonders of the World.*
>
> *December 13, 1942*

Outside, attached to the window is a mirror with an image superimposed on it to give the impression of a reflection of something happening in the street below. The image is that of a *razzia*, or roundup. The Nazis would cordon off a neighborhood and go door-to-door, rounding people up and loading them into green wagons. We know from the *Diary* that Anne was well aware of the terror of these *razzias* and deportations. And now, so am I.

There is nothing to do here and so few rooms that it doesn't take long to see them all. But the experience is not really about seeing an exhibit. The point, rather, is to stand here with Anne and Margot and Otto and Edith and the van Pels and old Fritz, to feel their isolation through Anne's words:

> *I can't help telling you that lately I've begun to feel deserted. I'm surrounded by too great a void.*
>
> *November 20, 1942*

Panels of information serve as guides on the way out, explaining how and when the eight were discovered. There is even a photograph of Karl Josef Silberbauer, the SS officer who ordered them out, into the wagon on August 4, 1944. Anne died of typhus at Bergen-Belsen in February or March 1945, just weeks before the camp was liberated. She was 15 at the time of her death.

*You never realize how much you've changed until after it's happened. I've changed
quite drastically, everything about me is different: my opinions, ideas, critical outlook.
Inwardly, outwardly, nothing's the same.*

March 25, 1944

I walk out into the street where a long line of people now winds along
the sidewalk, almost to the Westerkerk. I'm conscious of children laughing from their bicycles on the other side of the canal, of swans plying the
waters beneath the bridge, of tall, stately houses on the edge of the
Jordaan, one of Amsterdam's most fashionable districts. I shove my hands
in my pockets and look straight ahead as I walk. I am but one of over a
million people who come to this place every year, just another tourist, but
I don't want to be charmed with the neighborhood at the moment.
Besides, I can't quite absorb the sights and sounds around me. My mind
and heart are full of what I have just seen: empty rooms, a hiding place,
the haunting image of Anne's smiling face, frozen in black and white,
frozen in youth. After being *in there*, there is something unnatural about
being *out here*.

I walk away with determination, taking in the substance of something
unexpected, something pure and refreshing. I swallow it whole, this thing
they never breathed again once they entered those rooms. This is the taste
of freedom, the freedom to walk in the street, to call out across the canal,
to imagine a future, not just hope for it. Freedom fills my lungs and catches
in my throat. It pricks my eyes with the sting of unearned privilege. I walk
faster and faster toward the tram that will take me back to a safer place, any
place but this, for the house on the Prisengracht is no place.

Anne's "void" was inflicted on her by hatred. But there is another kind of
aloneness that has no source. In 1877, Vincent van Gogh was studying the
Bible in Amsterdam, hoping to become a preacher. His letters to his
brother Theo from this period reveal his view of himself as a "stranger and
a pilgrim" setting out on a long journey. He was fascinated by art, literature, and Nature. He was devoted to God to the point of fanaticism. His
deepest desire was to be "sorrowful and yet rejoicing" as one of God's servants. And yet he had already tasted failure and was beginning to develop a
sense of his own eccentricity.

I breakfasted on a piece of dry bread and a glass of beer—that is what Dickens
advises for those who are on the point of committing suicide, as being a good way
to keep them, at least for some time, from their purpose.

The tone of this comment isn't quite solemn enough to take seriously, but
within five or six years, his tone had changed. By the early 1880s, Vincent
was writing to Theo about "that loneliness—which a painter has to bear,
whom everyone in some isolated place regards as a lunatic, murderer, a
tramp."

Vincent's letters to Theo reveal his visual sensitivity, his yearning for
love, and his obsessive personality. He later referred to the period spent in
Amsterdam in 1877–78 as one of his unhappiest times, though in it we can
discern his deepest aspirations, his growing self-awareness:

The need is for nothing less than the infinite and the miraculous, and a man does
well to be satisfied with nothing less, and not feel easy until he has gained it . . .
Plumb the depths, that is what we must do if we want to make a catch, and if we
sometimes have to work the whole night without catching anything, then we do well
not to give up and to cast the net once more at dawn.

Amsterdam, April 3, 1878

When Vincent's dreams of serving God as a preacher became unattain-
able, he turned away from Christianity and toward the salvation of art.
From his vantage point as an art dealer in Paris, Theo became Vincent's life-
line, the one who would serve as a confidant and financial supporter, medi-
ator, manager, and protector, as the ill-kempt artist struggled alone to
realize his vision of self-worth that would, in time, bloom on the walls of
Amsterdam's Van Gogh Museum:

Well, right now it seems that things are going badly for me, have been doing so for
some considerable time, and may continue to do so in the future. But it is possible
that everything will get better after it has all seemed to go wrong. I am not counting
on it, it may never happen, but if there should be a change for the better, I should
regard that as a gain, I should rejoice, I should say, at last! So there was something
after all!

The Borinage, July of 1880

The collection at the Van Gogh Museum on the Paulus Potterstraat
traces Vincent's expressive work from the dark, earth-colored drawings and

paintings of the north to the sunbaked canvases that seem to burst forth from his time in Provence. The contemporary building that houses the collection originally amassed by the Van Gogh family includes a study area, an exhibit of the letters, and the work of other artists like Paul Gauguin and Emile Bernard. After all, Theo was an art dealer with a good eye; and both he and his brother had contacts in the Parisian art world in the 1880s.

Without Theo, what would have become of this young man, so eager to paint the hard-working people of the Netherlandish region? What became of him anyway? A life-altering trip to Provence; a suicide at age 37. Here is a record of feeling captured on canvas, but at what cost?

The profound solitude of Vincent's life hovers like a ghost as I pass the self-portraits and climb the stairs to the galleries. In a sense, the work that has become part of our visual vocabulary—sunflowers, a starry night, portraits of the postman—is the work of a displaced person dazzled by sunlight, an artist's artist who was alone not only in Amsterdam, but everywhere he went. The paintings rage with their thick lines, their furious strokes, their riot of color. There is something more orderly about the drawings in sepia ink or bold *conté* crayon. Perhaps this is why he, ultimately, turned to paint with its organic properties, its vivid liquid color. What other medium could possibly express the caged soul of this "stranger and pilgrim" on his chaotic journey?

After his voluntary time at a mental hospital in St. Rémy-de-Provence, the exhausted painter visited Theo and his wife, Johanna, in Paris. By the end of January 1890, Theo will father a son, Vincent Willem van Gogh, and his troubled brother will be living at a small *auberge* in the village of Auvers-sur-Oise under the care of Dr. Gachet. When Vincent shoots himself in July 1890, the staff of the Auberge Ravoux clears a room for the coffin made by a local carpenter. In the words of his friend Emile Bernard, his paintings are hung on the walls, forming "a kind of halo around him and rendering—through the brilliance of the genius that shone from them—his death even more painful for us artists."

⌐┐

On November 2, 2004, the grandson of the baby born to Theo and Johanna van Gogh in 1890 was murdered on the streets of Amsterdam by a 26-year-old Muslim of Dutch and Moroccan descent. Theo van Gogh (1957–2004) was a documentary filmmaker with strong opinions. Permissive and tolerant, the Dutch way of being does not get bogged down in political correctness. Frankness is considered a virtue, regardless of where you stand. Thus Theo van Gogh's well-known epithet for Moroccan Muslims, *geiteneukers*, or "goatfuckers," was freely uttered, even from his perch as a public person with a famous name.

But the motivation for the murder was more specific than a verbal insult. Van Gogh's most recent film, *Submission*, focused on the violent treatment of women by Muslim men, included a reference to Mohammed the Prophet as a "pedophile." It depicted abused Muslim woman in see-through clothing with anti-women verses from the Qu'ran painted on their bodies. For the accused killer, Mohammed Bouyeri, these offenses were the last straw. And so, as Theo bicycled to work along the streets of this city, he was shot in cold blood. Reports describe him staggering to the other side of the street before he fell. Was he dead? To make sure, Bouyeri slit his throat and affixed a five-page Islamic tract to his chest with a sharp knife.

In the wake of Theo van Gogh's murder, the Somalian Muslim screen-writer of *Submission*, a woman named Ayaan Hirsi Ali, went into hiding. Worse, there was an explosion of right-wing extremist violence in the Netherlands. Islamic schools were burned, mosques attacked 47 times, more than a dozen churches defaced or burned. But in Amsterdam I saw no burned mosques, and very few women in headscarves. Where would I find the one million Muslims (6 percent of the Dutch population) who live in this country? On my way to the American Café, a man with a beard and an orange turban asked me for directions to the Libyan Tourist Office. Watching him saunter down the Weteringschans in his white suit and tur-ban, it occurred to me that he might be the one with the directions that mattered.

The American Café at the American Hotel is an open, airy space notable for its Art Deco ambience: a vaulted ceiling, potted palms, and stained glass. And so it is here that I've decided to take a break from the Van Gogh Museum and read an article recommended by a friend about Oriana Fallaci's bestseller, *The Pride and the Rage*. Fallaci, 72, is one of Europe's best-known journalists. She is outspoken, opinionated, and influential, even in her self-proclaimed "rage."

This "screed," as one journalist calls it, was written within weeks of the 9/11 terrorist attacks in the United States. The book review I'm reading with a cup of incredibly delicious coffee and a generous slice of *apelgebak met slagroom*, or apple pie with whipped cream, makes "La Fallaci's" posi-tion clear. She views Islam as a religion that has not bothered to question itself in centuries. She, furthermore, considers Europeans to be blind to the threat of Islam and, frankly, incapable of defending themselves from the evil it represents. In response to the pope's apology to Muslims for the Crusades, she says, "Most Holy Father, in all respect, you remind me of the German-Jewish bankers who, in the 1930s, hoping to save themselves, lent money to Hitler and who, a few years later, ended in his crematory ovens." Fallaci speaks for millions. How else could this book have become a bestseller? Even my friend back in Boston, a Republican who wrinkles his nose at the idea of "celebrating diversity," believes she has put her finger on something that no one else has had the courage to say in our post-9/11 world.

I order another coffee and sit watching the ebb and flow of trams and tourists in front of the American Hotel. I try to make sense of La Fallaci's words in light of Theo van Gogh's death. I try to imagine the true believer's tract stabbed into the artist's chest. Then I close my eyes and return to the flowering orchards that Vincent painted in Provence, to the heavy heads of his sunflowers in a clay pot. Beauty competes with hatred and death in this place, though in truth they coexist.

In the days and weeks following Theo van Gogh's murder, Internet chat rooms fill with commentary. Some mourned his death, condemning his murderer as an "Islamafascist." Others blamed Theo as the instigator of the violence. "Goood riddance to a fat intolerant bastard," one Cybercritic wrote. The cover of the December issue of *de Filmkrant* features a pensive photograph of the great-grandson of Vincent's brother. I stare in vain for a family resemblance. Beneath this photograph, there is a statement in Dutch that seems to serve as the most complete truth that can be uttered at this moment: *Het laatste word is nog niet gezegd.* Roughly translated, it says, "The last word had not yet been spoken."

⌐┐

On the southeastern edge of central Amsterdam, away from the teeming foot traffic and tourist stops, around the corner from the art college, I find the rusty sign that marks the entrance to the Tropenmuseum where the roots of Amsterdam's hidden conflict can be found. Established in 1910 as the Colonial Institute, this institution is now part of the three-pronged Koninklijk Instituut voor de Tropen, or the Netherlands' Royal Institute for the Tropics. The now-independent "KIT" encompasses the Tropenmuseum, a theater, and a publishing department, all dedicated to "international cooperation, sustainable development, the struggle against poverty, and the preservation of the world's cultures."

It is a slightly anachronistic place. Halls echo; wooden floors squeak. In the low-ceilinged galleries, the curious tourist is greeted by dioramas of jungle settlements and coffee plantations, conglomerations of Oceanic art, small environments meant to evoke Caribbean homes or the inner sanctum of a mosque. A forest of wax figures represents colonial life with their glossy skin and glittering eyes.

I have come here to connect the dots of the Dutch colonial adventure, to trace the line on the map that runs between Amsterdam along the coast of Africa into the Indian Ocean, all the way to Sri Lanka and the islands of Indonesia and New Guinea. I sit in front of a screen and watch footage from the 1930s of two Dutch couples on a veranda. They look well fed and socially satisfied as Javanese servants pour tea from a silver pot. Another video shows a woman in a long Batik skirt and white ruffled blouse accepting deliveries on the steps of a large house while her lovely blond children play nearby. These are the people who maintained global commerce in spices, coffee, sugar, or—in Africa—diamonds. Many of them spent their lives in remote corners of the world, believing they were doing good. And surely, some of them did improve the world around them. But the Dutch hung on to slavery longer than most. And when it was officially abolished in 1863, they enlisted "coolies" from India and China and employed poor Javanese workers to do the hard labor required in their globalized society. It is not hard to sense the tension, anger, and uncertainty that colored Colonial life, for the colonized.

I leave the Tropenmuseum, craving air, and walk along the long boulevard bordering Amsterdam's Zoo, the Artis. All I can see from the sidewalk is a flock of flamingos tiptoeing through a murky pond. This area, called the Plantage, culminates in a small park where people are walking dogs and chatting with one another. The park features a stone memorial to honor the victims of Auschwitz. Parks, like the Plantage or the Vondelpark, offer open spaces to Amsterdammers and add to the walkability of the city. But parks, gardens, and plants are, like art, also part of the history of this place.

Just on the edge of this area, on the Plantage Middenlaan is the Hortus Botanicus, or "de Hortus," Amsterdam's historic botanical garden established in 1638 by the Amsterdam City Council. De Hortus was conceived as a resource for physicians and pharmacists who needed to master the curative powers of medicinal herbs in the wake of a deadly plague. Today, de Hortus grows over 4,000 species of plants, including herbs, trees, and flowers, behind its 300-year-old gates.

In November, a tangle of late autumn detritus has taken over, awaiting the meticulous care of the specialists who work here. It is a quiet time to roam through the curvilinear paths laid out in the nineteenth century, to see—as it were—the bones of the garden. A thousand golden gingko leaves float in a silent pool. A gazebo is covered in leafless vines. I follow a path through a small but thick bamboo forest to the Palm House, built in 1912 to appease Professor Hugo de Vries, who threatened to leave unless he got a better glass house for the rare palm collection. This airy structure houses the Giant Cycad collection, which includes a 300-year-old Eastern Cape Giant Cycad. There is a cinnamon tree in the Palm House planted by de Vries himself nearly 100 years ago, a prickly plant with two tufted "heads" called a "Black Boy" palm, and one of the crown jewels of the collection, an Oil Palm whose seeds arrived here in the early nineteenth century from the island of Mauritius before the plant was developed by the Dutch into lucrative palm oil plantations in Sumatra. Elsewhere, in the Three-Climate Greenhouse, there are rare flowers brought by the VOC from South Africa like the Clivia and the African Lily. The bog section of the same greenhouse contains an unusual selection of carnivorous plants with their sticky traps and alluring floral "pitchers" ready to grab and drown their prey. Metal walkways in the Three-Climate glass house are built high, enabling curious tourists to walk up into the tops of trees and look down through deep layers of sweltering green foliage. Next door, what was once a thriving orangerie, built to keep citrus trees content in winter, now serves as a coffee shop with a view.

Amsterdam's Hortus Botanicus, like everything else in this city, is a window on the history of the nation. One of its "crown jewels" is the coffee plant, of which there are now about 60 species. Originally, Arab traders brought coffee to Persia from Ethiopia. But it was the Dutch who resolved to cultivate the plant themselves and introduce it to Europe, partly to avoid the high prices being charged by Arabs. As the de Hortus website explains, "The first shipment of coffee seeds that were propagated by the VOC (in Java) reached Amsterdam in 1706." And, not surprisingly, these plants thrived in the Hortus Botanicus. And then, of course, there was the Turkish tulip bulb, arriving in 1554, whose cheerful descendants fill miles of open country outside the city.

Later, in yet another café, I sip the magical liquid that the Dutch harnessed from that first Ethiopian bean and then cultivated in tropical colonies. Outside, gray light has given way to rain showers that come and go, saturating the brown brick of tall houses, though people on bicycles hardly seem to notice. A blond child toddles past, holding her mother's hand loosely. She turns and smiles at the foreign lady waving from the window of the coffee shop, then walks off. The back of her red jacket is decorated with an appliquéd tulip.

⊔

On my last day in Amsterdam, I take a canal boat tour and walk through the center of the city one last time. Later, I stop in a pub on the Leidseplein for a glass of wine before dinner. I sit at the bar next to a young man with a large shopping bag and we strike up a conversation. He has just bought a new sweater, a new coat, and god knows what else. He is handsome, slim, and dark-haired. He doesn't look Dutch and his English is only slightly accented, so I ask him where he's from and he explains that his father is Italian and his mother Dutch. Pasquale works for an American company and has just returned from Chicago. He gives me his business card with an impressive title. It occurs to me that he is one of the new adventurers from this watery world, a global citizen with ties to many cultures. He travels easily, speaks four languages, works for an international company, likes to shop. His Italian girlfriend, who looks like a young Sophia Loren, soon comes along. She too works for an international company. There is something reassuring in the way these stylish young people represent the deep traditions of Dutch culture. I smile inside, imagining their portraits on the walls of the Rijksmuseum one day.

There are many ways to enter the soul of a city. In Amsterdam, many are drawn to noise and youth and music and shopping. Others, like me, feel the presence of lives shaped by a particular kind of solitude. To be alone in Amsterdam is to share that universal condition. There is Rembrandt, pushing each day to keep up with portrait commissions; Vincent, with his fanatical dreams of preaching the Gospel; Anne, learning that her family would go into hiding while walking these streets with her father and then, in a sense, ceasing to exist even before her death. Being here has allowed me to share their solitude, to meet the ghosts of tulip speculators reeling from their losses, to wink at the winners gazing quietly from prosperous houses onto ever-flowing waters. Like Paul Claudel, I've been lost in thought but grounded in layers of reality. Imagining the final thoughts of Theo van Gogh the filmmaker, I've felt the presence of an undercurrent, an agitation that—like still-life paintings in the Rijksmuseum—is anything but still.

Twilight now. I stop on a bridge outlined in tiny lights overlooking the Herengracht and trace the ripples of this watery world with my eyes until the canal curves and vanishes. Slowly the scene before me disintegrates as crowds disperse and each dark figure walks its own way, into the fullness of solitude. Just before the sky deepens, Vincent's words from an 1877 letter to Theo float back to the surface of my mind. He was alone again after his brother's departure: "What a good day we spent together in Amsterdam," he wrote. "I stayed and watched your train until it was out of sight." ∎

38

A Self-Portrait of a Woman Who Hates Cameras

Rebecca J. Butorac

Here is a self-portrait of a woman who hates cameras.

Here is a self- woman who hates taken, who hates other people, who tures of herself. portrait of a

portrait of a getting her picture taking pictures of hates seeing pic- Here is a self- woman who hates

photography, loves French food, Audrey Hepburn, and shadow dancing.

I have no fashion sense. Let that be known.

In my closet are clothes, yes, that's true, clothing that I've no doubt kept around for years: the pair of chocolate-colored pants with buckles that my now-husband, then-boyfriend bought me on a whim at a Gap because they made my ass look nice, because I swooned over them in the store. He bought them, and I wore them once, once on our next date, and then only for a few hours, and then never again, the pivotal "then" moment of fashion forever abandoned in a closet of men's jeans (because they're longer, more comfortable); sweatshirts with football team logos on them, football teams that I've never watched a game of, but they are birthday present sweatshirts; Christmas sweatshirts that my brother Aaron finds on sale, that he mails me "Fed-Ex, Next Day Shipment" because he can't bear the thought that a Georgia bulldogs sweatshirt, a T-shirt with Tigger or Grumpy with the phrase "I don't do mornings" will end up lost somewhere in the U.S. Postal system, a chewed-up package in the "unsalvageable" bin in the dirty back room at some hub in the middle of nowhere in Wichita.

And he never sends a receipt, so I can never return them.

39

I wear them on days like today when I'm cleaning the apartment, scrubbing caked-on piles of aqua-colored aromatherapy bath salts off the orange tiles in the bathroom.

There are more than sweatshirts, that's true. There are "vintage" clothes, too, I guess, because I've never bought anything for myself that wasn't on sale somewhere, that wasn't in some Salvation Army or Goodwill . . . clothes that never fit me quite right but cost five dollars for a pound . . . seriously, five dollars for a pound . . . kind of like five dollars for a bushel of apples . . . cram as many tweed blazers and plaid pants as you can into a five-pound bag, hope the lady at the register doesn't notice that your five pounds is more like seven. There are dresses that my mother sends me from Ann Taylor, nice dresses that I wear during the summer with cream-colored wraps that I bought on honeymoon in Greece, and that's such a nice phrase: "On Honeymoon in Greece." It just begs to be capitalized, muttered with a dirty Martini in hand, calamari, and filtered cigarettes.

There are these nice clothes, these wedding-capable dresses and slacks, interview clothes, clothes one wears to bridal showers and funerals, the standard black pants, black skirts in three lengths, an assortment of mix-and-match button-down tops.

There are T-shirts, too, T-shirts with sayings, with cartoon characters from ten years ago that no one really remembers, T-shirts that are slowly becoming "vintage" . . . my mother's T-shirts that I've stolen over the years, my favorite a much-too-large-for-me butter yellow shirt with a Kliban cat, a cat in a chef hat frying mice and cheese. I couldn't bring myself to lift her Kliban piggy bank, her Kliban kitty-bank of sorts, a black-and-white tabby with tennis shoes on his feet, a bank lodged on a shelf of outdated relics: a coffee mug shaped like Chewbacca, a bust of W. C. Fields, a pinkish Real McCoy vase that she kept irises in until I told her not to, until programs like *Antiques Road Show* became popular, a mustard-yellow Real McCoy pitcher and washbasin that she uses to sort her mail, a Kliban checkbook cover of a cat with a banjo.

> I love them little mousies. Mousies what I love to eat.
> Bite they little heads off. Nibble on they tiny feet.

To put it simply, she is a packrat, my mother. My father jokes that when she dies, heaven forbid, he's going to rent a dumpster, rent a dumpster and pitch it all, and I laugh. I laugh because *I* am not one to hang on to things, not one to save old papers and Girl Scout uniforms, an archivist of old accordions, scratched 45s of the best of Dick and Didi.

I just can't let go of the clothes.

Pictures?

Who cares?

Toss them.

I'm in the picture?

Toss it faster, rip it up and burn it in a coffee can, use them as kindling, any photo between the ages of 3 and 20 will do.

Here's a paper plate to fan the flame.

Here's some lighter fluid to finish the job.

And yet, I can't get rid of a shirt for David Lipscomb University.

Did I go there?

No.

Did any of my friends go there?

No.

Family? Parents? Any close ties or affiliation, some drunken, unchaperoned fling in the back seat of a Beamer with a Johnny Depp look-alike Church-of-Christer studying Biology?

No.

And the worst part is that the damn thing was free, a recruitment shirt from a school I couldn't afford to go to, a school that I would never dream of going to unless I was "born again," born again with a trust fund. I've worn it so much that it's become unwearable, holes in places that can't be mended, under the arm, around the collar. The closet is full of them, these unwearable, embarrassing things: that T-shirt my aunt bought me when I was 16 with three Greek goddesses embroidered on the front, wear a black bra and no one will notice that half of an eye is missing; the size six gray dress I got on sale eight years ago at Marshall Fields; old theater costumes, Queen Elizabeth, a background character in the Crucible; that Italian leather jacket I found at Goodwill for a dollar, the one with the sleeves too short for my arms, a cigarette burn on the cuff; those damn brown pants with the buckles, the pants I only wore once, only for a few hours at least.

And when they're unsalvageable beyond doing the floors?

Rags, rags for polishing furniture, for wiping down the car.

Old "Visit Las Vegas" T-shirts are coated in Armourall. Strips of corduroy pant legs are good for dusting, and old skirts make interesting quilt pieces, interesting additions to the base of a lopsided Christmas tree, a tree with nothing but berry garlands and fake birds, a family of porcelain bears underneath. No lights. No lights, thank you very much.

But the shoes, the shoes are different. They are new and old and used and worn and never worn and thrown out and donated and sold at garage sales and borrowed and indefinitely borrowed and broken. The shoes are private things that double as public things. I spend more time and money and effort on them: picking them out, lacing them, matching them with pants and shirts and belts and bags, scuffing the soles, stuffing paper into the ones that were on sale when I bought them, too big when I bought them, but too good to pass over.

In a way, too, I think I'm fashionless with my shoes, that I buy them at random, that I pamper my feet in a way that I deny the rest of me, the rest of the frumpy, dumpy, mismatched rest of me in tube socks and old soccer jerseys. Simply, demystifyingly: I am a woman, and I love footwear.

My feet mean nothing to me, though. I think it's because when I was a kid, I thought that feet were gross, ugly, something that humans needed to stay balanced. My mother said my toes were like my fingers; long, long enough to play piano. I think she meant my fingers, meant that my fingers were long enough to play the piano, but I can never be sure.

I am horrible to my feet. That's true. I've never treated them to a pedicure, a foot massage, a loofah . . . a pumice stone has never touched these heels. I have never allowed myself to walk barefoot, at least not since I've been able to remember. I have walked down a shoreline in flip-flops, keeping my toes out of the wet sand, out of grass and dew and dirt and mud.

MY POOR FEET.
ARE THOSE CRACKER CRUMBS?

My feet are only bare when I'm alone in my apartment . . . the one place I shouldn't walk barefoot, no doubt. I tread on sticky floors that I'm too lazy to clean; bits of cereal stick to my soles. I walk through spilled milk and cat puke and melting pools of ice on the floor. When I'm not torturing them, I hide them. I keep them camouflaged. I keep them in the dark.

MY FEET MUST HATE ME,
AND JEALOUSLY CRAVE BANANAS.

I imagine that my feet must hate me when I hide them like this . . . that they conspire tripping me over the rug late at night, that they long to run me into the hard corner of the bed frame, that they plan on tripping over each other to send me tumbling when I get up at four in the morning for a glass of water, for a trip to the toilet . . . no pun intended.

I imagine that they have minds of their own, and that the right foot, controlled by the left side of my brain, is embarrassed by me and my monkey slippers. I imagine that she considers herself an "artiste," a bohemian that longs to be painted in henna, longs to be wrapped in seaweed and dipped in wet cement with her initials, somewhere next to a poem about spring, a quotation from T. S. Eliot. I imagine that she is angry at me for "selling out," for buying slippers that are made with less than 100 percent organic material.

The left foot, the practical one, hates me as well, hates me because I have worn the slippers too long, long past the recommended shelf-life of slippers, long past the bottoms have worn down and have started collecting bits of string and fluff and trash, gum wrapper bits and popcorn kernels. She knows that it's only a matter of time before something bad happens, before some kind of bizarre accident involving bacteria and athlete's foot, won't be long before a wayward splinter finds its way into her hard and mistreated sole. She wants new slippers and new shoes and socks, and she hates it when I wear the same pair of socks over again when it's almost time to do the laundry . . . can't stand the thought of wearing last night's tube socks with this morning's jog. For her, there is no excuse for being unsanitary, for wearing things before you wash them, for wearing things after you've worn them.

I TRY TO SPOIL THEM.
UNGRATEFUL FEET.

Sometimes, though, I think I hate them more than they could possibly ever hate me. They ask for wraps and pedicures and massages, and they don't realize what a hassle they are, how big they are, how long and awkward, how fin-like and flap-like. Duck feet. Yes, they are duck feet, platypus feet, fish feet, fins. They don't understand that they are built for swimming, for swimming and running and jogging. They are masculine feet, athletic feet that were made for tennis shoes and golfing shoes. They are bowling feet. They are hiking feet. They want to be dancers. They want to salsa and do ballet. They want to pirouette to *Swan Lake*, but they don't realize that the best they could ever do is learn to play the music, that they are not meant to be graceful, but play gracefully. Although I would never tell them that it's too late for them to learn. I will instead delude them with promises of Mozart's *Requiem*, challenge them with *An American in Paris*, let them pretend. Let them play dress-up.

Playing dress-up is something they do often, something I let them do when we're alone, just three of us:

Just the girls.

They break out the dancing shoes, the little black pumps that are too small for them, awkward. Pantyhose and pumps and an old sweatshirt. They half-step in the kitchen while I boil macaroni, while I chop carrots and do the dishes. It is a scene of *Flashdance* meets Martha Stewart, and I indulge them.

I let them think that they are graceful, that they are sexy and good dancers, unpolished dancers, neglected.

In a bathrobe and '50s heels we "draw a bath" and "turn the tap" and say things that make us feel delicious.

As long as they never want to leave the house that way, I'm fine with it. I'm fine with Halloween parties and stage productions. Interviews. Weddings. Funerals. Once in a while I let them go for it, but never like we do at home, never as much as we pretend when we're playing dress-up.

⊔

I AM A ROCK STAR.   I AM A DANCER.   I AM JACKIE-O.
POOR FEET. THEY ARE DELUSIONAL.

They are not girly feet, that's for sure. They are meant for tube socks and tennis shoes. I have always worn tennis shoes, since I was a little girl. When I was in fifth grade, I wore tennis shoes with no laces. I wore tennis shoes and friendship bracelets around my ankles. I wore tennis shoes with tights and shorts, and the tights were always striped or checked or dotted with hearts, and the shorts were blue jeans that my mother cut when I grew too tall. They were jeans, and then they were high-waters, and then they were shorts; and I wore them with patterned tights and shoes with no laces.

In fifth grade, I was also good in math and English. I was good in science and got an A in social studies. I'm not sure exactly what constituted an A in social studies. And, looking back now, I'm not sure exactly what social studies constitutes. It was a mixture, I think, a kind of introduction to history for kids who weren't interested in history. It was history, and it was sociology. It was culture. Language. People and places. Times. Customs. Stories. Legends. Folklore. Irish Fairytales. Milk Cartons. Accounting.

It was Art History. Psychology. Journalism. Journaling. Journals. Journeys. Love Letters. Big League Chew and saltines.

It was an intensive six-week study on Hair Clips and Schoolyard Gossip. And, looking back now, I can't remember what the class was about, really. I can't remember the names or dates, and the only historical facts I remember are random ones gleaned from reading 20 or so Trivial Pursuit cards before bed so I could, one day, beat both of my brothers in sports and the sciences and geography and make them never challenge me to a game again, never laugh when I say that the Bears won the '72 Super Bowl because I like the Bears and they are my default answer to anything regarding football.

The only historical fact I remember from social studies probably wasn't a fact at all. It was probably the teacher in the sweater with the apples on it threw in there to get our attention because she probably didn't know what the class was about either, because it's hard enough to keep 25 kids' attention without candy and stickers, filmstrips and prize baskets for good behavior.

Women make their feet smaller.

That's it. That is the one fact that I remember. Women . . . *past* women, not so much "now" women, or when I was in fifth grade women, but past women, women that would have known the famous men that were in the social studies book *made* their feet smaller so they could wear smaller shoes.

They bound them.

They broke them and reshaped them.

They bid adieu to extra toes, big toes, sometimes pinkie toes too so they could wear tiny shoes with tiny heels to match their tiny waists and wrists, so that the men who were in the social studies books would fall in love and talk of things like "dance cards" and "high tea" and "revolutions."

Vanity . . . Vanity . . . All is Vanity . . .

And from that moment on, from the moment that I learned that some women make their feet smaller, I considered women to be very silly creatures. Furthermore, I decided that I would not be silly, and that I would rather be consigned to a dowagerhood before I tried my hand, before I tried my feet, rather, at being a princess. And so I wore the shorts that were jeans and tights without hearts on them and tennis shoes with no laces. And as I grew, I wore vests and boots and men's jeans. I cut my hair short. No more pigtails. No thank you, very much. And what of my feet? The men's size 9. The woman's size 9, sometimes 9 1/2, sometimes 10, 10 1/2 W depending on the store, the region, the quality, the 9 1/2 in cheap dress shoes, 9 in expensive . . .

They wear tennis shoes and bowling shoes.

They wear the same socks if I run low on laundry, and they step in wet things and on crunchy things and things stick to them. They deserve a pedicure more than any other feet I know, but I refuse to spoil them, refuse to get them accustomed to "that kind of life," to "that kind of treatment."

They wear shoes with long laces that I still can't tie the right way, that I still tie like a present the way my brother taught me to because I couldn't understand the simplicity of my second grade teacher . . . the rabbit running, running, runs, and the dog runs, and the rabbit runs, and the rabbit runs into a hole and the dog follows . . . and voila! a shoe is tied . . . and I got a U, a U for Unsatisfactory because I cheated, because I tied the laces like bows, and I still do, and I guess I am still Un-something.

My feet, they don't complain. They just trip me every now and then, run me into things in the middle of the night. They turn circles in heels on the living room rug, and sometimes, I admit, I squeeze them into an 8. ▄

48

Thoughts Occasioned by My Father-in-law, Garlic, and Montevideo's Mercado Modelo

Patrick Madden

For 20 years, since the man he shared a fruit stand with stiffed him, my father-in-law has worked as a simple middleman carting vegetables, mainly garlic, from Montevideo's giant central market to faraway cities and forgotten towns. He likes the easy pace of it, the chats with old friends at the market stalls, the quiet, jostling hours on the bus, the quick conversations with the terminal staff who watch his extra bags as he carries one slung over his shoulder to front-yard kiosks and corner bars, to steady customers who smile when they see him and offer him drinks and pay him when they can. He likes the card games and drinks at late hours in bars with fleeting friends his age and temperament who remember fatter times, and greener.

We left early in the early morning, dressed in flannel and jeans, walked to the bus stop near his apartment: concrete slabs in patchy grass and rusting metal tubes holding up a corrugated fiberglass roof. Light from the streetlamps overpowered the stars, or the clouds did, and crickets sang, or frogs, and a cat crossed our path and turned, paused, looked back menacingly, then continued on to the overflowing trash bins where it foraged for food, or slept. We waited in silence and yawns as other weary travelers arrived dressed in ties and slacks and dresses and yawning and silent and drab in the feeble light blocking stars and casting the world in dreary gray, and languor.

We hardly spoke, but I observed him, white with years and worn and wizened, his skin leather, his hands strong and curled from years of hauling his 50-pound bags of garlic—I, unaccustomed and soft with tender hands and worsening eyesight from reading books and people.

⎍

49

The plot today is we are going to Mercado Modelo, Montevideo's central fruit and vegetable market, where he will buy garlic to sell and I will observe and accompany and sit lethargically on boxes of apples eating dried sausage on crackers and fry bread as the sun slashes through the spaces between easterly buildings.

⊓

He is like so many other Uruguayan men, dressed in a plaid shirt and faded pants and comfortable *alpargatas*, canvas shoes with coiled-rope soles, with a white moustache and missing teeth. He is five-foot-eight but hunches over, he is overweight, he walks slowly and deliberately, sings ever so slightly when he talks, calls me "*mi hijo*," my son, and watches the world with piercing steel-blue eyes.

⊓

On the bus, the people scattered to empty benches to sit alone, but my father-in-law and I sat with each other, his shoulder jabbing my biceps, in silence. After a short ride, we arrived at the market, in the warehouse district in the middle of the city, north of the tall buildings, along Avenida José Batlle y Ordóñez, named after Uruguay's great social reformer president, who served twice in office from 1906 to 1910 and from 1916 to 1920. But the street name is ceremonial, perfunctory, and everyone calls the avenue by its old name, Propios, which means "ours" or "those who belong," because it once divided *Us* from *Them*. The market is on the Ajenos side.

I was struck immediately by the immensity of the conglomeration of merchants, the hustle of runners with hand trucks dashing through amoebic crowds, the sweet and pungent smells of fruits in all stages of ripeness and decay, stacked neatly in piles and boxes or trampled underfoot. I saw colors and blurs of movement in the darkness turned back by vapor lights strung high from vaulted ceilings. I heard echoes of a more glorious past grown too big and past its limits in the stalls and stands sprawled outside the original fading central building into smaller buildings and spilled over into alleyways and walkways, among the trucks and tarps and stacks and stacks of crates and boxes, everywhere.

⊓

I thought of the impossible complexity of interrelations. I grew up near New York City, 45 minutes west in suburban New Jersey. Life was simplified and compartmentalized for me and—for the trees or for the regimen,

I cannot tell—I never had to see far beyond my neighborhood or my schoolwork, and because I was good at school, I never worried. Life was a series of assignments and tests and time to play with friends, and home was stable and never wanting. I excelled in math and science and our high school science experiments were contained, assumed a closed system, and we spoke lightly of the unreality of a closed system, or of the problem of working within a system to test that system, as scientists must inescapably do, but it was theory, and reality was neat and ordered and I believed I could wrap my mind around it.

But New York, it seemed to me little by little and increasingly as I grew older and visited more frequently and paid more attention to the local news on television, was chaos with a veneer of order. It was a sphere atop a cone, waiting for the slightest provocation to send it careening down to destruction. Simple things—the garbage collection for so many people and businesses, the sanitation, the subway system maintenance—were incredibly complex, things I could never fit inside my brain. I considered the weight of buildings and people supported by the island, perforated like Swiss cheese by subway tunnels. I thought of the apartment buildings just inside Manhattan on the Upper West Side, where the George Washington Bridge empties out and which Interstate 95 dives underneath in a series of short tunnels on its way to the Bronx. Do the people above, watching television, doing homework, know that their building rests only on columns of concrete and rebar? The engineers have it all figured out, I realize, and the buildings remain standing, but my amazement at that fact always gets the better of me and something like an irrational fear grips me as I drive underneath them.

⊐

A List, in Spanish, of the Various Fruits and Vegetables Available at Different Times of the Year at Mercado Modelo, as Given Me by My Father-in-law Some Months after Our Visit to the Market:

papa, boñato, zapallo, calabaza, zapallito, berenjena blanca y negra, cebolla blanca, morrón rojo y amarillo [My computer automatically changes *morrón* to *moron* and capitalizes *Amarillo*. That we allow our programmers to insert such annoying functions in our software I take as a sign of increasing dependence on machines and willingness to surrender decisions and avoid thinking or knowing useful conventions.], remolacha, zanahoria, espinaca, acelga, escarola, lechuga verde crespa, lechuga manteca, lechuga morada, lechuga

morada crespa, brocoli, coliflor, radicha, zalsifi, nabo, nabiza, puerro, apio,
repollo blanco, repollo morado, repollo crespo, cebollin, albahaca, perejil,
hongos, espárragos, eudibias, brotes de soja, brotes de alfalfa, choclo, repol-
litos de bruselas, ajos, pepinos, tomates, arvejas, habas, porotos manteca fres-
cos, chauchas, chaucha alubia, cebolla colorada, sandía, melón, kiwi,
naranjas, tanjarines, bergamotas, pomelo rosado, pomelo amarillo, bananas,
frutillas, uva blanca, uva moscatel rosada, uva chinche, higos, manzana deli-
cia, manzana grani smith, manzana redelicia, kinotos, peras, duraznos rey del
monte, duraznos pelón, damascos, durazno blanco, ciruela betellita, ciruela
morada, ciruela blanca, gemidas, cerezas, frambuesas, ananá [not the typical
Spanish word for pineapple, but the one Uruguayans use and share with
German and Russian and Latvian and, I suspect, many other languages].

⌐

My father once told me about Robert Shields, a retired minister who tried
to keep a journal of everything he did. At the time, it seemed to me a
colossal waste of time, but I didn't ponder the impossibility of it all until
later. I imagine that he hadn't read Jorge Luis Borges's "The Library of
Babel," or maybe he had and hadn't felt the despair and futility of the idea
of completeness or total self-reflexivity, metaliterature, writing about writ-
ing about writing trapped forever unable to write more than "I am writ-
ing, still writing, writing, writing still" never doing except writing caught
in an infinite loop like Aureliano Babilonia at the end of *One Hundred Years
of Solitude* reading the moment he is living unable to escape the broken
record looping and looping while his town is obliterated and he goes on
reading, only reading.

The personal essay, according to Phillip Lopate, shows the activity of a
mind at work. It reflects discovery through writing. Its author better not
begin with a conclusion or epiphany already in hand. And yet, of course an
essay is artifice, somewhat inspired by the muse and somewhat formed by
conscious decision and revision and pruning to finally appear fresh and
reflexive of a mind at work. Yet this seems to me also an impossibility. One
must restrain oneself, heed the lesson of Apollo's son Phaethon: rein the
horses one can, avoid the horses one can't.

An essay is performative if its medium—words, sentences, tone, diction,
format, style—reflects its subject. Yet: an essay that ends up being *about*
chaos or entropy?

⌐

I wonder if he gets bored, walking alone so much of the time with his bags of garlic. I wonder what he thinks about, or does he think very little, is he simply content to be? When I walk, I walk to reach my destination. I am ashamed of my walks, purposeful beasts, in light of Thoreau and Hazlitt and now Sebald and so many other great walkers whose time was consecrated to the what-have-you, the come-what-may of a walk. I have bought into the hustle and bustle of everyday life in America, getting and getting to, arriving. Neil Peart writes, echoing the spirit of so many who came before, "The point of the journey is not to arrive." And yet for me, it is. And I am ashamed of that.

My father-in-law *does* walk to get to his destinations. He arrives at bars and grocery stores and restaurants and kiosks to sell garlic. Yet I see him not as an acquisitive product-oriented destination-seeker like myself. He is somehow above that, halfway translated to a calm oneness with the world around him. I say this because he never complains, because he moves about quietly and sometimes stares fixedly at nothing, as if lost in thought or at peace. But I also remember men who worked their whole adult lives in a tire factory that I withstood only one summer. They, too, seemed to have that resigned look in their eyes, and I imagined it was their escape from the atrophy of routine, from the heat of the tire ovens and the black dust of the air. My difficulty was my resistance: I couldn't not think and be miserable longing for variety and excitement and, I would have said, it was mind-numbing, and so perhaps their minds had been numbed, and the younger men spoke incessantly of the weekend and the lottery and of everything that was not work and would make work no longer necessary.

I have no proof that my father-in-law, whose walks are also determined by the market and his small part in it as distributor of garlic to small markets and restaurants in faraway towns, walks any differently than I do. I have no proof that he is anything like the ideal I paint of him with his peace and oneness with the landscape of the country he's lived in for 63 years.

He tells his past very infrequently, but when he tells, he explains that he was raised in the farmland north of the capital by humble parents whose struggle to live meant that children were expected to help with chores and planting and harvest. Early on he was an exceptional student, his children tell me. In the sixth grade, his teacher gave him a dictionary, which she signed, "To Uber, Best of luck in your future studies. You will do well." But his father needed him at home and he never went back to school. When I ask him about it, his voice seems a lament, but his words remain stoic with the inevitable fact of life in the 1940s in Uruguay where land reforms and social programs were enough to make people like his parents content to be working their own farm and in control of their own progress and prosperity.

꒦

Almost simultaneously, as I write, there appear in my mind two phrases, one from Lu Hsun and one from John Lennon. Respectively: "This, too, is life," and "Life is what happens to you while you're busy making other plans."

꒦

Garlic, historians believe, was originally native to mountainous eastern Asia, and was traded widely so that the earliest farmers, in Mesopotamia, cultivated it 10,000 years ago. The Greek historian Herodotus wrote of a memorial plaque dating from about 2500 B.C. on the Great Pyramid of Cheops at Giza that mentioned the cost of the radishes, onions, and garlic used to feed workers. When Tutankhamen's tomb was opened in 1922, archeologists found among the artifacts therein six dried cloves of garlic. In about 1500 B.C., the Children of Israel, recently escaped from slavery in Egypt, remembered wistfully the fish, cucumbers, melons, leeks, onions, and garlic they used to eat. It has long been a staple, if a disparaged one because of its breath-fouling effects.

All garlic is of one species, *allium sativar*, though bulbs do differ widely from one another in size, shape, texture, and other ways. Variations are called cultivars. In this way, it occurs to me, garlic is like people. Its Latin name, which has filtered into its common name in French, Italian, and Spanish, may derive from a Celtic term for "burning," and it shares a genus with onions, chives, shallots, and leeks. This last contributed to garlic's English name, along with the Anglo-Saxon word *gar*, which is a lance or spear: gar-leek, because of its spear-shaped stalk, reminiscent of a leek's.

Garlic has also been called, derogatorily, "poor man's treacle" or "churl's treacle," *treacle* being an antidote or cure-all, and *churl* being that ill-bred lowest class of freeman who has, it seems, the last laugh. While aristocracy from Persia to Spain despised the herb and forbade their courtiers to partake of it, recent research confirms some of what ancient Egyptian, Chinese, Indian, and Mediterranean "common" peoples have long believed about garlic's curative properties. Garlic can lower cholesterol and decrease a person's risk of getting certain cancers. Louis Pasteur, in 1858, discovered its antibacterial properties, and its diluted juices were used as an antiseptic during World War I.

Garlic then have power to save from death
Bear with it though it makes unsavoury breath

—John Harrington

We are slow and methodical in our research nowadays, taking great pains to reduce or eliminate outside uncontrolled influences on our subjects, so it may take us a while to confirm or refute the ancients' claims that garlic also stimulates the heart, fights rheumatism, and cures headaches, dog bites, earaches, intestinal worms, and throat tumors.

⊐

Every three months or so, my father-in-law brings home a fresh braid of large garlic bulbs tied with a red ribbon. He hangs it on a nail just outside the kitchen doorway for good luck, savory food, and health.

⊐

Once, as we rode standing in the back of a rusted pickup along a long dirt road north of Montevideo, my father-in-law spoke about his family, his wife's unpredictable temper, his son Fernando's bureaucratic tangles caught between the bike factory that had laid him off temporarily and the government that refused to pay him temporary unemployment benefits. He spoke about his happiness for Karina, my wife, though she lived far away and they saw each other only rarely. He spoke with pride about his daughter Graciela, who had recently graduated from the university and would be an elementary school teacher, though she had forgotten her ID on the day of the incoming teacher examination, had been unable to take it, and was thus relegated to substitute work for a year because all teachers are processed through the state system, not hired through interviews and common accord.

And then—how did we get here?—an allusion to his oldest son, Bernardo, called Lalo, his firstborn. He had played soccer in the minor leagues, and as a young boy had stood his father down those nights when he came home broke, drunk, belligerent; he had gone into the military for the sake of a steady paycheck and for the sake of his mother, who worked a factory job to keep the family afloat while her husband pissed away his own earnings in the cantinas of the Interior; he had excelled in marksmanship and horsemanship, earning an instructor's job at the training center in Colonia along with a blue-blood golden-boy sonofatorturer who was always a second behind, always a bit off the mark, except for the evening he shot and killed Lalo with one bullet, claiming it was a gun-cleaning accident and getting off, despite witnesses who heard him shouting, threatening. Now Lalo's military pension, ascended to that of a lieutenant's and awarded posthumously to his mother, keeps the family comfortable enough in these days of hardships and factory closings and my father-in-law returns home having sold only half his stock.

He says, "I've been through a lot. You know."

I do. The pause sits heavily, holding to the truck as it thrums, the whipping wind too feeble to lift it and carry it away.

⊔

The impossible complexity of interrelations, commerces, supplies and demands and imports and exports, middlemen and middlemen and an accessible price when the fruit is spit out the other end before I buy it, before I bite it. And only one thread, garlic, almost impossible to follow from a poor farmer in China during Uruguay's off-season when garlic must be imported, to an assembly line of women braiding bulbs together by their long spear leaves, to a man stacking strands between sheets of purple paper in cardboard boxes with *garlic* written in seven languages, to a boat across the ocean to a port in Montevideo to awaiting trucks to be stacked and delivered across town in the early morning hours to a stall in the market, bustling below the grayness of the night amidst the clanking of carts and crunching of boxes and the colors, laid on slats of wood in one of the rows and rows of labyrinthine paths, awaiting my father-in-law or somebody like him, to be carried in 50-pound bags in the underside of a bus from Montevideo to Rocha then distributed a few strands at a time to front-yard kiosks and corner bars to be sold to the customers to be used in the sauce for the pasta, for sustenance, good health, and good luck, at tonight's dinner. ■

Regrets Only

Susan Messer

SPRING

There she was, my daughter's piano teacher, beside the big blue mailbox, in this freethinking town on the edge of Chicago.

Let's call her Anna.

"Hey, Anna," I called, waving as I came up the street to the post office.

"Hey," she said, waving back. She was in her early 30s, and tall, lanky. I was in my mid-40s, and small. She was dressed in a plain, straightforward way—a white blouse, Gap chinos. Sensible shoes. I concluded early on in our friendship that, unlike me, she did not have two feather boas stored in her closet.

After her life turned the fateful corner, and she hated herself, she described herself as schoolmarmish. Before that, though, when she'd felt strong, grounded by the sense that she had chosen her look and her style, she said, "I don't like to think of myself as a *female*; I like to think of myself as a *person*."

"How are you doing?" I said once I reached her. Cars swarmed around the curb, jockeying for position, while we stood slightly outside the fray.

"I just dropped my bank deposit into the mail box," she said. People moved around us, up and down the stairs, into and out of the heavy old post office doors with their brass moldings and depictions of mail delivery methods over the ages.

"Oooph," I said. "What are you going to do?" It was a fine spring day, which perhaps lightened the mood around this little mishap.

"I don't know," she said. "I'll go in and tell someone in a while." She brushed her fingers through her short, feathery hair, a warm, light brown. Not fussy, but well groomed. "I guess I'm distracted."

"I guess so," I said. I thought of the bank deposit, all her piano-teacher income, lying amidst the confusion of letters. I thought of the unfriendly post office clerks—surly even when faced with the simplest request—despite the glorious marble and brass building they worked in.

"Do you have a few minutes?" she asked.

"Sure," I said. She wanted to tell why she was distracted: Let's call him Louie.

Louie lived in California, but he had come to town for a few days to hear Beethoven's *Ninth Symphony*. His brother was conducting, chorus and all.

If the regular rehearsal accompanist had been available and asked someone other than Anna to substitute. If Anna hadn't so loved the Beethoven. If Anna hadn't decided, in the last days of rehearsal, to sing in the chorus. If the conductor had not seen her in the crowd after the performance and called out, "We're going to celebrate. Why don't you join us?" If she'd followed her instinct (tired, sore throat) and gone home. If her throat had been even sorer (from singing all the high notes), perhaps she would have gone home.

Imagine an illustration in a magazine, she said as we stood by the busy post office curb. A dinner party, in gray, but two people in full color. Anna and Louie, sitting beside each other. She'd seen him in the crowd after the performance and thought, "There's trouble." But at the dinner, he seemed wonderful.

"Do you ever want to get married?" he asked as they sat beside each other, in full color.

"Sure," she said. Laughing.

"And kids? You want to have kids?"

"Sure," she said. Laughing some more. Perhaps her throat hurt less by now.

And he said laughing, "How many?"

"I don't know," she said. "Four, five, six, seven."

"That many?"

"Yes," she said. "I want a cacophonous house."

Anna lived in an efficiency apartment in an old brick courtyard building. Her piano, along a wall of the apartment's one room, was an upright, with a spectacularly high-gloss black finish. This was possibly her most flamboyant accessory. Her bed was a futon with a navy blue cover set on a wooden fold-out frame, not far from the piano. During the day, students waiting for their lessons or parents staying to observe sat on the folded futon.

After the technicolor dinner, Louie sat on the futon, then stayed on for a few nights in the efficiency. They unfolded and folded the bed. She played the piano for him. "Men always love that I can play the piano," she said. I could see why: the competence, the stately posture, the power coming up through the spine, flowing through the shoulders and arms into the strong, graceful hands and arched fingers like rainbows, like bridges. A woman who played the piano could fill a room with notes, layer on layer, adding up to something deep and rich. In graduate school, she'd entered competitions, practiced six or eight hours a day. She was masterful.

Louie was in his 40s. He'd dropped out of college in his last semester to follow a guru to India. Later, he continued his spiritual quest in Santa Cruz, where he learned to restore BMWs. Now he had his own business. He, too, worked with his hands.

"Maybe you better go see about the bank deposit?" I asked. I worried about the post office bureaucracy, the stone wall of rules they could concoct: no unscheduled openings of government property, no civilian presence at box openings, no civilian manipulation of box contents, no unorthodox release of unintended deposits. I imagined the forms, signatures, notarizations.

"I suppose," she said, unconcerned. And, indeed, when I called her a few days later, she said she'd gotten the money back. No big deal.

FALL

If I hadn't been so squeamish about conflict, so afraid of interfering. If I'd been less concerned with seeming joyless, or old-fashioned. If she hadn't seemed so defensive. If I had been more trusting that we could work through the clashing points of view. If I hadn't had so much wine. Or if I'd had more.

My husband, our daughter, and I went out with Anna one night—to Chicago's Greek Town for dinner. We liked the Parthenon in those days—a festive place, crowded and noisy, with the whooshing of the flaming cheese, the murals of Greek temples, inebriated diners at long tables with big baskets of bread, and overflowing family-style platters of meats and rice and salads. The sharp, salty tang of feta and olives. We ordered a carafe of Roditys, a blush wine, served cold.

Anna spoke of Louie. Since their first meeting, he'd been back to visit. They'd had a rendezvous in DC. She'd gone to California. A few days here, a few days there. He was house-sitting at a friend's apartment when she visited in California. Thanksgiving was coming, and Louie had planned on spending it with her but had to cancel.

"Why?" my husband asked.

"Oh, it's complicated," she said. "Some work release thing about parking tickets."

"Parking tickets?" my husband said.

"He gets a lot of parking tickets," Anna said. "It's not a big deal. Lots of people get parking tickets." There was a hint here that concern for parking rules was a bourgeois convention. I thought of the post office. No big deal.

"Maybe so," my husband said. "But people don't get work release for parking tickets. There must be something else." My husband is a lawyer, comfortable with giving advice, certain of his opinions.

"There's nothing else," Anna said. Anna, too, could be assertive and self-assured—the towering piano teacher.

Our daughter, seven years old, sat quietly, eating her dinner, while the Roditys had its way with us, and the conflict escalated between Anna and my husband. I agreed with my husband that Louie seemed risky—that the work-release story was suspect—but Anna was an adult. Who were we to tell her what to do or think?

"Jim," I said. "I don't think Anna wants advice." He sometimes accuses me of being too quick to censor him. And sometimes I am, running interference in conflicts simply because of my own discomfort. So he looked at me a little crossly, but then decided not to pursue it, and we moved on—to movies, perhaps, a safer topic, though the tension hung in the air like the fumes from the flaming cheese, burning a little at the back of the throat. Our daughter quietly picked at her dinner.

I didn't sleep well that night. My head spun from too much wine. And the *skordalia* had been too garlicky. Or perhaps I had eaten too much *skordalia*—or eaten it too fast in my nervousness about whether my husband was being pushy, whether Anna would like us anymore, what our daughter was making of all this, and what would become of Anna with her Louie.

About a month later, I picked my daughter up at her piano lesson. Anna admired a necklace my daughter was wearing. "Speaking of jewelry," she said. She held up her strong pianist hand with the power fingers. A big diamond ring. "We're getting married," she said, "Louie and I." She beamed.

"Wow," I said. "You don't mess around."

"And I'm pregnant." A hint of smile. She was due in the summer. They would marry in June.

"Wow," I said. "Congrats. But where are you going to live?"

"We'll figure it out," she said. "He's willing to come here. Or I could go there."

"Wow."

Children are often silent during these adult exchanges, and I'd often wondered whether or in what way they were listening or observing, absorbing, or whether because of their own needs and impatience to move on, adult talk was all a blur. But my daughter had heard this one. In the car, on the way home, she said, "I didn't know you could get pregnant without being married." She knew the facts of conception—the sperm and the egg, even the basics of insertion—but this muddle of biology and social convention was beyond her. I attempted to explain as we drove through the streets of our Midwestern town with its tall elms and oaks, its maples with the broad crowns.

If she hadn't become pregnant. If she'd been younger, say in her 20s. If she hadn't felt this might be her only chance to have a baby. Or if she'd been older, so that genetic screening was recommended. If someone had said, "What are you doing?" Her mother or father? A friend who knew her far better than I did?

Anna's body changed as her pregnancy advanced, and she wore large overalls and big T-shirts. She planned a church wedding. She registered for gifts at Crate and Barrel. "A matter of practicality," she said. "A way to make sure you get what you want." She chose dishes, white ones; and napkins, navy blue; and conservative, good-quality flatware. My husband and daughter and I were invited to the wedding, and we bought two place settings for the wedding gift.

SPRING

When Anna was seven or eight months pregnant, I received an invitation to a baby shower, given by one of her friends. On the day of the party, Anna drove over to get me. She wore a navy blue maternity jumper with a white blouse. I probably wore something bright—fuchsia or teal, gypsyish.

"Wow," I said, as she pulled onto the highway. "You can really drive." I admired her bold moves, her foot solid on the gas pedal, the strong thrusts with the gear shift, vrooming along with just a hint of muffler trouble. At

our destination, an old Chicago apartment building, a man wearing shorts
and a T-shirt sat on the front stoop. Anna greeted him. His wife was host-
ing the shower.

"So you think he'll show?" he quipped. Louie, he meant. Would he
show for the wedding? *Good grief,* I thought and pretended I hadn't heard.

"I can deal with it if he doesn't," she said with a sniff. They made it
sound like clever repartee.

Upstairs in the apartment that was our destination, tables and chairs filled
the living and dining rooms. One table was for the gifts, and I placed mine
in the pile: soft, cotton baby jumpers in non-gender-biased colors. Other
tables held pastries, finger sandwiches, crudités arranged on platters. Sweet
red liquid filled a punch bowl. Women talked in small groups. Louie's sister-in-law was there—the wife of the Beethoven conductor who had
invited Anna to the technicolor dinner. The sister-in-law joked about
Louie, how unpredictable he was, such a character. No one in the family
ever thought he would settle down. How lucky he was to nab a solid, high-
quality woman like Anna. Anna laughed. I think we all did. Anna's mother
was there, and she may not have laughed, but she did admire the gifts—the
tiny clothes, the blankets, the soft, cuddly toys. She held the little shirts, the
jumpers, refolded them and placed them in their boxes. She told us that she
had a name in mind for the baby if she was a girl: Liza. Anna didn't dislike
the name, but she didn't like being pressured toward any particular name.
So there was this bit of tension; nothing serious.

SUMMER

When we arrived at the old gray stone church, guests in groups of threes
and fours sat scattered among the pews. The sun shone red and purple and
blue through the stained-glass windows as my husband, my daughter, and
I found seats in the burnished chapel with its rough stone walls and arch-
ing wood-beam ceiling.

Accompanied by piano music, the groom walked down the aisle in a
dark suit. Guests craned their necks as he passed. "He arrived just last
night," someone behind me whispered. At the front of the church, he
turned. Our first look at him. He was handsome, with a good sturdy build,
thick black hair, and a craggy face. (*"There's trouble,"* Anna had thought
when she first saw him, but he didn't look troublesome right then. At least
not to me.)

Also in the procession: a maid of honor (Anna's best friend from New York). A best man (the conductor of the Beethoven). Then Anna. Arm in arm with her tall father. Together they took the slow, even steps of the processional. She wore a beige pants suit, the jacket smooth over her pregnant belly, a large bouquet of pink lilies in the elbow crook of her arm. Her head drooped to her shoulder as she walked. She closed her eyes, and tears drenched her cheeks.

As she drew near, Louie reached for her, and the father stepped back. My husband and I, seated with our daughter in the pew, exchanged looks, reassured by his tenderness. Louie held Anna throughout the service, arm around her waist, and she continued to cry—through the pronouncement of marriage, and even, perhaps, through the salty kiss. *No one raised an objection, even when the minister asked.*

The guests moved into the party room and sat at round tables, eating and talking. We listened to each others' stories of how we knew Anna, how we knew Louie. Louie circulated, greeting the guests, thanking them for coming, shaking hands. His hands were strong and callused, like tree bark or leather, axle grease under the skin looking like a permanent condition. Later, Anna stood with her new husband to address her guests. "Thank you," she said, "for being so supportive." *But what if we hadn't been?* Louie stayed in town for a few days and then returned to California.

If I'd voiced my doubts. If I'd said, "What's the hurry?" If I knew what role a friend should have in a friend's life.

About a month later, I called Anna's house, to see how she was, and Anna's mother answered. She was there to get some things to take to the hospital. When Anna's labor had begun, a few days earlier, she told me, no one could find Louie, not at any of the phone numbers they had for him. One rang and rang—no answering machine; another had been disconnected.

"You've got to wonder," her mother said.

"How's the baby?" I asked.

"A girl. The doctors are checking her out. There might be some problems," she said. "We just have to see."

The baby did have problems, a whole complex of problems that the doctors couldn't neatly categorize or name. Undeveloped or impaired cranial nerves. Weak swallow response, so she had to be fed through a tube.

Potential breathing problems, so she had to have a tracheotomy. This allowed a tube to be inserted in her windpipe, through which Anna learned to suction secretions. Possible vision and/or hearing problems, the doctors said; possible mental retardation. She remained in the hospital after Anna went home. Anna visited daily, absorbing everything she could about her baby's condition and care.

Someone reached Louie after a few days, and he did come, but he stayed only a short time. Anna gave the baby the name that her mother had suggested. Liza.

If she hadn't . . . If he hadn't . . . If someone had . . .

FALL/WINTER

Anna didn't teach for several months. During those months, her life was hectic, death-defying—the repeated trips to the hospitals, the medical emergencies—so I hadn't visited, as people usually do when a new baby arrives. I had dropped off food, done grocery shopping for her, checked in by phone. But I couldn't get her out of my mind, the life change I'd witnessed from start to finish. The joyous plunge. The crash.

When Liza was three or four months old, Anna began teaching again, and I took my daughter for a lesson. Anna was still in the efficiency, so the baby's crib had been added to the room with the piano and the fold-out futon. Also in the room were machines that blinked and beeped—checking Liza's oxygen level, rate of breathing. We looked into the crib, and there she was: her asymmetrical face, her misshapen head. "The flat-headed princess of coo," Anna called her with a laugh.

I suppose I did my best to be positive—she was a baby, after all, so she still brought out the coo instinct in me—but I felt tentative about leaving my daughter, now eight years old, for her lesson. If I wasn't sure how to behave in this room, how could I expect her to be? Later, on our way home, she told me that she'd felt scared, and that Anna had to get up several times to care for Liza.

In one sense, my family's relationship with Anna was a business arrangement: My daughter was her piano student, and the atmosphere of her apartment hardly seemed optimal for learning. It was also true that my daughter's lessons and the practice generated more conflict than pleasure in our home. Quitting the lessons, then, would be practical, perhaps even understandable. But the relationship wasn't purely business, and quitting might imply an abandonment. Certainly, we could quit the lessons and continue to be friends, but I wasn't even sure how to be Anna's friend now. I didn't know what to say to her, or how much.

If I hadn't felt so stunned and scared at the way life could turn on a person. If I'd been able to see something positive in her fate. If it hadn't seemed like a headlong plunge into tragedy. If I'd known the rules for what to say and do.

When we stopped my daughter's piano lessons, Anna did not seem surprised or offended—a mere blip on the screen, I suppose, in relation to the rest of her life. But I did keep in touch with her. Sometimes I brought dinner, after Liza was asleep, and we sat in the dim room with the piano and the baby. She described the trips in the middle of the night to the hospital, the hospital stays, Liza's breathing problems, the surgeries. She described these events and the caregiving skills she was acquiring in a straightforward, energetic, almost entertaining way.

She told me that Louie wanted her to move to California with Liza, that she'd left the baby with her parents for a few days while she flew off for a trial visit. It had not gone well. Louie kept busy with his work most of the time (avoiding her?), and since he was no longer house-sitting for his friends, he lived in his shop (didn't he even have a home?). The irony that both lived in their "studios" was probably lost on them. Not that a car repair shop is like a piano studio. . . But if it had been a better time between them, if it hadn't been for the reality of Liza, perhaps they could have laughed at least a little.

But. The pressure of their circumstances, most likely, made laughter impossible, perhaps even made love impossible. She feared leaving her familiar surroundings and especially her parents, who lived close by and were the few people besides her who knew how to care for Liza. She feared that if she moved and the marriage with Louie didn't work, she'd be trapped in California for the legal proceedings. He accused her of being cold, but she didn't see how she could live there. When she got home, she filed for divorce. She didn't want child support from Louie. She didn't want anything from him.

These were the stories she told me as we sat in her room: the light low, the thrum of the compressor that helped Liza breathe.

Anna told me about her best friend from college, who lived in New York and had been maid of honor at her wedding. This friend no longer returned Anna's phone calls or letters. Not even the one in which Anna wrote that Liza had almost died. Before this, they had been in touch almost daily.

Anna told me that she had found a new lover—a friend of a friend. He was interesting, attentive, but then he had pulled away, become unavailable, always busy. Like me, others backed off.

The conversation returned to Liza. Anna had great hopes for her. Perhaps she dreamed that the cranial nerves could right themselves, that the confines of Liza's life could fall away like a cocoon. She found Liza a speech therapist and a physical therapist. She hired a nighttime nurse. But then the insurance company complained about the expenses.

I was a willing listener, glad that this was something I could give. But what most surprised me was that Anna was a willing listener too. Preoccupied but not self-absorbed. She wanted to hear about me: about my husband, my work, about lost friendships, lost lovers, disappointment. But she seemed manic at times, exhausted at others, and the variable energy levels, my uncertainty about whether to stay or go, the noises from Liza's crib—the high-pitched electronic beeps, the waxing and waning drone of the compressor—created an odd atmosphere. A cacophonous home.

"You're dealing with this so well," I said. "I don't know whether I could." This was the closest I came to saying what I felt.

"What choice do I have?" she asked. "Just lie down and die?"

The years passed, and I dipped in and out of Anna's life. I saw her at the farmers' market, or driving by, or out walking, occasionally at a music or theater event. Sometimes Liza was with her. She had become a little girl, with the same feathery brown hair as her mother, the same creamy skin, standing by her mother's side, holding her hand. She was growing tall, also like her mother, with long thin arms and legs, but she had plastic braces below the knee. One half of her forehead and one eye were more prominent than the other, the mouth at a slant. And she had a small plastic receptacle inserted in her throat for the suctioning. A deep silence, and absence, surrounded her.

"Hello, darling," I said when I saw her.

"Can you say hello?" Anna said to her.

Liza spoke, or verbalized: sounds I could not understand, words only very approximately articulated. In school, Anna told me, Liza worked with computers. She'd undergone a number of surgeries, including one—which Anna described as minor—to put weights in her eyelids so they would close fully.

We talked about the odd coincidence—that the best friends of Anna's parents had moved into the house next door to us. These new neighbors also became our friends, which gave all of us (Anna, her parents, the neighbors, my husband and I) new perspectives on each other. Through our windows, we saw Anna's parents come and go, visiting for dinner in our neighbors' beautiful garden. I tried to imagine what they might say to these friends about Anna, how they would tell her story, what anxieties they might express. More open with their friends than with their daughter?

If we'd known how much was at stake. If she didn't get so angry when we offered advice. If we had even known what advice to give.

For a time, I became one of Anna's students, eager, I thought, to benefit from her expertise. By then she had moved to a larger apartment, and the piano had a room of its own. Liza was usually asleep when I came, though Anna occasionally had to check on her. I didn't mind that, I told myself. What I didn't like was the feeling of incompetence, of my clumsy fingers, stumbling over the keys. Then my father got sick, and in my preoccupation, I couldn't sit at the piano at all. I never officially stopped; I simply didn't schedule another lesson. Anna never said anything about it either.

A year or so later, my husband became her piano student. By then, she had moved into a small house. Louie's mother had come into some money and given Anna enough for the down payment.

Sometimes, when my husband went for his lesson, Liza was still awake, and he played with her, silly games, peek-a-boo. He came home and talked about her progress, her ability to interact. He told me how nice their little house was. That the doctors were going to remove the tube from her throat and see how that would go—a great breakthrough.

Over the weeks, though, Jim and Anna had problems scheduling lessons because of Liza's bedtime and Jim's work and commute. Some weeks the lesson time was uncertain, and he waited at home for Anna to call. This uncertainty was sometimes an annoyance, but the real problem was that he didn't care for the music he was learning. He told Anna, and she thought he might be happier with a different teacher—a jazz pianist she knew. Then, too, our neighbors, the best friends of Anna's parents, moved away, to California. And so those two connections with her ended. Not that I forgot about her, just that we didn't have convenient reasons anymore to maintain the friendship.

If I knew how to behave with her. If her life didn't spark so much discomfort. If I didn't feel I had to do something to make it better, to solve it. If I knew what would hurt and what wouldn't.

SPRING

I was out running, and I saw Anna, in her car. She waved and pulled over to the curb.

"How *are* you?" I asked. The obligatory opener.

She didn't make a pretense, not even for a minute: "Bad," she said. She held the steering wheel and looked at the windshield. "I've ruined my life," she said. She gave me a tight teeth-clenched smile. "I had so much promise, and I threw it away." She stared straight ahead: "I've foreclosed the possibility of ever having adult companionship."

She spoke in fragments: A man she met. He broke up with her in February. Couldn't deal with Liza. And Liza. She couldn't deal with first-grade, the inclusion program. She needed to switch to special ed at a different school. And Anna kept thinking about an old boyfriend—one she had before Louie. He'd been a perfectly fine person, but she broke up with him, thinking she could do better. *(If she'd only . . .)*

"Do you have anyone to help you with these feelings?"

"Yeah," she said. "But a therapist can only do so much. What can someone do about a wasted life?"

Find a way to make it seem not wasted, I supposed.

"I remember that night we had dinner in Greek Town," she said, "and Jim tried to warn me against Louie."

"I remember it too," I said.

"I wish I'd listened."

"Sometimes he comes on a little strong," I said. "It can make people uncomfortable."

"I think it's good that he does that," she said. "I just wish I'd listened."

I'll have to tell Jim, I thought. *It will make him feel good*, but then I realized, what's to feel good about?

A long pause. "I've thought of giving her up," she said. "It's hard to find a placement though—because of the feeding tube. And then there are long waiting lists—three, four, five years for the good places. Then there's foster care," she said. "But I couldn't do that to her." Cars whizzed by. "If she stays with me, though, the whole thing is ruined." I didn't say a word. "I'm sorry," she said. "This is so embarrassing. I've been such a fool."

No, no, I said. But fool/not fool, I was still terrified by what had happened to her.

If she hadn't thought she could do better than that earlier boyfriend. If she hadn't loved the Beethoven. If her throat had been sorer. If the conductor hadn't seen her in the crowded lobby. If the telegraphed "there's trouble" had been a warning and not an enticement. If she'd listened to Jim in Greek Town. If Liza had been . . . normal.

"Are you playing piano?" I asked.
   "No," she said. "Not now."
   "Are your parents around to help?"
   "Yes," she said, "a little."
She asked about my husband, his lessons, my daughter. I felt relieved to shift from her life; maybe she did too. So I told her this and that—how much my husband enjoyed his new teacher, how difficult it was to be the parent of a teenager. Good news, bad news. But it all sounded to me like prattling, and potential insults, injuries.
   "What I'd give," she said, "to have problems like dealing with a teenaged daughter."
   "Can I do anything?"
   "Not really."
   "I know," I said, "What if I bring dinner? A big pot of something."
   "Okay," she said.
   "I could stay and we could talk."
   "Liza goes to sleep so late now," she said. "It's impossible."
   "Well, then I'll just drop off the food."
   "Okay," she said.

A few days later, I went to her house with food: a huge container of vegetable chili, cheddar for grating on top, and a bag of pistachios. Liza was asleep, and we sat in the living room. She looked good—trim and young and fit—though she didn't believe me when I said this. I asked if she felt any better since I saw her in the car that day, and she said no. She told me that this morning, after getting Liza off to school, she'd crawled back into bed. A bad choice, she said. Because once she's in, what's to get her out? No piano students until much later in the day. All those empty hours. She kept asking herself the same questions: *How did she . . . ? What made her . . . ? Why had she felt so desperate to have a child?*

Around her voice, the house was quiet, and the light was dim. The piano stood across from us, against the living room wall. Still sleek and glossy. "Sounds like you've gone over this material quite a bit." Down into the dark murky roots.

"Oh, yes," she said. "It's definitely become an unwelcome guest."

"Do you know other people in your situation who you can talk to?"

"There's no one like me," she said with a tight smile I'd seen before. "Most people who have children like Liza also have partners."

"You have an important story to tell," I said. "Some day you'll find a way to tell it."

"Like those people who go on the road and say 'don't drink and drive or you'll end up like me?'" Again, the tight smile. It wasn't meant as funny, but I couldn't help laughing, just a little. She's so smart.

She said, "You know those people who say everything happens for a reason?"

"Yeah."

Well she couldn't think of any reason for this—for what Liza has been through, for what she'd been through—though she'd certainly tried to find one. "It's not like I had to learn compassion," she said. And she told me about elementary school, when she was the only kid to stand up for a ridiculed classmate. She described an article she read in the paper, about a minister whose daughter had died tragically, who said he'd lost his faith after the death, who said how hard it would be for him to find his way back to belief.

"About time," Anna said. "All these years he's probably been counseling his parishioners to hold to their faith. About time he learned."

If she hadn't had a passionate fling. But many women have passionate flings. *If she hadn't gotten pregnant.* But many women have unplanned pregnancies. *If she'd terminated the pregnancy.* But many women, even unmarried ones, allow an unplanned pregnancy to run its course. *If she'd had genetic screening.* But many women her age forgo genetic screening. And genetic screening can't detect or explain everything. *Then if she'd chosen a better partner.* But many marriages fail, even when the partners know each other well, when they're "better" people. And many partnerships founder under the weight of a child who has a disability. *If she hadn't run into such a heart-wrenching, unearned, soul-testing stretch of bad luck on bad luck on bad luck.*

I remember the chalk drawings I used to see on the sidewalk outside Anna's old apartment building. I was certain Anna had drawn them—the pink and yellow and green outlines of umbrellas and guitars and musical notes and trees. I was certain, too, that Anna had drawn them for Liza, with labels, so she might learn. I could easily picture the two, seated on the concrete step—a mother and daughter—heads bent over the drawings. A shaft of sunlight.

"Yellow umbrella," Anna says. Easy to draw; hard to say.

"Lel la la lell la," says Liza.

"Very good," says Anna. ◼

Dam

Nicole Walker

My mother does this:

She bites her pinkie finger when she's upset to make herself not cry.

She drinks Chardonnay.

She always says what she means even if that means telling my friend Todd that she doesn't like the red pants he's wearing or my friend Jeff that all writers had tortured lives and if they didn't they can't be real writers or telling the waiter that the music is too f-ing loud.

She doesn't swear except to say god or damn or jesus. Usually in the same phrase.

She expresses her disgust by throwing her head to the left and pushing a *th* sound out from between her lips.

Sometimes the head shakes back to the right. Sometimes eye rolling accompanies the sound. If her shoulders get involved in a sort of humping shrug, her whole body is involved and you know you've committed a seriously egregious faux pas, like saying it's OK to put a shoe with gum stuck on it in the freezer to freeze the gum to get it off. Something like that may even make her shoulder twitch.

The main lesson at the dinner table was restraint. Singing was prohibited. As were elbows on the table. You must cut your salad greens into manageable bites. Eating too quickly or talking with food in your mouth—not allowed. Nor was salting your food before tasting it. Dad would always tell the cautionary tale of the guy who was interviewing for a job at IBM and they took him out to lunch. The guy salted his food before he tasted it and did not get the job. Apparently because he didn't look before he leapt or made decisions before he had all the facts. Or they thought he'd get high blood pressure and the cost to insure him would be too high. He never mentioned whether ordering a glass of wine before the other guys could have cost him the job as well. When I was interviewing for jobs, seven different people warned me to wait until my hosts ordered wine. Then I could drink up.

After we were done eating, my sisters and I had to ask to be excused and take our plates to the dishwasher. All good lessons, in the end, I think. We ended up to be relatively well-mannered people, conscious of how we appeared to others. My dad, though, had a problem with mustard. Maybe he had a problem with condiments in general, but in particular, whenever he'd get mustard on the side of his mouth, my mother's shoulder would twitch and eyes would roll. Jesus, she'd swear, and reach over to rub the offensive yellow off his face, like she was scraping gum off a shoe.

It was one of the few things she felt she had over him. He made the money, was supposedly the "smart" one, did the taxes, drafted blueprints for the hot tub room. But she outclassed him with a refined etiquette and a distaste for mustard.

⌐

The building of the Glen Canyon Dam began in 1956, when my mother was ten. By the time I was born, it was finished and finally nearing capacity—3,700 feet above sea level. The Glen Canyon Dam website boasts that "[t]he controversy surrounding the construction of the dam is often cited as the beginning of the modern-day environmental movement."

Cited reasons for said environmental movement:

Changes

Glen Canyon Dam has created a new Colorado River. Before the dam was built, water temperatures in the river fluctuated seasonally from 80°F (26°C) in the summer to near freezing in the winter. Now, the water temperature below the dam averages 46°F (7°C) year-round. The Colorado River was once filled with silt and sediment. Now, the river deposits its load of silt as it enters Lake Powell near Hite, Utah. Water released from the dam is clear and the Colorado River is muddy only when downstream tributaries contribute sediment.

As the habitat has changed, so have plant and animal species. Native fish, unable to survive in the colder water, have left the river. Five species are now endangered. But this new habitat now supports a healthy trout population. Before Glen Canyon Dam, spring run-offs built and rebuilt beaches and sandbars and scoured away riverside vegetation. Now, sediment is trapped in Lake Powell and the dam prevents high river flows. Riparian vegetation now grows along river banks, creating habitat for mammals, birds, amphibians, insects, and reptiles.

http://www.nps.gov/glca/watergo.htm

Who would argue with these changes? Green grasses? Riparian riverbanks? Five species of trout to fish for instead of the near-extinct chub. Who wants to eat a fish called chub, sucker, or squawfish anyway? Whoever heard of Chug Amandine? These changes confirm what we value—constancy (in water temperature), greenery (in idylls), an end to flooding (predictability), and clear, see-through water (cleanliness). Glen Canyon Dam made a little slice of heaven beneath it. The dirty Colorado has been reformed. Once, the Colorado River menaced seven states and Mexico with its unreliable, unproductive, silty water.

The effects weren't all so ideal. The silt that used to be distributed throughout those seven states and Mexico is now backing up against the dam. The turbines move more slowly every year. The river used to empty into the Gulf of California. Now it serves those seven states and Mexico with potable water and some electricity, but reaches its delta in a mere trickle. As the river ends further and further from the shore, you'll be able to hear the clanging of empty pots as the seven states, plus Mexico, clamor for water.

When I was eight and my twin sisters five, our family and another family, the McDonalds, rented a houseboat on Lake Powell, the lake that Glen Canyon Dam makes. We five kids were already in our life jackets, waiting for the *Eagle One*—the houseboat that would take us to Rainbow Bridge, to Anasazi ruins up Moki Canyon. Our boat's wake would lap against 2,000 miles of red-beach shoreline. Blue against orange are savage colors together. The *Eagle One* that we had reserved was a deluxe houseboat—two stories, two bathrooms, and a waterslide attached to the back. Unfortunately, by the time we got down to pick it up, it was sinking toward the bottom of the lake.

We took a dinghy out to check it out. A corner of the *Eagle One* still angled out of the water—you could tell by the smoothness of the paint and the purpose with which it seemed to sink that this had been the nicest boat in all of Bullfrog Marina. Sandy McDonald wanted to get a closer look. He asked my mom to steer the dinghy. She'd never driven a boat before—she pulled too hard to the left and the boat went in fast circles around the *Eagle*

One. Sandy took over controls. Good thing we were wearing our life jackets already.

We had to drive 95 miles south to Wahweap, the marina near Page, Arizona, to pick up the only houseboat left in all of Lake Powell. This houseboat was not so deluxe. It was a blue, bargelike thing with a camper kitchen and only one bathroom and beds that pulled out over the kitchen table, over the pilot's seat, over the lavatory. In fact, the whole thing smelled like one big floating toilet to me. Every time I flushed, I would turn to look down the drain and see the blue lake opening up like a big eye. I felt bad for peeing on the eye. I felt bad for everything that I imagined was at the bottom of the lake— sunken houseboats and toilets and their attendant disposables, batteries, and outboard motors. Even though the water is more than 500 feet deep in some places, I could hear the sound of metal on metal. I rushed out of the bathroom to see if we had run across the sunken *Eagle One*, but it was just my mom, standing at the smelly fridge, Lysol in hand. She was hitting the can on the side of the door to see if she could get more to come out.

Everybody else was changing into their suits to go swimming. Sandy stopped the boat as my dad watched from the deck, drink in hand. We jumped into the sun-soaked lake. We floated in our faded life jackets, felt the air bubble up by our ears, evaporating, and smelled the diesel of other boats wafting by.

Over the sounds of motors, I could hear my dad asking Sandy if he could drive. I could hear my mother say if he wanted to drive the boat, he shouldn't have drunk an entire bottle of wine before dinner. Sandy tried to explain that as a meteorologist, he had more experience steering boats. Dad was a good swimmer, Sandy explained. Maybe he should keep an eye on the kids. My dad emerged from the cabin to watch us play in the water, a new drink in his hand.

We never vacationed with another family after that.

Filling Lake Powell didn't only erase petroglyphs, wind impressions, and water expressions, it erased the names of places too. Kane Creek. Hidden Passage. Dungeon Canyon. Last Chance Canyon. Tapestry Wall. Hite Ferry. The places may still exist under the murky water. What strikes me most about the photos I've seen of before Glen Canyon was filled is how varied the landscape is. Some of the photos remind me of other national parks like Zion or Bryce Canyon or Capitol Reef with their narrow canyons and red turrets and wind-painted rock walls. Other pictures remind me more of what the Mississippi River must have looked like more than 200 years ago when there were no levies or locks or other flooding and transportation management plans. The Colorado River, wide and meandering, looks like it has the patience, if not necessarily the power, to carve the Grand Canyon.

Even if they take down the dam, which some people want, there would still be water left behind, a large bathtub ring, and all the *Eagle Ones* that had ever sunk. Congress would never fund removing the dam completely, only letting the water sink to its dead-pool level—below any of the out-flow tunnels. And while many of the canyons underneath have changed, the promise is that desert vegetation, wildlife, and sediment deposits will restore the canyons to their original beauty. Some things are permanent. Sometimes even water.

Growing up, we lived behind a mortuary, a cemetery, and a Mormon church. The prospect of death seemed to follow us throughout suburbia. Even the Mormon Church, which had been built on a lot that promised to be kept "Open Space," carried the specter of death. To my dad it meant patriarchal oversight, judgment, and offended his rationalistic atheism. To my mom it meant patriarchal oversight, abuse, Republicans, and offended her cosmopolitan sensibilities. When a mother would show up with six kids in tow, the oldest looking to be seven or eight, she'd shake her head and whisper "birth control" under her breath.

But when we lived behind the cemetery, no one complained about the neighbors. They were quiet and accommodating. The cemetery was one of the modern kind where no headstones stuck up so the lawn mowers could drive their Toros from a chair without needing to edge or weed-whack or turn until they reached the fence that ran behind our house or one of our neighbors'.

Right behind our house, a small reservoir collected mountain runoff, enough to keep the cemetery green all summer long. A tall chain-link fence surrounded the concrete-reinforced pool, making it look as sculpted and manmade as the flat headstones that surrounded it. But maybe it was a natural pool, fed by a spring rather than a dammed-up little stream. The street we lived on was named Silver Lake. Maybe the reservoir had once been a beautiful shimmering lake. As I learned later, there are pockets of natural ponds all over Salt Lake Valley. Some are filled with mountain runoff but others seem to have gathered in their depression with rain and snowmelt and a rupture in the aquifer. The cemetery's reservoir must have been made of the last kind because the dirt I dug in the backyard to build castles and moats felt more like soil than sand, more drenched than desert —maybe it's why they built the cemetery there (thank God we moved before the movie *Poltergeist* came out and all those dead bodies emerged in the swimming pool)—the houses would have sunk in the swamplike ground.

Plus, a natural natatorium would explain the salamanders. I don't know how old I was when I discovered them or how I convinced my younger sisters to crawl down into the window wells to dig for them with me, but during the summer, I would spring up from out of the tin-lined trenches that kept land from house with a salamander a day. As my mom canned peaches and pears, apricots, and pickles all summer, I would charge out with an empty Mason jar and back in with one full of a brown-speckled amphibian. Mom would punch holes in the gold lid to let in air and warn me to get some grass and water so it wouldn't starve or die of thirst. I'd take the salamander back outside and play Wizard of Oz with him. I'd put the captive salamander at the top of the path my dad had dug into the wall of dirt that separated our yard from the cemetery. And then I would follow that path, singing that direction-filled song the only direction the path led. The salamander was the wizard because he would have disappeared by the time I made it to the end of the song. I swore I'd screwed the lid on tight, but then, Mom was the last one to have touched it.

If salamanders were coveted, then the frogs were more so. My dad and I would sit out on the back patio and he'd list constellations and we'd listen to the frogs croaking from inside the fence of the reservoir. The crickets chimed in with frogs and the stars kept their names for the duration of the melody. My dad tried to explain about triangulation and how we knew how far away certain stars were but the stars seemed closer to me than the frogs did. I was eight years old and I had never seen a frog. I'd seen a star. I could draw a triangle.

I convinced my friend Kim, who lived three houses up, that if salamanders were so easy to catch, frogs couldn't be much harder. It was accessing them that was the difficult part. The frogs had smartly cordoned themselves off from Mason-jar-bearing kids. But the fence was not perfect. In one section of the perimeter, the metal had been wrenched up, leaving a gap between the fence and the ground just big enough for nine-year-old girls to slide through. I handed Kim the jar and tucked down to slide in first. I got my head through no problem but my shoulder got stuck on the wires. I tried to slide forward. I really wanted a frog. I tried to slide back out. I really didn't want to be stuck. Or to get caught. I pushed and pulled and cut my arm on one of the links but there was no going anywhere. The frogs had eluded me.

Kim went to get her dad. Her dad went to get my mom. Kim's dad lifted the fence while my mom dragged me out. Of all the stupid things, she kept saying. You could have drowned, she kept saying. I'm not sure how I could have drowned if I was caught up on that fence like a scarecrow. The worst that could have happened, besides getting caught and getting no frogs, was that I could have been stuck there like the one time the salamander hadn't escaped from the jar. I didn't show this one to my mom and the air holes I had made were mostly cosmetic. I'd left him in the sun in the jar for a few days and he'd turned all white and desiccated. His flaky skin made my own skin itch.

The cervix is an amazing body part. Unlike the heart's perpetual motion, it moves only occasionally. Yet like the heart, as part of the uterus, this is one of the most powerful muscles in the female human body. The cervix has the power to hold in a nine-pound baby and its attendant placenta and amniotic sac while at its weakest— the closer a pregnant woman gets to labor, the thinner the cervix becomes. Some inverse relation occurs that when the unpregnant body needs to let sperm in or menstrual fluid out, this strong muscle moves only millimeters to allow passage but when the up-to-40-pounds-per-inch pressure weighs most heavily, it stays zipped tight like a corset. Until it performs its next miracle.

Once the water breaks, the cervix goes from a pair of tight, puckered lips to gaping mouth in a matter of hours. From the size of a gaping mouth to the span of a gopher hole, the cervix dilates in another hour. From there to a breach large enough to fit a baby's head can happen in a few minutes. Very few other parts of the anatomy change so fast, so violently, so pro-ductively as the cervix. The heart beats or it doesn't. The blood flows or not. Over a lot of time, skin sags, fat cells grow. But the cervix, handy elas-tic that it is, stretches wide enough to turn a body inside out. And then it turns back again into little puckered lips.

It used to snow a lot more. We walked to school in a tunnel of snowplow. We could barely see over what the shovelers had stacked between the side-walk and the curb. When it snowed that much, my mom usually picked me and the twins up from school. As we drove interminably slowly through the 20-mile-an-hour school zone, my mom started yelling at the kids on the sidewalk ahead who were alternately throwing snowballs at the cars that

passed and at a small kid, Jeff, in my class that I played with after school
sometimes but rarely at recess, in public. The snowballs burst against the
metal of the cars. They bounced hard and small off of Jeff's back as if they
had rocks in them. My mom yelled "Stop it" again. Of course, the kids
couldn't hear her. The windows rolled up against the 20-degree cold. But
they could hear her when she pulled over and got out of the car.

"What in the hell do you think you're doing? You could break a window. You could hurt that kid. Poke an eye out. Give him an aneurysm."
The kids squinted at her, snowballs in hand. My mother walked over to Jeff
and rose up to her full height—which was almost six feet tall. She blocked
Jeff. She could have blocked six of him.

"Go ahead, throw." Her eyes grew thin.

The kids scowled at her, but unconvincingly. One of the kids turned to
look at me. Threatened "the next day." I shrugged right at them.

"Throw."

The kids ran away. She scuttled Jeff into our car. She didn't stop yelling.
"I don't know who the hell those kids think they are. I'm going to drive
you guys home every day while it snows. I'm calling their mothers. They
throw one more goddamned snowball at anyone . . ."

She didn't finish the threat. I think Jeff was more scared of her than of
the kids with snowballs. As she drove home, I rolled my window down and
glared at the running kids as we drove by. I wanted to yell "goddamn" at
them like my mother had, but I didn't. I was sitting safely behind her. I
could have, but I wasn't as strong. ■

Final: Comprehensive, Roughly

Desirae Matherly

NAME _____

Final: Comprehensive, Roughly

I. MATCHING

Instructions: *Using what you know about words and the way they work, match the word in column A with the word in column B with which it shares the most in common. Write the matching word beside its mate in column A. If you suffer from test anxiety, go directly to Part IV.*

A		B
crypt	_____	bear
commentary	_____	stream
quality	_____	class
bare	_____	selection
soul	_____	quantity
Descartes	_____	momentary
current	_____	cryptic
election	_____	currency
channel	_____	sole
class	_____	Dehorse

II. FILL IN THE BLANK

Instructions: *Fill in the missing word, number, or phrase.*

1. _____ is too much to pay for one week's worth of groceries.

2. I consider myself a(n) _____.

3. When I spin in place with my eyes closed, I feel _____.

III. TRUE OR FALSE

Instructions: *With a magic marker, blot out the statements you consider to be true. In ten words or less, classify the statements you consider to be false in the space at the bottom of this page.*

You can't always get what you want.

I've been a miner for a heart of gold.

I was sinking deep in sin, far from the peaceful shore.

There's pow'r, pow'r, wonder-workin' pow'r in the blood of the lamb.

The fool on the hill sees the sun going down.

I'll fly away.

It took me four days to hitchhike from Saginaw.

You know me, I'm your friend, I'm your pusherman.

I've flown the house of freezing steel.

You've got to pick up every stitch.

I've seen him in the watch-fires of a hundred circling camps.

IV. MULTIPLE CHOICE

Instructions: *Choose the best answer*

1. _____ A better title for this exam would be:
   a. Shaking the Tree of Knowledge, Seeing What Falls
   b. Literati Pedagogico: The Final Exam as Literary Genre
   c. _____

2. _____ Where is America?
   a. East of Eden

   b. Under the Table and Dreaming
   c. Below the Salt
   d. On Top of Old Smokey
   e. In a Prepositional Phrase
   f. Over the Edge
   g. $y = mx + b$

3. _____ The Poverty Line:
   a. divided an estimated 12.7 percent of the households in the United States from the other 87.3 percent in 2004.
   b. termed a *threshold*, is set at \$9,570 per year in 2005 for one person living in the United States.
   c. may lie close to what some Wal-Mart associates earn, after paying health insurance deductibles.
   d. equates to \$797.50 a month, \$184.03 a week, \$26.21 a day, or \$1.09 per hour of life in a year.
   e. is still more than what the majority of the world lives on, with poverty estimates worldwide usually measured as less than a U.S. dollar a day, relative to local economy.
   f. is an abstraction, regardless of the Dept. of Health and Human Services and the Census Bureau.
   g. is a convenient organizing concept for policy makers.
   h. does not inspire compassion among those in the upper 87.3 percent.
   i. is all of the above, and more.

4. _____ Art is:
   a. true
   b. beautiful

V. TRANSLATION

Instructions: *Working collaboratively, find the English equivalences of the following.*

1. à la belle étoile:

2. alter idem:

3. Selbstbildnis:

4. El llanto:

VI. ESSAY RESPONSE

Instructions: *Using yourself as a primary source, and the lives of other people you love as secondary sources, construct a 3–5 paragraph response to three of the following questions. You may not use a separate sheet of paper, and your answer must appear directly below the question. Therefore, you must write tinily. Please don't ask me questions of clarification, as I feel that I have made this exam perfectly clear. In addition to the three elective responses, everyone must answer #4.*

1. I was in a high school trigonometry class when I first realized I had something on my mind that I needed to get down on paper. I had made the connection between two words: *Revolution* and *Evolution.* I spent the entire class covertly filling up the margins of a failed exam on the Cartesian coordinate system, explaining how the two words shared a connection deeper than nine letters. I don't know what I intended to do with my thought of that day, but I know that I did not perceive the writing of that moment as important enough for anyone else to read. Earlier that year I had begun to keep a journal, or more precisely a diary, whose pages I filled with utter drivel—"Went to the mall today, didn't see J. there," or "I love J.! I wish I could tell him how I feel." Now that J. exists only as a character I had mostly invented, I wish I could shake the 16-year-old me and explain to her the importance of time, and how little there is to write in. She should not have wasted those two years on a diary whose pages succumbed to the tortuous fancies of her teenage heart. She might have actually read that volume of Aristotle she checked out of the library, or she might have finished *War and Peace* and thought about it, or she could have at the very least noted some of her finer thoughts, which I am sure she must have had . . . the shape of her day, or the feeling of her body as it pressed out into the world. What are some of your finer thoughts for today, the ones which you will not write down?

2. We know that Montaigne read voraciously, and that his margins became overfilled, and it was because of their surplus ideas that his library's pages bred more pages, and his writing drifted from the margins into blank space, empty counties for his ideas, which were utterly original hamlets. We value this originality, his commentary on the thinkers before and of his age, because we can only hope to experience the world as uniquely as he did, though most of us have no inclination to put down those thoughts which are profitless. But if we did record those profitless realizations, we might

find something more valuable in them than either money or fame. If we were to follow the private thoughts of our days, we might find that they accrue into a sort of publication, and our words into a type of commentary. When we shout at the TV for showing us visions of idiocy or cruelty, when we mutter to ourselves about our neighbor's unkempt yard or barking dog, we are in the realm of our judgments, each active moment an evaluation of our experiences which we must have constructed in private, or with the help of those we converse with (that is, if we haven't simply bought them ready-made at the store of ideas). Somehow an inner dialogue is shaped that we appear to have no outlet for unless we channel it into our work. Ours is no less a philosophy because it is personal; the ideal is not so awfully separate from the practical. What better work then, than to be pundits of our own lives?

3. The day I began to set these thoughts down, I decided to not take a shower. I brushed my hair, which I never do, and tied it back in a scarf. I made oatmeal for my husband and myself while my son played on a blanket on the floor. We sliced up bananas to have on the oats, and sprinkled cinnamon, sugar, and raisins on top of that. This was a good moment, though I did listen to the news, to someone else's commentary on that day, which was *never* just about oatmeal and babies and cinnamon. While I ate, I philosophized at my husband, who patiently nodded without arguing with me. He went to work, and I washed dishes, did some light grading, and filed some papers away. But my most important act was the smallest, and took the lesser part of my morning. I took the scrap papers I had jotted spare ideas on, and recorded them in my journal—putting them back for the lean times to come. Now my baby is a four-year-old child, my husband and I have divorced, and I live a day's drive, *three years away* (the greater distance) from that morning. Still, I have these notes. Can you describe the least wasteful process for cooking these ideas into a dish worth consuming?

4. The most important political act of any artist is to draw the middle edge of public opinion away from itself. Is this statement true? If you think so, explain in your own words how the homogenous compensate for their banality by creating the appearance of happiness, wholeness, difference, and creativity, and how poverty has become a romanticized ideal for those who collect raw and beautiful ideas. If it is not true that the artist draws the middle edge of public opinion away from itself, explain in 50 words or less why

the only *safe* and ambitiously artistic citizen in a selfish society paints pretty pictures.

5. I used to believe that there was a hell in the center of the earth where people went when they were bad and died before apologizing. Since then, I have taken geology. Have you heard the story of the samurai who visits the Buddhist monk, and asks him where hell is?

   a. If you *have not* heard the story, tell me the joke about the man with the parrot who goes into the bar (you know, the one with the three blondes, the Catholic, the Jew, the Black Man, the Gypsy, the Indian Chief, the Hindu, or the Feminist) instead.

   b. If you *do know the story about the samurai*, relate to me the version you have heard, and be specific. In my version of the story, the monk scoffs at the samurai and says, "Why should I tell a stupid jackass like you where hell is?" to which the samurai rises, face on fire, drawing his sword. At this the monk says, "THAT, is hell." As the samurai lowers his sword, and sinks to his knees in realization, the monk quietly remarks, "and THIS is heaven."

6. Should Texas be granted diplomatic relations with (the) US?

7. One of the more serious and secretive responsibilities of the teacher is grading his or her students. I have always despised this aspect of my job. "Grading" is something we do for those things which are related to consumption: tobacco, dairy products, and restaurants. A friend of mine, a fellow essayist and teacher, introduced me to a website called *pickaprof.com*. Myself and many other instructors I know are listed there, along with the averages of the grades we've given, reviews, and other tidbits interesting to students wanting information about professors in advance. For a long time, I was one of only two English instructors at my school who had an average of 4.0 in the grades they give their undergraduate students. This fact still embarrasses me, and makes me feel that I have wronged my students by my acceptance of their work. Even though this representation of my grading history levels out A minuses, it is roughly true, though I know that a good deal of data has been omitted. Looking through my master file, I see that over a period of five years, I distributed five F's, one D+, one C+, one C, and nine B-range grades. But I've always felt violated by Pick-A-

Prof!'s evaluation of my teaching. Among the more private subjects people may keep to themselves—income, religion, politics, aesthetic desires, fears, regrets—how we evaluate the work we do must be the most private of all. Our labor transmits our secrets, if anyone would care to listen. My grading (of writing) is based upon originality, effort, sense of humor, serious revision, and philosophical maturity. These things are not quantifiable. To the contrary, when I taught Introduction to Logic as a graduate student in philosophy, my students' grades were like a bell-curve buffet. My grade book revealed A's as rare as chocolate-coated strawberries, B's like the wine that disappears early, C's like the cheese we expect. And the F's—try as I might, despite my elegantly honest multiple choice exams, even for a final that required them to demonstrate an ability to complete logical proofs, my F's were like napkins that every one of my students carried discreetly beneath their plates, hoping no one would notice. And it could have been that there was only one way to classify categorical propositions, because no one real lived in them anyway; "Mexican Hat Dancers" were simply those nouns that lived in a Venn diagram to the exclusion of "Griffins" or "Unicorns," and these metaphorical populations would never mingle or converge except syntactically. (Choose C or D if A or B seems unlikely, True or False *can* answer your question, and yes, your grade will be expressed as a decimal.) Logic and math seem honest enough I suppose, at least going into them. Spelling was that way for me, long ago, until I learned about the effect of Norman French on Old English. But then, there is a decay in American English when we must rely on quantitative expressions to describe qualitative relationships between people, places, things, or ideas. When I say *class*, do you think of tax brackets, school divisions, or that certain strain of self-respect that was once believed to accompany nobility, but cannot be purchased for the love of money without cheapening it?

8. I spent seven years of my life in a trailer, three of those in Sinking Creek Trailer Park. Lot rent there was $75 a month. There were probably around 30 trailers in that park, and the landlord, Mr. Fisher, harvested almost $2,250 a month. Mr. Fisher lived behind the park, on the other side of his cornfield. He was a farmer, so he allowed his tenants some garden space, which in hindsight is remarkable. For three years I lived in Nelsonville, a mostly dilapidated Victorian town that chokes a major highway (Rt. 33) running between the Capit(o/a)l of Ohio and the brick-street college town of Athens, which is 85.2 percent "white" according to the 2004 census. There are few gardens in Nelsonville. Our house payment during that time

was $373.21, something my husband and I could afford. It was $100 less than the two-bedroom apartment we used to rent in The Plains, which is approximately seven miles southwest of Nelsonville. It seems ironic to me that a house payment could be cheaper than rent, especially since I estimate that I threw away $30,600 over the time I spent as a renter before my marriage, which was about six years. That amount was 72 percent of the cost of the house my husband and I lived in, and I have nothing to show for those years, except expired leases that outline what our finite freedoms were as renters. The people who lived across the street (and beside us) were renters, among them the bleached-blond woman who was on a well-known talk show several years ago. Her husband proposed to her after he had exposed his butt-crack to national TV while pummeling her unfortunate boyfriend on stage. This woman, and the family that lived next to her in the duplex, were slovenly, loud, rude, vulgar, and not at all the abstract and invisible "poor" that I like to imagine living in economic theories I am sensitive to. Someone paid the rent, but who? I remember checking the HUD website for income limits in Athens County, Ohio, and finding that my husband and I were considered "very low income." When I would peep out through the Venetian blinds at my neighbors, I often wondered what made our families different, and what "class" really must have meant to that sad, overripe Victorian street. TWO-PART QUESTION: What is it about my former neighbors that I am trying to escape, and where is hell?

9. Sinking Creek Trailer Park was in Johnson City, Tennessee, about one mile (as the crow flies) from the grocery store where we bought our food, which is directly across from the controversial regional landfill, which is 500 yards away from the Hourglass Lounge (a "gentlemen's" club a.k.a. topless bar), which is 500 more yards away from the Keystone Projects, which is a good mile (the crow tells me) from the ostensible center of Johnson City, whose northern border has been developing rapidly for the past ten years or more. Cow pastures have been parsed into luxury home lots to house the influx of doctors into Johnson City, which grows because of the thriving medical industry there, and the lawyers are close behind, gypsies that they are. It seems that the only people who stay in one place are the people who are trapped where they began. But for the nomadic professional, compassion doesn't grow while just passing through, trying the dials on the radio to find something tolerably local. I might as well mention that the main radio station in Johnson City is WQUT (101.5 FM), a station that plays mostly classic rock from the '70s. My stepfather had a huge record

collection from the '70s, so between WQUT and my stepfather, much of my musical education involved '70s rock. I still listen to '70s rock because it relaxes me. This is because I only remember the latter half of the seventies from the perspective of a young child, and the former half through my mom's high school memories. When I find myself humming songs to which I have forgotten the words, they are usually '70s tunes, and only recently, '80s pop, or its short-lived inheritor/antithesis, '90s alternative. Despite this transdecade auditory education, I only remember the words to Baptist hymns, as I was inundated with them for the first 15 years of my life, until I became old enough to resist going to services and no one argued. Music is an art form available to everyone, so it must educate our aesthetic sensibilities in ways we rarely consider significant. For that matter, magazines must do the same, if only for their ubiquitous presences in the grocery lines where we find ourselves corralled for minutes every week (unless we pay someone to deliver our groceries, unless we go to the natural foods store or the farmer's market . . . *unless*). Magazines spread us out at the same time they spread themselves open for us. Do we take the test to see how sexy we are, do we measure up to the idols offered us, do we . . . but I get ahead of myself. THREE-PART QUESTION: When we reflect on what art most influenced us, what do we remember? Do we recall the Titians and the Bachs, or the *Vogues* and the Stones most, or, if it is holy art that we have a taste for, where are our stripes? Specifically, what are the best dressed gods wearing this year?

10. A wise teacher once asked me, how would philosophy have been different if it had followed the manner of Montaigne instead of Descartes? Descartes' dualisms all arise from his ability to say "I think, therefore I exist." That he *can* say this referentially, of himself, amuses him enough to follow out the deductive consequences of this primal truth. We must have a mind and body that are separate. Not to belittle Descartes' realization, but big fucking deal. I have been realizing that "I exist" since grade school. Sometimes it would just hit me, in the schoolroom cafeteria, or in class, at my desk. I would suddenly feel unattached from my surroundings, look around, notice that everyone else was paying attention to the teacher, or doodling, or passing notes and whispering—and I would have my existential moment in utter loneliness and silence. I usually wanted to jump up and shout "Hey! I exist!," but the fear of punishment kept me quiet. In the lunchroom, when I would say, "I'm having the funny feeling like I'm alive," friends would roll their eyes and say I was weird. After high school,

whenever I met a potential boyfriend, and we would be lying somewhere peaceful and sweet, I would ask him if he had ever felt himself existing, you know, in a *serious way*. (Like all time stops and everything in you becomes still though the rest of the universe keeps moving—and there you are, just existing along, and you can do anything you want to with this realization, anything at all.) A Buddhist might say to prolong this moment as long as possible, because it is a moment of pure and perfect clarity. If we could have this clarity with us all the time, the world would reflect the difference. What a much better form Descartes' realizations would have taken if he, like Montaigne before him, would have simply said, "I think, therefore I digress." Having no need then to posit any kind of truth beyond himself, he would have simply acknowledged his thinking as a movement forward that cuts through the truth of the world like the bow of a ship, would have pressed aside all of the deep complexities that threatened to sink him (in effect being buoyed up by them), and skated across a significant volume of shit, that though truthful and logical, does not deserve to be pressed into service as philosophy, to be emulated by drones after him, like so many shakes of a bee's ass. Descartes might have found better uses for his time then, than nailing cats to tables by their paws so that he could cut them up alive, and he might have recognized their agonized howls as something more than the sound a clock makes when hammered into a thousand pieces. Or maybe I would have had the opportunity to read Spinoza instead of Descartes, or any number of neglected thinkers who had humbler truths to offer the world. *I have no need* for the truths of Descartes unless they exist in his mathematical principles, where lines can safely cross and uncross themselves like rapiers, or better yet, good Catholics, and put themselves to sleep with clean consciences. In the expression $y = mx + b$, what do we hear? Solve for m.

11. Aside from my concern that exams never accurately measure a student's range of knowledge (whether it be a 5-week, 10-week, or 16-week course, or a degree-long adventure ending in a PhD, or that swampish range of time between birth and 30 years or so), there is something to be said for those most pious of pedagogical tools: the question and one's memory. Memory alone can only offer sensibility, so our answers count for something when they begin with a jerk and a rattle to move across a page like an old Ford Model-T. But by the time we are going into our answers we wonder if we haven't left some integral piece behind. We want to be comprehensive in demonstrating that we have understood. But comprehensiveness is an

impossibility, and only an impossible question can approach it. We could say,
"There are three things you must understand before we move on from
here," or "It would be best if you read so-and-so on this matter," and finally,
"Your test will cover all of chapter 3," but we might as well be saying,
"Reveal to me how much this matters to you, because if you do not see the
value of knowledge in and of itself, then you have no right to claim it." (But
we have already lost our way, and cannot tell the teachers from the students
anymore. If we fail the Final, we have forfeited a wealth that cannot be taken
away, and have assumed a poverty that will not wear off, be bought off, or
stay secret for long. With a reading list as long as all our days and nights, we
have no time to wonder whether the library has been exhausted. Having
been born beautiful, rich, or sad will not keep us safe, and all the stars will
turn their backs on us when it is time to turn in our answers.) TWELVE-
PART QUESTION: Do we always think of hell as being exclusion or separation from God, or the good, or the beautiful/true, or do we sometimes
simply say "hell" and mean someplace permanently uncomfortable? Is hell
private or public, do we hide in it secretly or do others peek through their
blinds at us in it, shamefully turning away when we look them straight in
their eyes? Do we ever look at one another at all? Is there a brutal homo-
geneity overtaking the world, or is this a myth—that there is more even-
ness in the world than there actually is? How much of our thinking is
thought out of us, before we ever ripen, before we ever make it to that final
examination where we are classed and filed away? Or is knowledge fed on
its own increase, like a viral pap sucking its own openings and closings and
growing despite all weathers? When we examine ourselves in the Socratic
manner, do we find our lives worth more? Or do we decrease and waste,
Solomon-like, turning in the wind of our own pinings for some lovely
innocence that died too long ago to even be lightly remembered? If dying
people are burning libraries, why do we encrypt their final secrets instead
of letting them waste in view? Do we know what happens to flesh or do
we have it on good faith that it rots away, like paper rots, and plants rot, and
pages too? Does our knowledge rot on the vine the longer we let it rest
unharvested? Or do we care at all that our best minds fall quietly to the
ground unnoticed by civilization, quieter for having not argued anything at
all, softer for having always yielded, and closer to being gone than the sunlight at evening, when dusk thickens? ▪

Big-Shot

Jan Shoemaker

My father began dying a year ago this Labor Day weekend. It would take him six months to work his way out of the world but we, my sister Sue and I, didn't know that when we found him lying on the floor beside his bed. "Dad," I asked gently. "What happened?"

"A big-shot slipped me a mickey," he groaned, trying and failing to heave himself up. *Big-shot? Mickey?* Had he been watching old gangster movies on cable during all of those insomniac nights that had followed one another over the past few years, gray and vaguely threatening, like suspects in a lineup? "He *thinks* he's a big-shot," my father continued, sure of his facts, "but he's not."

Sue and I told the paramedics who arrived a few minutes later about the big-shot and we told the nurses and the cardiologist at the hospital and most of our friends—and we laughed about it edgily and sometimes hysterically and often weepily through the ensuing miserable months and we laugh about it still. We should all give our stumbling families in our confused, final days so preposterous a gift—some mad claim or delusion for them to cling to and laugh over—and so draw breath again.

We buried my father amid a cluster of small trees in a flat, suburban cemetery that holds the remains of so many people I have loved and love still. I leave notes on the marble slab that marks his grave as if it were the Wailing Wall, notes that have always disappeared when I return although the small stone I slip them beneath remains. Contrary to the claims of that old children's game, stone covers paper—and outlasts it, like Housman's enduring bone.

I don't suppose endurance is everything—God love the Buddhists for helping me try to see and believe this again and again. Nevertheless, most of us hang on for as long as we can. Even Douglas, the one tomato plant I

potted this past summer, (my family names everything), threw his lot in
with existence—proclaimed his enduring Douglas-ness—with what was
surely a heroic effort after my husband, Larry, halved him with a shingle
while he was reroofing our house. Douglas lived to pass on his seed with
Darwinian determination in the form of half a dozen ping-pong ball–sized
tomatoes and so placed a claim on the future—Dougla-fying it. Douglas,
in fact, persisted in living in a rickety way straight through September,
looking a lot like an old man I often see at my favorite bookstore—spindly
and stooped—but dressed nattily in just the way I have threatened to dress
Larry some day if his senility strikes before my own—in a cardigan sweater
with elbow patches and a small, smart cap. Douglas and his contemporary
bibliophile—both bent on making it another day.

In the wood bowl full of birds' nests (which I so often find just where
I'm about to place my foot) that sits on a table in my living room there is
a phial of blue sand from a Buddhist mandala. Not long ago four Tibetan
monks, *bikkhus* from Dharmasala, the Tibetan refuge in India, visited the
university in my town. For a week they sat silently on the floor of the college art museum, one on each side of a square mat the size of a card table,
blowing brightly colored sand through thin pipes into intricate patterns
surrounding the sacred image of a beloved bodhisattva—a buddha of compassion. We—the members of the community who went to college and
know how to treat art and support its preservation, ogled it and murmured
our praise. We crept up until our toes touched the mat but the monks, who
create these fragile mandalas as a form of meditation—a study in impermanence—paid us no mind. They blew silently, tapping their slim pipes,
and when they had finished, when the mandala was complete and perfect,
it seemed, as Michelangelo's *Sistine Chapel* or Monet's *Water Lilies*, they
lifted the corners of the mat and indifferently destroyed it. Bottling up bits
of colored sand for those of us in the room—someone must have tipped
them off to Americans' love of souvenirs—they trotted the rest of it down
to the river and flung it in, emblemizing in a gesture: *anicca*—the impermanence of all things.

"Everything is temporary!" Vincent Gardenia, who plays a plumber
troubled by the encroaching imminence of his own death, yells at Cher in
the movie *Moonstruck*. When I've had enough of this poor old world
where every creature is scrambling to retain his own skin and identity and
not to be recycled indifferently into the all of it, I sit down and watch a
stack of my favorite movies—nothing heavy: *A Room with a View, Chocolat,
Sense and Sensibility*. "Chick-flicks," I suppose—a disparaging term, like

Rambo merits apologetics or a table of talking heads. I fill up a tray with a pot full of tea and a plate piled high with toast and settle onto the couch and hit Play. Then the world steps back and Lucy Honeychurch and her tiny waist defeat the prejudices of class and concede her love to George Emerson and his broad shoulders. Right there in my family room passion and truth bubble up and spill over and I let them wash me away. My students sometimes try to bully me into watching serious *films* (I only watch *movies*). "You should see *Battle Royale*," they say or "You *have to* rent *Requiem for a Dream*." Sometimes I evade them by explaining that I don't watch movies with subtitles—ever. It worries me that this is probably something I have in common with George Bush—a taste for movies that are easy, that never trouble your mind and that you can eat through, but there you have it. They don't get it, my serious-minded students—that life *will* do us all in, that even as we speak it is *fixin'* (as my southern relations say) to deliver us up to our individual deaths—to fling our atoms into void so they can be reassembled into fresh forms, whole new bunnies and geese and hairdressers and violinists who will, in their turn, scramble to stay alive. "We *live* confounded and desperate—who wants to see it at the movies?" I ask them. They shake their heads at me, disappointed; they'd hoped for greater depth from a literature teacher. But I am resolute. "I only see movies that make me laugh; now open your books and explain to me just how Hester's scarlet letter has become her passport to freedom." But ultimately even my retreats into the prettiest and most docile movie worlds are in vain. Because it's there too—the hint of impermanence. Vianne spills the pot of her dead mother's ashes, which are grabbed up by the wind, and the Miss Dashwoods' wedding parade winds through a churchyard of mossy tombstones. Those old skulls painted into Renaissance landscapes—they're still everywhere you look.

My father's dying was difficult. When it became obvious that he and my mother could no longer live in their house Sue and I moved them into an assisted living apartment complex close to our homes. There followed a succession of calamities physical and emotional involving falls and ambulances; there was bitterness and blame and despair but there were rich moments as well. A couple of months before he died I sat beside my dad, a meat and potatoes man, drinking red wine and looking out his picture window at the November twilight. It was snowing hard and the power was out; my mother was one high-rise floor below us (I'd gone looking for her with a flashlight) sitting under a silent hair dryer with her wet hair full of curlers—she was waiting for the power to come on. I piled cheese and crackers onto a plate and set it between my dad and me and I refilled our glasses from time to time. "Best dinner there is right here," he declared. "What more do you want?" Nothing. Just a life filled with moments like this—moments of reconciliation and small kindnesses and a little red wine. Two months later he was in the hospital again with congestive heart failure. When his nurse called my school during third hour to ask about life support the school secretary naturally put the call through to my room. Thirty sophomores listened as I declined the technologies that would hold his life inside his body and make him fit enough for transfer to a nursing home. "Just make him comfortable," I said. He died a few days later.

What is it that endures? That's the question the religions scramble to answer. *Nothing*, the Buddhists say. *But then again*, they add gamely, *we never really existed as separate selves to begin with*. "But I seem real," I recently told Ajahn Kemensanto, the abbot at the Wat Dharmasala Monastery in my town. We were sitting cross-legged on cushions in front of a gold-painted Buddha the size of a Victorian armoire. "My father seemed real. My husband and children seem real."

"Ah—*seem*," Kemensanto replied, nodding at my error—he'd heard it a million times. In the East it is not sin but ignorance that separates us from what Ultimately Is—call it God, Brahman, Nirvana. Recognizing It, merging with It is what releases us from our personal finitude and claims us for eternity—without the disqualifying baggage of "I" or "me" or "us." The Western religions, arguably with the exception of Judaism, regard the discrete and eternal soul of each person as a fact and concern themselves with where that soul will go after it's finished its short business with the unglorified body it occupied in this life. In keeping with ancient Gnostic traditions that predate Christianity itself, the Christian church articulates a creed that a person must believe in order to gain heaven and so endure eternity comfortably. *What* endures is not a question for a Christian or a Muslim; *where* is where the drama is.

I do not know what, if anything, endures of our lives after we die. I only know how desperately I love the temporary forms of this world—my gentle husband, my precocious daughters, my wise old golden retriever who, in these his final days, collapses unexpectedly and refuses to eat anything but Fig Newtons—and I sense how devastating it will be to lose or leave them. There may be a Big-Shot, as my father testified, taking us all out in our turn for reasons of his own; I don't know. If it's true, I remember thinking the last time I visited his grave, then everyone in that cemetery, everyone who has ever died, in fact, has the same story; one way or another a Big-Shot slipped them a mickey.

The poet David Ignatow said, "In the next world, should I remember this one, I will praise it above everything." I would like to be so large, so able to magnanimously allow the return of all the ones I love to the Void, the Tao, the Source—call it what you will—from which they came; I would like to celebrate the Eternal turning out its finite forms and the Eternal receiving them again. But I am no detached yogi, no wise arhat, no faithful Christian willing to fall backward into the arms of her unseen Lord like people do in those trust-building games. I have not handed it over to Jesus—the burden and heartbreak of my willful love for perishable things. The best I can hope for at this time and probably for a long time to come is the courage to love them well enough despite their devastating fragility and their nonnegotiable term limits. The best that I can pray for is the faithfulness to love them like they need to be, like they love to be loved. ▄

98

What Has Happened to Charmaine?

Eve Abrams

Bobby is not an evacuator. He's usually low on cash, has two dogs and no car, and seems faintly precarious outside of his habitat. More than ever before, New Orleans is the water, and Bobby is the fish.

Not long after turning 30, I decided I needed a break from my life. I had a short list of places to go for a while, and at parties or during long-distance phone calls, one kept emerging from the rest. Faces lit at her mention. Love was sworn. Voices changed tenor and pitch. I was given names and numbers to call, exultations of meals eaten and music heard. When the ex-girlfriend of one friend secured me a carriage house, and another promised me her parents as surrogates, I loaded up my Honda with my clothes and computer and fat cat Jack, and hit the road. There was no choice to be made. New Orleans it was, without question.

Before leaving, I asked Jonathan, a New Orleans devotee, how I was going to buy marijuana. He pulled out his phone book and gave me Bobby's number. "He's a really good friend," Jonathan told me. "He's a great guy."

Last week, four plus years later, I dialed that number over and over again, day after day. Of course, I wasn't looking for pot. When I was lucky enough to get a ring—rather than the efficient mantra *All circuits are busy*—I tried to picture an actual phone ringing at Bobby's place, two blocks from the Quarter, slightly below street level, and therefore, I calculated, no more than a foot under water.

In the great expanse of time before the harsh wind known as Katrina blew ruin upon the Gulf Coast, Bobby lived in a beautiful, warm, sensual city, whose offerings—music, food, freedom—immediately brushed along one's nerve endings; there were no laborious paths through the intellect. "We're about the lower chakras," he once told me. In this city charged with sex, deep into flirtation, and kept afloat in alcohol, Bobby's life ran on cash and paid no taxes. Its base of operations lay behind a tall picket fence, thickly covered in flowers, which served as a visual obstruction to the traffic of quotidian illegalities that were the source of his income. To enter this fortress, you pulled a string through a hole in the door connected to a bone (Bobby's nickname is "The Bone"), which caused bells to ring and his mini pinscher to bark. Bobby might eventually answer this call, depending on his mood and whether or not he was conducting business and with whom that business was being conducted. In the parlance of his native city, Bobby's home was known as a "shack," and this shack was part of a pipeline sup-plying goods to the fine people of his city. While passing time in the shack, underneath a string of tinkling bells, hanging bones, costumes, feathers, and ornate clocks that no longer worked, I met a former mayor's brother and the musicians I saw perform the night before and a girl who ate fire for a living. I learned about astral projection, and I listened to hours of delib-eration on politicians and Palestine and human nature, on motorcycles and gurus and the art of winding speaker cords. The air in the shack was filled with the sounds of WWOZ, spinning records, eight-track gospel record-ings, and improvisational strummings; grown men crooned along to Earth, Wind and Fire and Tammy Wynette and Earl King's *Trick Dog*. On more than one occasion, Bobby leaned back and crossed one skinny leg over another and commented, "Hard day of work. Sitting here, playing music, making money."

Bobby was, of course, a musician. Long curly blond hair gone a bit to gray, sideburns like the ends of lightning rods, slight goatee, stubble. When I met him, he was in a hipster cowboy phase and wore a straw hat, pur-chased down in the Quarter and curled just so atop his ponytail. Black pre-scription sunglasses with the lenses tinted dark blue; rhinestone bone dangling from his neck, fingers full of rings. Sometimes he wore his hair out, a billow of curls; a smile showed teeth slightly parted like the Red Sea. One night, when he had a gig at Checkpoint Charlie's, he wore red leather pants with blue stars up the side, a tight white T-shirt, and his fleur-de-lis key ring hanging from his pocket. With his collection of guitars and his penchant for strut, the stage was his most unshakable addiction, the place where his raw soul shot out on the arrows of loud southern rock. Bobby liked to talk about the evolution of his music, as well as his different looks, and the phases of his life they represented. When I met him he was wear-ing a lot of white. Not long after the breakup with his shiksa babe wife, he'd gone to a spirit man—a reader of bones—who'd instructed him to stay away from black and wear as much white as possible.

What can be better than being in love in a land of sunshine where the buildings have grille work and the trees drip forsythia? Bobby opened doors and rolled perfect joints. He was a backyard philosopher, a brilliant thinker who never finished high school, read everything that crossed his path, and had expansive opinions continuously informed by new ideas. He called me *Baby* and *Darlin* and so what if it was New Orleans and everyone called everyone these things? He picked me confederate jasmine and bought me oysters at Felix's and pralines on the ferry to Algiers; he took me to see the Indians on Super Sunday and once, when I slept over at the shack and the next morning realized I had therapy by phone in ten minutes, he took the dogs out for a walk so I could talk about him in private. When he returned—his phone battery dead ten minutes already—he found me talking to my therapist on the pay phone on Frenchman Street, and he brought me a cup of coffee and a chair. "Don't worry, Baby," he said. "It's the neighborhood's living room out here."

Bobby's perimeter was the bikeable radius from the shack. For the first month I knew him, I lived in the Lower Garden District, and though we saw each other nearly every day, he never set foot in my place. I biked through the Garden District, the CBD, the Quarter, and a block of the Marigny to pull the bone in Bobby's fence and have him open it and call me Baby. But the day I moved to a rented shack of my own in the Bywater, Bobby was there. "You're finally on the right side of Canal Street," he explained.

When I first met him, Bobby's VW bus was parked outside the shack, and the city of New Orleans had stuck a notice on it some months before telling him it had to go. The problem was it couldn't. Anywhere. Bobby also owned two motorcycles, Hondas, but those didn't move either. He got around on foot, usually at the tail end of two leashes, or by way of his bike—a cruiser so low with handlebars so high that the first time I saw him on it I could not remove my eyes nor stop laughing and ran my own bicycle straight into a metal garbage dump. Bobby got rides to band practice, and I was the one, once or twice a week, who drove us over the Mississippi to Pho Tau Bay in Gretna for Vietnamese food.

Inside his perimeter, Bobby couldn't turn a corner without seeing someone he knew. *What up? Where y'at? What's happening?* People were always coming by the shack. Bobby's was a stop—for some a daily stop—in the living of their lives. Our friend John declared the shack the closest thing New Orleans had to a New Amsterdam coffee house. In addition to the regulars, there were people like me—people who periodically activated a connection to New Orleans—people for whom a visit to New Orleans included, by necessity, a visit to Bobby.

I fell in love—first with New Orleans, and second with Bobby—and after a while I didn't know the difference. At the end of three months, I left. I came home to the North, to the land where people work a lot, and where we make plans to meet for dinner two weeks from Wednesday at eight P.M., not knowing if we will be hungry when that hour arrives. Men did not open doors for me. No one called me "baby." People walked by without making eye contact—even when I looked cute, even on the day my bicycle fell on my leg and blood ran down to my ankle.

I feel just awful using the past tense. These days, when otherwise thoughtful conversationalists use the word *if* in reference to the rebuilding of New Orleans, or when they terminate their comments with question marks, or even when they declare how unharmed the French Quarter was—the anger and sadness rise in me like all that putrid water. In place of the politicians I'd like to tongue lash are these people, powerless citizens like me, residents of a country whose indifference and/or incompetence has caught us all off guard. They are speaking logically, but New Orleans was not a city built on logic. And what may not be substantial to them, but what I'm so terrified of losing, is the living organism, the hive, which is New Orleans. Bobby, and New Orleans' vast cadre of iconoclastic denizens, cannot survive long outside their habitat. They are fragile flowers kept alive by a gumbo of sunshine and wickedness and creativity that is the Crescent City. Left too long out on the vine, they will wither and die.

What has happened to Charmaine, who yelled and cursed, night and day at the top of her lungs at no one at all, save the demons she could see, from the corner of Mazant and Burgundy? What has happened to the old woman on the opposite corner, the one who lived in the pink, shuttered double shotgun, who opened those shutters once a day, and once a day only, to throw scraps of bread to the pigeons? What has happened to 49 and 64—two men with bad hips and porkpie hats—who refused to explain their names, whom I met on the stoop of John's house on North Robinson in the Treme? What has happened to Jason, the young, sweet, blond hoodlum who lived on Dauphine next to Vaughn's?

One day in the Bywater, long before Katrina, Jason sat with me on my rented lawn. Overhead, the live oaks spread wide under the five o'clock sun, and across the way, Charmaine was ranting. Jason smiled, and full of love, declared, "Charmaine." In his Ninth Ward accent, which sounds like South Brooklyn on Southern Comfort, he said it plain: "Wouldn't be New Orleans without Charmaine."

What has happened to Charmaine?

When I called Bobby from New York, it was usually landline to cellular.

"Evie, baby," he answered, long after I'd ceased being his baby. "Striker! C'mere boy."

I pictured him perfectly, walking along the neutral ground on Esplanade, the wide patch of dirt separating the Quarter from the Marigny, shaded by live oaks and smelling of sweet olive and honeysuckle; his mutt Striker ambling by his side, smelling, peeing; his mini pinscher Simon pinging from tree root to shrub to passing car, barking at every sign of movement, adrenalinated like a fly on cocaine.

"Are you happy?"

"You ask the weirdest questions."

"Just answer."

"Striker!"

It was two-thirty in the afternoon his time, and when I'd called, Bobby told me he'd just woken up. I could feel the humidity over the phone line, and I pictured Bobby's long curly hair set into a ponytail, his fingers without rings, fresh from sleep, not yet on anything save a cup of chicory coffee.

"I like the way I have evolved," he said. "As an individual. Spiritually, metaphysically. I like who I've become. But the infrastructure could use some work."

I thought of his cracked walls and concrete floors and the kitchen sink whose water never ran. I didn't ask if he still had rats. Once upon a time it all seemed so romantic. What you get out of life, given good weather, when you don't work too hard. What you need—so that you can enjoy life, so that you can make music and art and mischief. For Bobby didn't spend his energy building stability; he spent it living. Crafting, playing, performing, partying. This disposition—what my friend Chris refers to as "the Caribbean mentality"—makes New Orleans what it is. The lifestyle that created jazz. The environment in which music, until just a short time ago, was as ubiquitous as air. It's why people outside call it "The Big Easy," why we flock there to revel or relax or be something new. Bobby's way of life is a bargain made with fate: trade in stability for possibility, for serendipity, for the miraculous. He makes the sacrifice; we get to visit and enjoy.

Given his line of work, Bobby thought about what-ifs. He'd spent nights in jail. He knew how to play it—how to *yes officer, of course officer*. One time he summarized the essentials of evacuation, what to grab in case of emergency: "The stash, the cash, and the dogs." But this life preserver will only last so long.

Days passed and I'd heard nothing. I dialed numbers in the 504 area code and trolled websites for information. Jonathan and I convened in Brooklyn, and he assured me that Bobby was fine. "He's a survivor," Jonathan reminded me. And though I knew this, I worried. Reports of shootings and bands of thugs with guns filled the newspaper stories, and my anxieties lapped over the seawalls of my senses. I finally tracked him down via his sister-in-law in Texas. Bobby was alive, and well, and still in New Orleans—in the Quarter, in fact—living "on the edge of civilization" with ten other people.

"Having the time of his life," his brother shouted in the background.

I was right about one thing: Bobby wasn't an evacuator. Not even Katrina could get him out of his habitat. It was easy to picture him cavorting in the aftermath. Bobby loved being an outlaw. He fantasized about getting a pilot's license and becoming a smuggler. He thrived in the fuzzy margin between what you're supposed to do and what you can get away with. Clear that space away, and Bobby disappears.

Eliminating the likes of Bobby might be okay for some people. People who choose hygienic, orderly Singapore or Houston, people who are fine with gum's being illegal, or who are happy without the squeegee guys. But I like a bit of mess in my life. That gritty, messy part is where the art comes from, where the intellect gets fed, where ire and resolve grow strong as weeds. In the margins, there is the time and there is the freedom from expectation to create the unexpected. I don't want a world without mess, without creativity. I don't want a world without New Orleans. I can't even bear to think about it.

The latest news on Bobby is that he's back in the shack and blasting music by way of a generator from the balcony upstairs. He's calling it "Radio Free Marigny" and his straggle of remaining neighbors, along with the 82nd Airborne and the border patrol, love it. All this I learned on a blog and via email, for there's still no power, no phone lines, no running water. But thanks to resilient Bobby, son of New Orleans, once again, there's music.

I love Bobby, but that's not why I'm writing about him. I'm writing about him because I'm a preservationist, and at present, he's an endangered species. The line between romantic dilapidation and misery currently seems slim. Having slid into one, can you reclaim the other?

We are Americans; we don't suffer nature lightly. *No hurricane will drown one of our cities!* I can practically hear the chauvinists cry already. The city will, in some fashion, be rebuilt. But as what? This container called New Orleans holds a very particular cup of life. Through sunshine and neglect, New Orleans had a habitat where you could be yourself without having to work too terribly hard to support it. There was always housing to be found, albeit a bit rotting and tumble-down. You didn't need heat; you could go without air-conditioning. It was a fragile ecosystem, but it functioned.

Sure, Bobby will survive. He's resilient and resourceful and full of pluck. But where will he flourish? On top of the thousands of lives gone and still precarious, there is this to worry about: the collective. A New Orleans ecosystem is in peril.

What will happen to the soul of New Orleans, inhabited by all those people, sent hither and thither, with little prayer of coming home to a home that is anything like what it was? Forgive all the tenses. Time has jumbled into a knot. What will become of Bobby? What will become of them all? ■

Kano, and Elsewhere

Brad Comann

But while we are intent upon one object we already feel the pull of
another.

R. M. Rilke

Upon waking early on December 8, 1980, Mark David Chapman
signed his copy of *The Catcher in the Rye* to "Holden Caulfield" from,
in his own hand, *Holden Caulfield,* and wrote underneath it, "This is my
statement." Apparently he would give no interviews after the shooting. As
planned, that afternoon Chapman, the antihero, took his infamous combat
stance and fired several shots into John Lennon's back only to pace the sidewalk, gun in one hand, *Catcher* in the other.

A few months before, in
September, my girl friend Wendy accepted a teaching position at Bayero
University in Northern Nigeria. Since I've never liked being left behind,
and she felt anxious without a man, off we went to Africa as though married, practically romantic. I too hoped to be hired as a lecturer in their
English Department, but none of that would really work. Meanwhile, in
that relentless sub-Saharan heat Wendy's blouses looked thrown against her
body, sagging like damp bread, and I can remember my shirtsleeves rolled
to the elbows, heavy as a marsh.

As Lennon was dying in the front doorway
of the Dakota Apartments, we stood at a window trying to make out those
sounds coming from the Old City. Sounded like gunfire. Later, we were told
that outnumbered local police had set off smoke bombs in the attempt to disperse a Muslim gathering of the Maitatsine, a renegade group who were led by
a self-declared prophet named Marwa. In response, near the emir's palace,
Marwa's following had retaliated with machetes, arrows, and daggers. The police

retaliated with their service revolvers. Within hours four Kano policemen were beaten to death and 13 government vehicles burned.

During a 1992 interview with Barbara Walters, Chapman cites *The Catcher in the Rye* with a reverence more commonly saved for religious texts—for example, the Diamond Sutra or the Koran. He identified with Salinger's work, in part, because the phoniness that Holden perceived applied to John Lennon's "sell-out" to the ritzy world of limos and places like the Dakota Apartments. Chapman's idol had turned into a materialist, no longer on a lotus blossom, no longer true to his own lyrics: *I don't care too much for money, money can't buy me love.*

When we heard of Lennon's death on the BBC, it fit, oddly, with everything else going on within earshot, although the Kano riots triggered on December 8th continued for three weeks and would claim roughly 10,000 times the number of lives.

On December 9th, on the front page of the *New York Times*, below the photo of terrorized Yoko Ono outside the hospital where John Lennon has been pronounced dead, is an article on president-elect Reagan's fundraising for his expensive "transition team." To the right of Yoko Ono's face is a piece on the 13-month-long "hostage situation" in Tehran. We know now that John Hinckley, also a big reader of *Catcher in the Rye*, will soon try to murder the newly elected Reagan with a Saturday Night Special, a revolver commonly dissed by those in the arms business as "trash," so poorly made that it could give handguns a bad name. Hinckley's .22, although considered a lesser version of the .38 used on Lennon, has a compact two-inch barrel and a great reputation for never jamming. But few of us in the States knew that Muslims in the Middle East were not only having a say in Tehran, but that other messages would follow.

According to the *Oxford English Dictionary*, the prefix "dis" from the Latin, from the Greek, primarily means "twice" or "two ways," with "dis" the opposite of "con" : discord, concord; disjunction, conjunction. The mythological God of the Underworld was Dis, the one of separation, undoings, and we now have hundreds of forms, in print and elsewhere, including the slang verb "to dis," for "disrespecting" someone. It's no fluke that the word came into use between 1980 and 1985. Given the reversals, in this World of Dis, John the target becomes John the triggerman. It does seem to fit, after all, if *I am him as you are him as you are me and we are all together.*

After three months in-country, by early December, I was either writing poems or repairing Nigerian Volkswagens (parts from Brazil, assembled in Lagos, the capitol). Then to hear of Lennon murdered—of all people—made me see red: how can some displaced guy get confused over the LP *Revolver*! For God's sake, gunning down a *Beatle*? Fucking A. Later the shame took over: one of our *own* murdered him. I really wanted to dismiss Chapman as one more nobody who wanted to be noticed, as a deadbeat that no parole board would have to busy themselves with—like Manson, the guy would be in for good. But Lennon's death then felt like *our* doing, America's, including me, and maybe that's the reason why it has taken so long for me to write this piece.

In fact, I'd nearly given up until in Prague, in 2000, after eating a gyro at the west end of the Charles Bridge, I found myself suddenly before "The Lennon Wall." As everyone does in Prague, I had followed one medieval-thin street after another with no point in mind. As if I'd turned my mind off, relaxed, and floated down the smooth cobblestones, this memorial to Lennon just seemed to appear. As public art, it is a non-wall, separating nothing, perfectly positioned in the capital of the Czech Republic, within the long shadow of the Berlin Wall. To eastern Europeans, Lennon died as a victim of social violence, beginning with manufacturers who block handgun legislation. It's never about one man's pathology. Lennon was silenced as so many freethinkers and nonconformists have been before him. He died a martyr to peace and, as we say in the same breath, to "democracy." So Lennon, like a dissident, like an enemy of the state, like a union member at a shipyard (Lennon *was* increasingly active in labor union causes), or like a persecuted poet, gave his life. I notice, between the hand-painted daisies—the kind I always associate with that Kent State photo of a woman decorating a National Guard's rifle—there's "Give peace a chance." I also see lots of yellow and red peace signs, and words that I can't follow as though written in Indo-European. Midway, there's a huge long-haired Lennon with wire-rimmed glasses, surrounded by homage from every hand, adding up to a kind of focused graffiti with penknife, paintbrush, or felt-tipped marker, including initials, acronyms, sayings in Arabic. "Let It Be" is very big, and "There will be an answer . . ." but passages of Bertolt Brecht and Sartre and Salvador Dali have also found a home. The tenor is consistently that of opposition to hate, war, institutional thinking, and indifference. "Lennon Lives" one tourist has argued, and maybe she is right. At the foot of the wall votive candles burned. Bouquets wilted in the shade. A thumbtack managed to hold a snapshot of some teenager, assumedly killed by a terrorist, maybe on the West Bank: gun bomb knife boot. The next day, near the same castle that K. would never access, although tour groups do in hordes—informed by audio tapes in eight languages—I bought a John Lennon T-shirt, his picture taken from the wall, complete with Jesus-long hair. It was to be a high school graduation present for a colleague's son whose hair is as long as Lennon's when "Imagine" hit the charts.

In 2000, a newspaper column explains that Chapman finished serving the minimum of his 20-to-life sentence, so the parole board met for his hearing. I realize Chapman's in New York State, in Attica. Living in Pennsylvania, I'm not far from him. A paragraph notes, matter-of-factly, his request is denied in part because of Yoko Ono's testimony of continual fear of what Chapman might do with his freedom, and in part because of the tireless efforts of Lennon fans who presented to the board petitions signed by many thousands, asking that Chapman remain in prison, where he is known to write Christian short stories. Two years later I read a much shorter piece about Chapman, who was again denied parole. Every two years will be the same.

Then the disintegration of the World Trade Center by Muslim terrorists reminded me of Kano. All those thousands killed in New York City, DC, and Pennsylvania, whom I never knew personally, were suddenly stacked up against three times their number who were killed in 1980, but people you would never hear about until now.

The failure of the Kano police to protect and enforce common law reminds me of police in cities like New York that also fail to safeguard even its leading citizens. Everywhere it's true: when religious zeal and political greed and delusional insanity take over, a place breaks into violence. Could be on the small scale that has enormous repercussions, as with John Lennon's death, or the large-scale loss of human life, in the thousands, that makes no measurable dent in the metallic hearts of those who read newspapers—although those Kano riots would foretell the events on 9/11, or so I would argue.

How many dead Muslims have the same emotional weight as one Lennon? That obviously depends. The New York Times on December 29th, three weeks after the "riots" started, on page A5, includes a 100-word report taken from Reuters monitoring of a radio broadcast picked up in the Ivory Coast, sent from Lagos, explaining that "some religious fanatics" were responsible for the "unrest." Fanatic, from the word "fan," sounds like our guy Chapman.

Of course, John Lennon had a name, even in West Africa, and his life is a particular loss. As you might recall, Joan Didion claims in *The White Album* that the '60s ended with the Sharon Tate murders, but to me the '60s ended with a murder in 1980, with four or five bullets pouring into the back of Lennon's jacket. The '60s ended precisely with what they, at a firing range, call a "good shot group."

Chapman admitted that his preparatory prayer went "to Satan for the strength to kill Lennon." This Christian bent is disconcerting and disingenuous because the shooter has since found Jesus, like so many inmates who hit bottom. Murderous Religion is always a kind of either/or movement. And perennial. In Kano and elsewhere.

The Japanese Zeros in the Pacific Theater, where my father and uncle both served during World War II, *The Big One*, were terribly feared because of their fearlessness, their kamikaze commitment so unlike the Western idea of patriotism, sacrificing one's life as a necessity to save a fellow soldier, but the body itself was never a weapon. Maybe the Japanese established the prototype of today's suicide pilot—the cockpit taken over by bearded men with box-cutters.

Chapman was a killer in the rye, intending to save future children from falling off the cliff into a secular underworld of new money, billboard fame, and shallow affluence. In contrast, Chapman has moral focus and takes "five steps toward the street" before "firing five shots into his [Lennon's] back." What methodical work, what conviction, so the world would have one less phony. And after the deed, Chapman stays at the scene as if waiting for his punishment, to be as dead as John, like a car bomber having set the timer but lagging around in the neighborhood to see the outcome. But perhaps more accurately, Chapman would confess to Barbara Walters, after shooting Lennon, "it was like the film strip broke."

A subway station was close by. "He could have run," as one New York policeman observed, but Chapman himself was like blood on the bricks, pooling. As killers go, is there a similarity between Chapman's reading of *The Catcher* and Marwa's textual interpretation of the Koran? Both heard a higher calling, to disrupt the comfortable lives of the wealthy, the dissemblers, the materialists, the phonies. Dislodge them from their luxurious rooms, disembowel those who, on the outside, have it all—but who have no interior, only a smattering of small pleasures that they call good. Here, in Dante's words, we have *The Land of Dis* that does not die out: two years after the Kano riots, the *New York Times* covered, briefly, additional unrest in northern Nigeria, sparked by the Maitatsine, again to protest the "dilution of its Islamic culture as Nigeria uses its oil wealth to become more urban, industrial, and secular." Islamic fundamentalism and Nigeria's economic and political decay combined destructively while Western forms of decadence and the growing materialism of powerful politicians and businessmen networked with American oil companies, which radicalized a growing number of educated Nigerians, often Muslims, who were suffering from soaring food prices, high unemployment, environmental problems, and corrupt leaders who failed to take care of such problems. Religiously speaking, materialism was winning out, as the disinherited have sometimes put it, and this fall from perceived grace is evident in the privileged and the poor. Ironically, John Lennon, as the archetype of the '60s, was outspoken against forms of opportunism, not only environmental erosion resulting from a lack of corporate responsibility, but also "the system's" opposition to the civil rights movement and its crass support of the Vietnam War. In short, '60s ideology was about questioning materialism and supporting social change. That is why Chapman, the failed Romantic, went after Lennon for turning his back on those days of idealism and activism—becoming *one of them*. However, Chapman overread Salinger and we know well enough what he did to Lennon.

When I look again at my old passport, issued in 1980 and filled with colorful visas to Nigeria, Niger, and Algeria, I see a full black beard on a man in his mid-20s, olive skinned, seriousness to the mouth. I remember saying to friends both before and after traveling to Africa that I looked like a terrorist, laughing a little at my commentary because as we all knew those extremists with their oily skin and headwraps formed cells only in places like Damascus, wherever that was. Then I read in a 2003 *New York Times* that five young Muslim men in a suburb of Buffalo, not 45 minutes from my house, had been arrested for being an al-Qaeda cell. One of the suspicious moves on their part, within the past year, was growing their beards long.

There was no foretelling that roughly two decades later, in an Oxford cloth shirt, short gray hair, pale skin caused by a long Pennsylvania winter, and a herniated disk from doing nothing more than bending over to pick up a kitchen plate, I would find myself on a Southwest Air flight from Buffalo to Oakland, by way of Phoenix. My only relief from the back pain resided in slowly pacing the aisle. Whenever the pilot turned off the seat belt sign, I was up. The

FAA had recently passed a new regulation, which I wasn't aware of before, that no passengers could stand in the front galley, either to chat or to wait to use the toilet. But while I stood there in the galley, along with two women about my age, the new regulation was spelled out on the intercom and all three of us began returning down the aisle to our seats. I took my time and looked at the various sleepers, readers, and talkers, some who seemed to give me dirty looks. I am not foreign to such looks; I have always had a tendency to turn some people the wrong way without saying anything. Anyway, one in-flight attendant, a woman with pinched eyebrows and small ears, stopped me in the aisle as I soon paced to the front of the plane to tell me again that I couldn't wait in the galley although I was only half way up the aisle of the 737. I reassured her that I would stop short of the galley, and that my back hurt. With lower back problems so common, I figured she was familiar with passengers needing to stand and walk. But moments later she bounded toward me from the first-class galley to give me the command that I must sit down. *Why?* I asked. *Stop hassling me*, I said and moved past her toward the front of the plane, still 20 seats away from the pilots behind their locked door.

Not too long after the plane touched down, all but five of us deplaned in Phoenix; unfortunately, we would have to stop in LA as well, to finally reach Oakland. It began to feel like I was flying to Osaka, but then two federal agents, a PR guy from Southwest Air, and a plainclothesman with a German shepherd were coming up the empty aisle toward me. *How are you today?* the PR guy asked, apparently trained to calm intruders with a harmless question, apparently so that I wouldn't think to run for it. I simply stood there, unmoved by the show of force, *like a pro,* I thought later. *Can I see a form of identification?* he went on before I could tell him how my day was going. I gave him my driver's license, and he retreated into first class to cell phone in my data, surely to run a background check. The other members of the crisis management team held their positions and said nothing. The PR man had a brief but apparently positive chat with someone who said I was—what exactly? Not of Middle-Eastern descent? No former member of the SLA or Shining Path? I will never know how much the federals know about me. The guy then tells me the in-flight attendant informed marshals on the ground that I was hostile and threatening. *You should know that on a flight the attendants are god*, he explained. I stared back at him. "God" was a trope that I never expected to hear, but he seemed to understand that his unscripted term was confusing to me and he reworded his claim, patiently explaining, *Whatever they say goes*. My medical excuse for pacing the aisles was neutralized by his adding, *other passengers also complained that I looked like a threat to the safety of the aircraft.* Then it came to me: *The passengers themselves felt terror.* Had I looked as I did 20 some years earlier, I might have been one of those detainees that you don't read about, that are held somewhere dark without bail, legal representation, or human rights. But truthfully, if you would happen to see me sitting at some restaurant table, I would remind you of a plain old mid-level manager of a Wal-Mart on his day off, someone on the tall side, piebald, a cleft chin. Someone whom America has been good to.

Lisa Belkin in the *New York Times Magazine* (August 2002) explores the apparent link between events, or the science of coincidence and whether there is more than probability going on, as put forth by Mel Gibson in *Conspiracy Theory* or by Squire Rushnell in his book *When God Winks: How the Power of Coincidence Guides Your Life.* Political conspiracies surround Lennon's murder and the Maitatsine riots. Although Chapman denies as "hogwash" the theory of a CIA-backed assassination, with him as their shooter, the theory was given book-length attention in *Who Killed John Lennon?* by Fenton Bresler. In addition, Marwa was assumed by some politicians to be a front man for Khaddafi and funded by the Ayatollah, although both explanations have fallen off as unfounded and unconvincing. The simultaneity of death, one Beatle, thousands of Muslims, seems merely an anomaly. Of course, we *look* for patterns and connections. Remember circumstances after 9/11: a microbiologist's "suicide"—an expert named Don Wiley who worked with Ebola, influenza, and anthrax—became a "murder" committed by the new Islamic enemy that targeted our major scientists. Or was there a logical fallacy at work: post hoc ergo prompter hoc? Finding connections, causes, is one way we make sense of the senseless, the coincidental, the unknown. This is how "we fill in the factual blanks," argues Lisa Belkin. We want, and even more importantly *need*, to find connections between times and places. For instance, early cartographers were at a loss for how to render, and to scale, the greater Sahara and borrowed the local term *Rub Al Kali* meaning "the empty quarter," which was in both a military and mathematical sense. It seems, at minimum, we must name what is immeasurable or impenetrable to make it less so.

Every Monday in a neighbor's Volkswagen we would do errands down unmarked roads, often disoriented on traffic circles that the British engineered. Often they gridlocked, forcing us to breathe the diesel breath of huge trucks called mammy wagons and watch goats in some soccer field chew wrapping paper, as brindled dogs cower to the side of a cook fire and pull-carts on the shoulder carry a green liquid that swishes badly in its glass containers.

Three days after the Kano violence began and Lennon was gone, I drove as usual down Zaria Road. Next to me sat Wendy, Wendy Bishop, whom I married the following year and divorced less than three years after that, a brilliant woman who would go on to write over 20 books of scholarly work as well as creative nonfiction and poetry as a faculty member at Florida State—only to die a few years ago from cancer-related complications. She was only 50. But on that day she was still 27, unworried that the Old City might be overrun by Muslim followers of a new Muhammad. We were low on food and the supermarket is just three clicks to the south. Plus we needed to exchange our "empties" for a new case of Star Beer. The safety of Bayero University gave way to the city's promise of cinder-block buildings half-finished forever, and that architecture gave way to treelessness and flying sand. Even before the Kano riots we disliked the campus mosque except as a religious curio; its round spire of gold and well-swept tile floors seemed like local color, but this naïveté melted into ancient Christian dread when we discovered that Zaria Road, although a divided highway connecting the campus to the city, was a pathway to the hereafter for Muslims who might be running late to prayers, thereby driving on the wrong side of the road to avoid traffic, believing that to die on the way would instantly take them to heaven and to Allah. If we as beer drinkers and humanists are taken out in the process, it's unfortunate—but not to them. That's what can happen if we get in the way.

So we timed our drive. Prayers were not for another two hours. And the gunfire we've heard in the background was said to be between Muslims, although Muslim-Christian conflicts would surface often in the months and years to come, long after we'd take off across the Sahara for Algeria and France. But the new Muhammad was in town. Obviously, this "Marwa" was a false prophet and not to be tolerated any more than a preacher would be in Atlanta who claimed to be Christ himself (not even as the Second Coming). But as Westerners, we knew almost nothing of what was taking place, street level. Only later would we hear that police bullets failed to kill rioters. Instead, bullets had bounced off the radical Muslims, which caused the police to panic, understandably, and their dropped weapons would fully arm the growing numbers of Maitatsine. Anyway, we figured it was all "Islamic" and we as *Bature*, white people, were neither here nor there. We couldn't have known that the military from Lagos was starting to "mortar" the old city where "extremists" had set up headquarters. In response, additional Maitatsine followers with stores of automatic weapons were suspected of coming into Kano by way of Zaria Road, causing government loyalists and traditional Muslims to set up roadblocks.

Within a few minutes of leaving campus, without another vehicle in the rearview, a swarm of figures appeared before us. A discarded truck tire and a 50-gallon oil drum and branches from a baobab tree littered the two-lane road. In support of the military, volunteers without a naira to their name—on the same day that our millionaire icon of peace was murdered—waved crowbars or broom handles, or cradled stones in both hands. They looked like some early species of *Homo nigerius*, as rendered at a low-budget museum. The only good news was that their eyes widened in surprise to see two white people instead of Libyan-backed supporters. We slowed down and stopped. Through our car window the road-blockers speak in Hausa, then English: "Out, out of the car." Wendy and I obey as their weapons are bobbing shoulder-high, warming up like athletes with javelins or shot putts. Then they point at our shoes and say in Hausa, then English, "Off." *How bad is this going to get?* I ask myself. *So this is what you do when Nigerian locals stop your borrowed car. If they want your shoes, you give them over. Socks too.* Barefoot now we had to bend our legs like horses to show the bottoms of our feet. *OK, but why?* Later on we hear that rebels would draw some kind of symbol on their feet to verify their allegiance to the Maitatsine. Next the volunteer force checks under the bonnet and back seats for bombs. *Or missiles?* Suddenly we are allowed to go as a second car approaches, a Peugeot with real Black Muslims inside. Our moment had passed. We were left to go buy beer. The colonized were finished searching the colonizer (being white, it was assumed we were British). The incident gave me the sense of now-you-see-what-it-feels-like-to-be-each-other. Wendy and I, afterwards, tell ourselves to be less stupid: just open expired boxes of macaroni and play another few days of Scrabble. Wait for the corrupt military to close ranks.

Not long after Lennon was murdered, spontaneous mourners in Atlanta joined hands in a park, ever-widening their circle until five football fields made up the interior, close to the size of Kano's Old City. The willingness of the Nigerian government to raze the heart of Kano reminds me of how high the stakes get when weaponry and religion join forces. The jewel of Kano, an ancient city at the junction of trade routes that went almost everywhere and brought in about everything, a city of merchants that had every conceivable ethnic and religious and cultural heritage, was gone. Muslim against Muslim, Nigerian against Nigerian (though Marwa was Cameroonian), neighbor against neighbor, it was self-destruction. But if Islamic followers could go against their own like that, how readily would they go against others, in their foreign countries?

I don't remember buying a photograph of the Maitatsine leader from some vendor at a traffic circle, but Wendy told me this detail decades later. She thought she still had the photo but never did find it. Our friend Stewart Brown, then at Bayero and now at the University of Birmingham, says in an email what I also don't remember, that Marwa's body would not decompose, and this rumor was proof to many that he *was* a prophet, *the* prophet, Mohammad.

It had been many years since I held the letters I had written home, letters given back to me when my parents recently moved into a retirement community. To my surprise they contain a bevy of details: the Harmatton air finally gives way overhead from its own weight, plans to see Yolo and continue south to Calabar. And the manual typewriter's ink readable now as ever. I also gaze at a photograph that Wendy took of Stewart and me standing in the doorway of a traditional Housa building, perhaps the front of the emir's palace, ornately painted stucco, heavy window frames, my white button-down shirt, arms akimbo, jeans too thick for the hot weather, feet planted with the confidence of an untrained boxer. I barely recall that day. But maybe it's best to have amnesia when you've lived like an imp.

The pocket-small journal I took with me to Nigeria that September is not much help. In fact, there's nothing at all to go on after an entry in transit, during a layover in Amsterdam: merely a sentence or two about the flat, imagistic poetry in some issue of the *London Review of Books*. Then, after arriving in Kano, notes on where to find the elusive Government Coastal Agent, the Hausa word for "broom," and the name of our first night's hotel, The Duala. That was it for the next four months of living in West Africa, proof of my self-identification as a postsymbolist poet, obviously in the tradition of Rimbaud, gunrunner extraordinaire. My best work was already behind me—as an MA thesis archived in the library at UC Davis? This stance of mine was captured, unbeknownst to me, in my copying out a few lines by Thomas Hobbes:

> For what is the heart, but a spring;
> And the nerves, but so many strings;
> And the joynts, but so many wheels . . .

As I write now, I'm grateful that not *all* was lost on me. My preference for bodies of conceptual knowledge including my trust in causes and effects would transform into finding solace in Buddhist commentaries and explanations of karma.

I am teaching a course at Penn State–Erie called Introduction to Buddhism. While trying to prepare a lecture on the Six Ox-herding Pictures, I read that December 8th is considered by some to be the date of the Buddha's awakening. The author goes on to explain the "unconditioned," the right view of what is before us, unobscured by concepts, simply this moment as is. Such "unknowing" reminds me of what is found by new travelers on their first day in-country, seeing the place right off despite their background reading in a *Lonely Planet Guide*. Our first time ever where we are, as a beginner open to what there is, unfiltered in part because we don't know what's what. Just face the unfamiliar—what is irreducible to a phrase on a postcard. But also, preparing for class, I ran across this sentence by Sri Nisargadatta: "I have just heard of New York. To me it is a word."

Meanwhile, Wendy would continue to run her body like a vehicle, cranking out book after book. Late in my 40s I came to accept this bag of skin with its seven holes, though I too would suffer from a bad wheel and heart-valve problems. However, back in 1980, hobbled by the genre of journal-as-quarterly-report, my next entry was four months later after Wendy and I had left Kano to cross the Sahara, heading for Zinder to the north on a bus, on February 4, 1981: "The bus fare was 10 naira," I noted, which in U.S. dollars equaled, well, I forget now. But within hours a fan belt snaps outside of Dambata, a place not found in our library's atlas but where teenage soldiers looking for contraband rifled through our belongings spread out beside the gravel road. I acted nonchalant and bored, like a Frenchman.

Those four missing months, as the calendar equivalent of the *Rub Al Kali*, began to find me one afternoon when hanging up a curtain in my guestroom, when the word *guesthouse* occurred to me, the common name for "hotel" in West Africa. The tie-dye curtain I held, as if for the first time, pictures a turtle with a shell of white and pink circles, and is signed

"E. Lere" and dated 1980. Although my having this cloth was living proof of where I'd been, those four months without a journal entry make me wonder about all the other emotional *Rub Al Kali* in my life, all the other uncommonplaces I've been to that were thought "empty," maybe 25 percent of them seen.

Like everyone in this country, I look forward. Not necessarily to progress, although that's a nice idea, but to what is next, what is within reach, what's ahead? We'd rather not linger on bygones. Why look back? As our current president has said, "I think that we all agree, the past is over." So whatever *really* happened is anybody's guess, and secondary. A kind of relativity infuses the past although the details of what took place yesterday or the day before can be generally agreed upon, if it is important enough to agree upon. Much beyond that, last month, two years ago or a decade, it's pretty inaccessible. We settle on imprecisions, our individual selections from the swirl of infinite details. Those who travel together know this multiplicity, know their later narratives are all variations on what can never be set straight. My family tends toward the less problematic future, which no one with any sense at all would claim is real, or discernable. Forthcoming details may be likely or counted on, but are far from given. As Americans we believe in letting go of the past while hanging on to our hopes. As the saying goes, *the past is past.* From the impact of Alex Haley's *Roots* on suburbia, and the outcrop of family trees that resulted from reclaiming where we came from, Africa or Ashtabula, the Census Bureau offices across the country were inundated for a few years. Even my father and I elbowed our way among the crowds. But predictably the "who's who" lost its staying power, like autumn leaves from a water maple, and the paperwork of names and who begot whom was given a file folder, or at best made its way into a safety deposit box. We all got back to making plans and moved on. But what I remember still is how our climbing the family tree ended with a depressing detail: according to the 1830 Census, our family in Virginia owned two slaves—probably taken out of Nigeria. At first I thought *only two?* But I quickly thought better of that, resorting instead to the soothing truth of how socially conditioned we are, and that my family members were victims of nineteenth-century practicalities—to make a go at farming. *Let go of what's gone.*

Toyin Falola's book *Violence in Nigeria* has the best sociological study of Kano's religious upheavals that came to a head in December 1980. Falola calls his chapter on Northern Nigeria "A Reign of Terror." Now three years after the derivation, "terrorists" has taken on new meaning for Americans, I am reminded of how much is already under way, remotely, elsewhere in the world, already in motion yet unfolding in such small increments that we won't bring them into focus until they are upon us, as the next unforeseen event. This creates a history of finishing touches. However slowly the changes are taking place, we are slower to see them. As Suzanne Doyle writes in one of her poems, "We carry with us, unaware, / The certain shape of our own ends." Wendy would have taken to those lines.

So when America's greatest boxer changed his name from Cassius Clay to Mohammad Ali, and when Black Muslims had a "cell" operating in Oakland, and when every major city in America had demonstrations protesting our foreign policy in Southeast Asia, we as a nation should then have known that someday the message would go from Molotov cocktails to fully-fueled jets. Had the Kano upheaval of 1980 been seen for what it was, and not reduced to the work of Islamic "radicals" or fanatics far off, elsewhere, we might have figured that the self-serving *us* would meet the sacrificial *them*, and that our New York City skyline is not unlike the once vital city of Old Kano, a center that colonialists thought to name *The Mecca of Saharan Trade*. ▪

I Met a Man Who Has Seen the Ivory-billed Woodpecker, and This Is What He Told Me

Nancy Lord

THE WOODS

The swamp forest is only a corridor between rice fields, but the ancient cypress tower there. Winds the week before had bared the trees, laying a carpet of tupelo golds, sweetgum reds, the rusty cypress needles. It was possible to walk dry-footed among the fluted trunks and spreading knees, the wet-season watermarks waist-high on a man.

WOODPECKERS

The usual woodpeckers were all there: their bouncing flight, the sounds of rapping, scrabbling on bark. They called *keer-uck* and *querrr-querrr, pik* and *peek, yucka, yucka yucka*. The downy and the hairy were there, the red-bellied, the yellow-bellied sapsucker. The pileated was there, the largest of them, the red crest, drumming like the pounding of mallets, loud. It was a birdy place: the wildness of trees in every aspect of life and death, with pecked-out cavities, with beetles, with peeling bark.

WOODPECKER!

This is the word he let out as he grabbed for his wife's arm. He knew what he was seeing, and he could not believe that he was, in fact, seeing it. If for 60 years something has been missing, it takes more than the sight of a large, utterly distinct flying bird to convince a man of what is possible.

EIGHT SECONDS

One for the bird flying toward him from deep forest. Two for the bird landing 12 feet up a cypress trunk and clinging there in profile. Three for the bird sliding around to the back of the tree, hiding itself. Two for the bird flashing back the way it came, a single whomping wingbeat and all that white.

COLOR

The colossal male crest, of course—the brilliant flame so inescapably, unignorably red and pointedly tall. The white was more the surprise, down the neck and across the shoulders like a saddle, and the two large wedges shaped by folded wings. And the black, the black that was not charcoal, not ebony, only the absolutest of all blacks, and blacker still beside white.

SOUND

He never heard the bird, not the *henk, henk* of its call, not its tooting, staccato song, not the double rap that distinguishes its tree knocking from any other woodpecker's. The early naturalists described ivory-bills as social and raucous, but whatever birds have survived have had to be shy and wary, as quiet as bark. They live by stealth.

WHAT HE MISSED

Not the bill, not the length, which he showed me, holding his fingers apart—"Three inches." Not the thickness of the bill—this time, making a fat circle of forefinger and thumb. What he forgot to notice was the pale color of the bill, the look of ivory. In the blitz of recognition, he missed that, as he missed the very yellow eye.

THE QUOTE

No puny pileated but a whacking big bird, he said, quoting Roger Tory Peterson, who witnessed the ivory-bill in 1941 and called that occasion the greatest birding moment of his long birding career. Peterson kept a page for the bird in his guidebooks, hope against hope, for years after others had shifted it to the extinct category. But a decade ago, even Peterson con-cluded that the bird had reached its end, like the woodlands it had inhab-ited, and no longer existed except in memory.

After

For a long time, he had to sit on a log and not say anything. He played the image of the bird over and over and over in his mind. It was too great a thing to comprehend—that he was there, and the bird was there, and he and the bird were breathing the same air. After the descriptions and illus-trations by Catesby, Audubon, and Wilson; and after the photos and films from the Louisiana swamps in the 1940s; and after the late but extensive Tanner scholarship about life history and habitat; and after Peterson's pas-sion and despair; and after the fleeting white of new video and all the talk about the ghost bird and the grail bird and the Lord God bird; and after his dead father's lifetime of desire and his own matching but far-fetched desire and all the desire of the world; after all that, the ivory-billed woodpecker was still more than a person could imagine. It was as beautiful and as per-fect as only it itself, its living being, could be. ■

The Lear Years

Richard Katrovas

I am too old to raise an infant daughter, but I do not regret, in any station of my psyche, her presence. She was a surprise, a jolt, a double take over the pink-tinged double stripes announcing her emergence from the void. She's a beauty, a keeper. She will be my Cordelia as I enter the Lear years, though I hope my two older daughters do not duplicate the proud king's other offspring. I hope to be doted on by all three, to whom I'll gladly give, in equal portions, all.

But, though I'm not certain if she'll "keep (me) young" as some say happens in such instances, I can testify that she doesn't make me *feel* young; I feel my 51 years more acutely when I hold her, coo into her face. I have never been quick with numbers, but one needn't be a math maven to know that as she's graduating high school I'll be 69; I'll be 73 as she's moving the tassel on her college mortarboard and beaming as she traverses the stage. I'll indeed be in my Lear Years for most of her adolescence and young adulthood. Then I'll die, while she is still young.

I run; I lift weights. I'm quite strong. I'm a type-two diabetic, but control the condition with diet and exercise. A lot of people on both sides of my family lived into their 80s, but they were mostly females; I don't know much about male mortality on either side, partly because there simply weren't that many males and, besides, I've lost contact with the extended families.

Dying's one thing, preparing quite another. It is strange to want to live less for yourself than for certain others, but that is the primary existential feature of parenting. When I catch myself being a little reckless, driving the freeway aggressively or walking a street most folks would consider dicey, or

From *Raising Girls in Bohemia: Meditations of an American Father* when the turbulence on a trans-Atlantic flight becomes extreme, what blazes through my mind is not an image of my doom but rather a tableau of my children in mourning, my daughters processing my loss.

I considered myself young for too long. I know I speak for many when I say that becoming not young, though it is a gradual process, can feel sudden in its effect.

A respected writer referred to me in a blurb on the back of my first book as "the best of the new poets." He was being too kind, indulging in the sort of inflated rhetoric that characterizes almost all blurbs, but I didn't stop considering myself a "new poet" for many years after. I don't mean I consciously thought of myself that way, but rather that it was an unconscious assumption into my 40s that I was a "young" poet, a young man.

As a young man I worried about being a coward, which meant of course that I was a coward, and the coward's classic defense is to tempt fate, ostentatiously but in a calculated fashion. My teenage daughter will matter-of-factly announce, "Tata, I'm scared," after viewing something troubling on TV before going to bed. She is frank and unequivocal about the effect of *The Blair Witch Project* or a UFO documentary on her psyche. She is unashamed of her fear, and I envy her that, and am proud to have encouraged such a lack.

The main difference between my young self and my present one is that I am now at least a little comfortable with my cowardice, thought not as comfortable as my daughter is with her fear. Fear and cowardice are fundamentally different. Fear becomes cowardice only when lying about one's fear is a strong compulsion, when acting and speaking other than how one feels seems necessary. It's a guy thing. Machismo is the lie that transforms fear into cowardice, even or especially for the man who manages to act bravely.

As I age, my gendered identity becomes more ironic. I'm not afraid anymore of being laughed at. I'm not afraid of being thought a fool or a clawless monster. I'm not afraid of failure, not really. I'm not afraid of being neglected, ignored, at least in a professional sense. I'm not afraid of young men; I've met few I've calculated to be of much physical threat, but over the coming years I'll feel, of course, more and more physically vulnerable. As I age, my terror of extinction mellows, and I believe that this must be something chemical; surely the organism prepares for death. Perhaps, as Eros mellows it also becomes a little fuzzy and attendant, like a pet, or a loyal fool who speaks in puzzles.

I love and admire those of my parents' generation, especially writers, especially poets, who have remained fierce, folks in their 70s who are still on the make in the fame game of the arts. They are the sort who, as they expire, will feel that they ran out of time, left things unfinished. One should hope that none—and I'm thinking of three or four who have been friends and mentors—feels bitterness; all will have completed significant works, won significant awards, fashioned a legacy in the hearts of people like me who will be committed to keeping their good work alive as long as we are, and indeed passing it on with whatever portion of our own work warrants transmission, on the ether, via the hearts of the young. I hope to remain fierce, fiercely engaged, involved, unto dénouement.

But, more importantly, I hope to age in such a way that my daughters, and now especially the infant Ellie, perceive me as a fount of life, of vitality, of affirmation that there is never a good time to retrench to the garden, that the good fight is always preferable to tending the garden.

Unless they are the garden, in which case I'll tend to them by being fierce, fiercely alive, involved, engaged, like Lear but without the royal hubris, I hope.

In New Orleans, in the mid-'80s, when I lived in the apartment between Bourbon and Dauphine that my landlady swore was the original House of the Rising Sun, a retired Filipino sailor, my neighbor, Bob, entered dementia quite suddenly. He was a wisp of a man, moving with unintentional stealth each morning and night by my back door, across the gangway overlooking the lush courtyard of our landlord and landlady. He occupied a "slave quarter" apartment, a single room and a bathroom that could not be accessed from the street. My apartment was three large rooms with 15-foot ceilings; my three floor-to-ceiling windows overlooked Rue St. Louis. Bob's only view was the courtyard, which I also had access to from my kitchen window and door. He and I shared a view of that bricked garden at the far end of which crouched a two-century-old voodoo shrine covered with charcoal X's, its crown lined with blue candle nubs. In season, the garden was resplendent with magnolias, and the odor from the gangway, the narrow balcony Bob and I shared, would be dizzying. Ferns, green fireballs, dripped from clay pots along the 30-foot mossy-brick walls. Sometimes I'd lean on the dubious railing, newly whitewashed rotting wood, and smoke. I'd glance left and spy Bob staring down into the verdant decay, the funky little paradise of the courtyard.

No one ever visited; I'd have known. He lived on a pension from the U.S. Navy; I discovered later that Judge Levy, the 93-year-old owner of the House of the Rising Sun, whose 40-something wife, Darleen Jacobs, insisted that the building had, indeed, sheltered the storied brothel, rented to Bob for a pittance.

I responded to the first howls clutching a serrated kitchen knife; I could see Bob through his window naked under the kitchen table, the four kitchen chairs lined up on their sides as a kind of barrier. I scanned the room; no one else was there. The bathroom door was open. Empty.

I tapped on the window; his eyes caught mine and trepidation shaded to terror. I was holding a foot-long blade, saluting to peer through the sun-blazed glass. Even a sane person would have been frightened.

He would leave his hovel clothed and impeccably groomed each morning, and return in the evenings to be crazy, howling and chattering in three languages. One day he did not transition to well-groomed sanity, but remained ensconced in madness.

On the third day of his howling, his screaming at demons and ex-wives, at an executive officer who had humiliated him, and at an actual ghost, that is, something he called a ghost, I phoned the police for at least the fourth time since Bob had begun the slide; once again they were useless, insisting that they couldn't take him away if he wasn't hurting anyone or himself. I pointed out that he'd been barricaded in that room for three days; I'd seen him eating saltines, drinking water from the tap, but surely he would soon run out of food and then, by virtue of being unable to negotiate the trip to the store, would begin to starve. Wouldn't that indeed constitute his hurting himself? They told me to call when he began to starve, otherwise I should search out his family; only family could have him committed if he had a domicile, wasn't dangerous, and was able, even minimally, to sustain himself.

Bob didn't have a phone; all the mail for the three apartments in the House of the Rising Sun got shoved through the same slot; he never had any, not even junk. I peeked again through his window; he was huddled under his table, wearing only skivvies, scraping the edges of an all-but-empty peanut butter jar with a spoon. I looked for photos, family pictures; there were none. Only a faux oil landscape, a lake and trees, in a gaudy golden frame hung on the wall. There was a transistor radio on the fridge, a little TV at the foot of his bed. I considered entering and rummaging through his drawers for contact information, but didn't want to set him howling under such a circumstance. Technically, I'd be breaking and entering. I'd be committing a crime.

That night he wept, unceasingly. He didn't howl; he didn't admonish demons or wives, argue with a ghost. He wept hugely through the night, moaning names, begging forgiveness. I couldn't sleep. I attempted repose on the couch, with the bedroom door shut, but his sobs seeped through the oak, and so I smoked and listened, and watched from my darkened living room with the high ceilings and the high windows, from the midst of diaphanous shadows, the dregs of the French Quarter flow in and out of the Roundup, the cowboy/biker/transvestite bar on the other side of Rue St. Louis.

So this is what it comes to, I thought. These are the Lear years, the years of wretched solitude unto madness, of wandering in a storm of remembrance, of losing, losing everything.

That week, I was showing the BBC *King Lear* to my sophomores; I showed a Shakespeare play at that point in each semester, toward the end. It took four class periods, so it was a nice break from lecturing and Socratic class discussions. My students had a *King Lear* study guide I handed out each semester; they were answering questions, constructing little essays, frowning through secondary materials.

I'd taught other Shakespeare plays in that poetry and drama genre course for sophomores, *Hamlet* and *Richard II*, but had settled on *King Lear*, and taught it consecutive semesters. I was still young enough to identify with Hamlet, but Lear, I felt even then, spoke to my future. And as Bob the retired sailor sobbed at the end of his life, poured forth his boundless remorse, I realized that if his dementia had been inevitable, such loneliness should not have been. Where were his children? Where were the sons? The daughters? The issue of bad marriages, the issue of the ex-wives with whom he still argued, against whom he still raged in his demented heart?

Should I act as a son, take hold of his life, secure what succor may still be available in such a world? Should I play Edgar, the good son?

I spoke to Judge Levy, who was at least 15 years older than Bob but incredibly lucid, in control of his every sense, and decent, deeply and quietly decent. The ancient fellow was married to a large, loud woman 50 years his junior, one of the most colorful and feared trial lawyers in New Orleans who could turn on the "Y'at" (from the Ninth Ward salutation, "Where y'at, Brother Man!") and woo any local, predominately black jury. Judge Levy, still on the bench (he would literally be forced to retire), was fully engaged in all of his business dealings, though Darleen ran the show. Judge Levy and Darleen Jacobs took control. They found out that Bob was indeed estranged from a scattered family, but that he had veterans' benefits that would cover his hospitalization, the extended care he would require. They were powerful people. I assumed they knew everyone, the mayor, the city councilmen, the police chief, everyone with power. Darleen Jacobs made a couple of phone calls and Bob was gone when I returned the next afternoon from the university.

In better days, Bob and I never spoke, but he'd watch from his window as I'd feed my birds, mostly mockingbirds I'd raised through fledge into adulthood, when I'd set them free in batches of three to seven, in the same number and company as I'd received them from the Bird Rehab Center at the New Orleans Audubon Zoo. For several seasons, my first wife's friend, an anorexic Up-Town woman who did volunteer work at the Rehab Center, would give me batches of birds to rehabilitate, local babies who'd fallen from nests. I'd keep them in boxes, feed them by hand for weeks, clean their feathers, teach them to fly in the house, then set them free from the balcony overlooking the courtyard. Some got eaten by cats, but most would return to that balcony for many days following their release; sometimes four or five grown birds would arrive at precisely the same time early in the morning and beg to be fed, and I'd pad out onto the little balcony holding an open can of moist cat food and drop a pinch or two down each gullet before they'd flit away.

Bob watched, sipping coffee, and sometimes he'd dip his chin to me, not so much, it seemed, in admiration as recognition. ■

Post-Mortem

Peggy Shinner

After my father's funeral, his ladyfriend Rose said he'd had a good send-off. I knew what she meant. Piser-Weinstein was packed, hardly an empty seat in the house. The rabbi, unknown to my father but briefed by my brother and me, was warm and well-spoken. He was Rose's rabbi. My father was not observant. The rabbi had graciously met with us the day before the funeral at my father's apartment. I was impressed that he'd make a house call, to strangers no less, and on a Sunday. Tell me about your father, he said. I'd compiled a list of his traits on a yellow legal pad. In the den I read them off. Occasionally my brother and I disagreed. He was con-tentious, I said. Contentious? What do you mean contentious? Argumentative. Okay, argumentative. The next day the rabbi stood before the assembled mourners. Nate was charming, the rabbi told us. He was funny. Hardworking. Frugal. A stickler. Yes, he could be argumentative. And the mourners, in agreement, laughed. He was, on occasion, hot-tem-pered. They nodded again. He was a simple man, not ostentatious. He loved his children. He loved the White Sox. He will be missed.

My father's brain is in a jar. That's how I imagine it. The curly mass squeezed in a Ball jar, sitting on a subterranean shelf somewhere in the basement of Evanston Hospital. I imagine it this way in part because I put it there. My father died on November 25, 1988, at five in the morning, Evanston hospital, Evanston, Illinois, a month after he had a stroke on the Dan Ryan expressway, and I, as one of his two closest living relatives, con-sented to an autopsy.

There was nothing unusual about my father's death. It was not a med-ical mystery. He'd had, as one of the residents put it, "a major bleed." To paraphrase another, he'd suffered a medical insult. Or, as he himself said when I entered his cubicle in the emergency room, *I had a strake*, which felt, as I saw him slipping, no less than that the gods of fate had driven a stake through his heart. There followed a craniotomy, tracheotomy, pulmonary embolism, mucous plug, brain death, pneumonia. But when, four weeks later, in the light of early morning, the attending physician asked, as part of the routine post-mortem protocol, about an autopsy, I felt what I can only call, even after 16 years, a twinge of hope. My father was dead, but maybe the autopsy would explain it.

The pathologist-cum-essayist F. Gonzalez Crussi, writing about autopsy, talks about "the familiar Y-shaped incision," and I feel a catch in my breathing. Familiar to whom?

Like a would-be scientist I entertain thoughts of discovery, causes, the seat of disease; but like the daughter I really am I blanch at the flash of a blade, the whir of a saw.

Autopsy is a dissection—an invasion—of the human body. If I didn't know that then I know it now.

Then, five-fifteen, five-thirty, the hospital corridor dim, dawn not yet breaking, a bleary-eyed resident asked if we would consent to an autopsy. It was part of his job, his checklist. There were four of us. My brother Gary, his girlfriend Jill, my lover Ann, me. We were children, all of us, and unaccustomed to making these decisions. We had spent the night at the Holiday Inn, not wanting to leave the hospital, not wanting to stay, a limbo night, awaiting one man's death. We'd asked the nurse to call us when it was time.

The Holiday Inn looked more like a parking garage than a hotel. The front entrance seemed like the back. The four of us were almost giddy. Two siblings and their lovers spending the night in a hotel together. Did their parents know? An ill-fitting shirt, cheap navy blue tie, the desk clerk was a college student—that's how I assessed him: from Northwestern—and I felt like we were pulling something over on him. At the same time I wanted to include him in our conspiracy. Our father's in the hospital, I told him, meaning me and my brother; we're expecting a phone call. He looked frightened, somber, perhaps a little confused; or maybe that's just how I wanted him to look.

We got a double double, and charged it on American Express. None of us even had a toothbrush. A placard on the dresser suggested we call the front desk if we forgot something—toothpaste, a razor—but none of us did. Ann and I heard rustling from the other bed; clothes flung on the floor. This is weird, one of us said. The last time I'd slept in the same room with my brother I was ten.

We arrived back in the room in time for my father's last half-hour of breathing. We surrounded his bed. A man across the hall died too, and they wheeled him out on a gurney, a woman hovering over him. We were all witnesses to the newly dead. I stirred at the offer—it was an offer, wasn't it?—of an autopsy. To help others, the resident suggested. I wasn't interested in others but I kept that under wraps. I had other motives, murky even to myself. This was solely a seduction of my own making. Jill and Ann demurred; my brother was uncertain. My father was still in his room but not for long. There's no dallying with the dead. I plied Gary's uncertainty; pushed forward; signed the necessary form.

Somehow I got the impression they called you. After all, we'd embarked on the procedure together, doctor and next of kin, we were co-conspirators of sorts, or if not conspirators, explorers, charting the hidden terrain, the buried byways, of the human body. I, of course, was the armchair explorer, waiting at home by the telephone, while the doctor, my cohort, was out in the field. But I was the one with the vested interest, the one for whom the results really mattered.

What was taking so long?

Dr. Eller, neurologist, brain surgeon, head honcho, didn't call. Three weeks after the funeral, after my father's burial, I left a message with Dr. Eller's answering service.

I own *The Jewish Book of Why*. Its format—a question posed, a question answered—is simple, straightforward. The Jews have been known to be a querying people. *Why is blue a Jewish color? Because the Mediterranean, the largest body of water near ancient Israel, casts a blue hue. Because blue is a reflection of God's throne, which is believed to be decorated with sapphires.* The book itself has a dark blue cover and flyleaf.

Years later, it is to this source that I turn. It spares no words. *Jewish law forbids mutilating the body. Kavod ha'met*, the prohibition against the desecration of the dead. My body, the one that reads this, flinches. The afternoon of my father's death, when I told my great-aunt that he was undergoing an autopsy, she said, Cut him up? Never. Her blue eyes, legend in our family, flashed like sapphires.

There are, *The Jewish Book of Why* says, some exceptions. Autopsy is allowed in cases of homicide or where there is suspicion of homicide; and when the findings are *certain* to contribute to the body of medical knowledge. This principle is called *pikkuah nefesh*. Saving a life.

Certain? The criteria are exacting. Daughter or doctor, who would pass muster? Are you ever wrong? I asked Dr. Eller a week before my father's death, when a mucous plug lodged in his throat and stopped his breathing, cutting off oxygen to his head. Yes, Dr. Eller conceded after a pause, but what daughter, though grasping at whatever straw she could, could fail to hear the unspoken words, *But not about this.*

1994: my friend Nora and I are both orphans. We're both in our 40s, both Jewish, still children. We talk about our parents. Hers: New Yorkers, sophisticated; her father irascible, opinionated; her mother—on a budget—fashionable. They listened to music. They had a cabin in upstate New York. My parents: sellers, of clothes; dresses, suits, my mother in the showroom, my father on the road; he went to Nebraska, walked through hotel lobbies full of dowagers, only he pronounced it dew-wadge-ers; this before I was born; later, they washed diapers, other people's clothes, they owned and operated a laundromat, my mother talked about the smell of shit. What did I know of them? As a child, my mother tormented a cat by sticking its whiskers up the kitchen faucet. My father, I learned, fathered a child with someone other than my mother. All that remains, 40 years later, when my aunt told me, is the name of the obstetrician. There are many facts, but these parents are all dead now.

Nora and I talk about how much we want them back. Like good children, we miss them. We bargain. What would we give up to get them back? What would we put on the table? We go straight to the body, our most coveted bargaining chip. Would we give up a leg? The stakes, it seems, are high when bargaining with the dead; a body part for the entire body; no, neither of us would give up a limb. What about a hand, a foot, then? Would you relinquish that? We look at each other. Our eyes film over; our voices waver. We love them, we miss them. Each of us, we're remembering; our whole lives pass before us. But no, if the price is a hand or a foot, we would not pay it. We shrug our shoulders. We want to remain intact. Nervously we laugh. This is ridiculous but does that stop us? Okay, then, one of us continues, the test apparently not over; what about a finger? Would you give up a finger to get one of your parents back? Each of us looks inward. I do not know what she sees inside but it does not take us long to answer.

Not even a finger, it turns out, would we give up to get our parents back. Not one single digit.

I have in my possession my father's death certificate. I dig it out of a plastic bag filled with other accountings: birthday cards my father saved and dated; legal papers authorizing his name change from Shinitzky to Shinner; something called the "Ten Commandments of a Winner," homespun homilies to shore yourself up when you stand in front of the mirror wondering who you are and what you've become. "A WINNER says 'I'm good, but not as good as I ought to be.' A loser says 'I'm not as bad as other people.'"

Issued before the autopsy, the death certificate is a document brimming with possibility. I know what it says but I'm sure it says more. It's layered, if only I could read it. Part of its power lies in the fact that it remains. It stands in his stead. *Nathan Shinner. Male. White. American.* An incomplete rendering is better than none at all. This is an official document; a certificate; a ceremony on paper. He was the son of Anna and Isadore. He served in World War II. He made his living in the furniture business. On the lower right-hand corner the certificate is embossed with a seal that looks like an emblem or crown. The state notices your comings and goings. It takes an interest. The original is filed with the Office of Vital Records in Springfield.

I study this piece of paper, which is, I tell myself when I feel the need for the leveling effect of reality, a photocopy. I've come back to it again and again. My father died of (a) bronchopneumonia, due to or as a consequence of (b) illegible, due to or as a consequence of (c) intracerebral hemorrhage, *c* being the last and underlying cause, the certificate says, and the first of the insults. It's signed by one C. Laurie Brown, Local Registrar, who, in a slanted, authoritative signature, certifies "that the foregoing is a true and correct copy of the death record for the decedent" that she certainly never met.

A month after my father died, I got together with his younger sister Zelda in a kosher pizza parlor on Devon. We met there to talk, but we were not close. There'd been a long-standing battle over my father that probably began 40 years earlier—the day he left Albany Park and the apartment above his family's dry cleaning store and married my long-waisted, melancholy mother—and had surfaced yet again at his *shiva* when Zelda, Orthodox, argued with the rabbi, Reform and chosen by my brother and me, about his right to assemble a *minyan* and preside over my father's passing. This was more than a theological parting, two branches of Judaism duking it out in one diminished family; this was, at its very root, proprietary. *Who owns this man?* Who, among his survivors, shall stake their claim and secure the body? Zelda had left my father's house that night, gone back to her own, and for the rest of the week, placed her couch cushion on the floor and sat *shiva* there. At the restaurant, both my parents dead now, she was going to tell me how it was.

I ordered a slice of mushroom pizza, rubbery disks toppled from a can. The table was the same color as the mushrooms. Even though it was winter, Zelda drank iced tea. She looked like my grandmother, who, when my father—firstborn, beloved son—was drafted into the army, tried to kill herself: gray bristly hair, eyelids folded like draperies, a jaw that might have been excavated. Her voice had the same yawing energy. Do you know about Margie? she said, wiping a napkin over her profuse lips. My father might as well have been served up on the table between us.

Margie? That gentile name, so like my own, sounded like a recrimination.

In that dung-colored restaurant Zelda was lit from within. *You think he's so good but I know better,* she flung across the table. I tried to ward her off, protest that of course he wasn't perfect, making reference to his argumentative nature, his capacity for meanness, as if I were admitting to my own faults, but my efforts were useless. Grief had vitalized her, given her an added edge. She would wipe out my father, as I knew him, and replace him with a version of her own. She plunked her arms down and proceeded.

The facts were few and simple. My father dated Margie after the war, *before your mother,* Zelda made it a point to add, in order, it seemed, to preempt her. Margie wasn't Jewish. He got her pregnant. There was a baby. A boy. Here Zelda paused, and in the momentary silence that filled the space between us, the baby materialized before me, fully sprouted and squirming.

He paid all the medical expenses, she said, but beyond that she had no idea what happened to either of them, Margie or the baby, nor did she know the baby's name; all she remembered, as she delivered this news across the table, was the name of the obstetrician; and all I remember, as I write this years later, is not the obstetrician's name, which I looked up once in the phone book and have since, regretfully, forgotten, but the name of the baby, the name I gave the baby, slapped on as he appeared that day in front of me, sudden and unexpected, at the kosher pizza place on Devon, slick from the labor of his birth: Little Marvin.

Little Marvin? This half-brother, at least four years older, has always been a baby to me, his gestation complete over the course of one lunchtime and his growth terminated during that same lunch as well; I cannot imagine him as a man. I try and he turns beefy and old, like other middle-aged men on the street, nondescript, ordinary, and I prefer to keep him as a newborn. Or perhaps he becomes too real, his paunch overhanging his pants, his face dark and stubbly, needing a shave; better the soft-skinned, milk-fed face of an infant, benign and ubiquitous. He appeared soon after my father had died, and, I suppose, just like my father, he'll live on indefinitely, haunting the fringes, a spectral presence.

In hospitals, there are hierarchies of waiting. The day lounge, the surgery lounge, the intensive care family room—in each you wait successively, agonizingly longer, because, of course, the procedures you are waiting to hear about are increasingly invasive and complex. Once I waited with my mother, for her mother to come out of surgery. At the time my mother was dying of thyroid cancer but nobody was ready to admit that yet. As we sat in the waiting room—volunteer dressed in a blue smock, framed silk-screen of choppy waves, clock reminding you the doctor said surgery would take three hours and now it's been four—my mother told me about a woman she'd recently heard of who had parked her car by some railroad tracks and walked in front of the train. Do you feel like a train is coming? I wanted to ask but couldn't.

And while we're waiting? While we're turning to the picture of choppy waves? They're cutting the body open. For now it's *they*—us and them, we and they—that objectified mass of muggers (don't they, in a dark corner of our imagination, put something over our loved one's face to knock her or him out?) and cutters and slicers to whom we've entrusted our parent, child, lover, or friend. First they numb it, a part of it or the whole, and then, tools in hand, they make the cut. Scalpels, forceps, hemostats, clamps, retractors, drills, saws, sutures, staples, swabs, sponges, scissors, scopes, lasers. The list of instruments, to the uninitiated, is staggering and often arcane. Some are frighteningly familiar—the saw—and others, like the surgical robotic arm (one model is named da Vinci), the latest in modern technology. How many of us have not seen a TV representation of an operating room, *Dr. Kildare*, *Marcus Welby*, *ER*, or more recently, *Scrubs*: the raised gloved hands, the sterile scrubs, the monitors, the tray of gleaming instruments, and the doctor, hovering over the covered, recumbent, sedated body, turning a fraction toward the nurse, extending a hand, and bidding, "Scalpel"?

Informed consent. That's the covenant binding most surgeries: the healer duly informs, the supplicant knowingly submits. We want to be cured, we want to be fixed. But at its root, its most elementary, consent is consent to cut. Break the skin; enter the body. Permission to come in and have a look. It's not permission lightly given, nor, says the essayist Richard Selzer, himself a surgeon, easily received. In a sense, surgery breaks a taboo against seeing into the body. "Even now, after so many voyages within, so much exploration, I feel the same sense that one must not gaze into the body, the same irrational fear that it is an evil deed for which punishment awaits. Consider. The sight of our internal organs is denied us. To how many men is it given to look upon their own spleens, their hearts, and live?"

When they opened up my father's brain after the stroke, to relieve the swelling they said, I didn't really understand what was happening. *They were going into my father's brain.* I could not, literally, imagine it. But then again, perhaps it was not for me to imagine. Not for me, even figuratively, to gain access. We grant that responsibility to someone else. The surgeon makes the cut, and then the poet, suggests Selzer, figures out what to make of it.

So, along with Ann and a few friends, I waited in the intensive care family lounge at midnight. There were cartons of Chinese food from The Pineyard. The television was on: home-shopping. Down some corridor, past some outsized metal doors, in a theater brightly lit, the neurosurgeon and his crew picked and probed. Past the skull, the dura mater, into the cerebral cortex—the seat of movement and speech and thought—the doctors would see what neither my father nor I had ever seen before, and they would see it not in a picture or on a screen, but in the actual living flesh. They would seal off the ruptured vessel, clean out the blood. When they were done, they would close him up.

In the '70s I volunteered briefly at the Emma Goldman Women's Health Center, a storefront clinic that advocated a woman's control over her own body—her sexual and reproductive organs—but I always felt like an impostor. I could never quite get the hang of it, putting in the speculum, getting the cervix into view, holding up the mirror. I was clumsy, and not quite enthused. And once I managed to accomplish all this maneuvering, what, exactly, was I seeing? I would put the discharge on a slide under the microscope, as I'd seen the other health-care workers do, but I couldn't identify the shapes that seemed to shift under my unsteady gaze. Still, I kept at it for almost a year because I liked going to the biweekly meetings, where we argued whether doctors were necessary.

Ann, however, had steered clear of the self-help movement. Jokingly, but not a joke, she says that maybe there was a reason we'd never looked inside before, kept ourselves hidden, a reason beyond the conspiracy of doctors, mostly male, who presumed to know what we did not. She, for one, had had little desire to insert a speculum and see her cervix reflected in a mirror, and her disclaimer now, years later, is accompanied by a kind of shudder. Is this a distancing from our bodies so complete that all we can do is shudder in response, or is this respectful, proper distance, an innate recognition that some things are better left unseen? Look within, we tell ourselves in times of self-assessment, but that is only metaphorical.

Once I saw a video of the inside of someone's body. It was part of a one-woman show by Palestinian artist Mona Hatoum at the Museum of Contemporary Art. I entered a dark, curtained cubicle, not knowing what to expect, and watched a continuous loop video showing the sinewy trails of Hatoum's innards. There was the squish and glisten of organs, a sense of pulsing and jostling, a moist display of orange viscera. Sound accompanied the video: gurgling, bubbling, belching; preliterate sounds: the body has its own voice. Watching in the darkness of the cubicle, I had the distinct impression of being *in* something; surrounded. Skin, the identifying layer, the protective filter, had been removed, the skeleton as well, and I was immersed in the body. This was the life within the life, the body we often take for granted. Hatoum's body, but it could have been anyone's, it could have been my own. I pulled my coat closer around me. You feel so mortal when the body is exposed.

On my driver's license, next to my picture, it says DONOR. I've agreed to be an organ donor. I agreed to this the last time I renewed my license, on my 51st birthday. The back of my license informs me that THIS IS A LEGAL DOCUMENT UNDER THE UNIFORM ANATOMICAL GIFT ACT. I see, now that I look, however, that I haven't signed the form. I haven't indicated if my whole body is ripe for the taking, or only certain specified organs. You get to parcel yourself out if you want. *Take my cornea, fine, my kidneys too, but please, oh no, not my heart.* Is the document legal without a signature? Is it binding?

Ann and I went to renew our licenses together. When they asked if she wanted to become a donor, she said yes. I did too. But I agreed because she did. I followed her lead. I didn't want to be thought of as ungenerous, although I don't think Ann would think of me that way. Ann loves me because of, not in spite of, who I am. I guess I felt, in some cosmic appraisal of my own devising, I would fall short. The pressure's on to be an organ donor. The ad campaign says it's the gift of life. (Or is that blood? I have, for the record, given blood.) Who could refuse? Former Bear running back Walter Payton died because there wasn't a liver available when he needed one. He was a sweet guy with a high-pitched voice, thighs that could plow through anything, and a prankster's sense of humor. At 45, he was the fallen athlete. I suppose I was so moved by his death, not only because it came too soon, but because his descent, from heights far greater than the rest of us will likely attain, was so precipitous. As an organ donor I could help someone like him and, added bonus, pat myself on the back in anticipation of doing so.

The unsigned license is a reproach, but I make no move to sign it. Alone and unobserved, I casually demur. I'm nonchalant about it, like it's an oversight I might eventually correct. Jews give money, I suddenly say to myself, not organs. When a person dies, we give to a charitable organization in his or her name. As proof I make a quick perusal of the *New York Times*: in lieu of flowers (Jews don't give flowers either), donations can be made to the Ronald McDonald House, the Multiple Sclerosis Foundation, Hadassah, the Alzheimer's Foundation, etc., etc. Never mind that my assertion echoes similar ones my father used to make, assertions that used to infuriate me with their blind, dismissive, self-congratulatory virtue. *Jews don't drink, Jews don't beat their wives*, and now, apparently, in continuation of that same line of thinking, Jews don't give organs.

So here I am a hypocrite: invoking my religion when I don't practice it, signing up to be an organ donor when I don't mean it. Profligate at times with my money, it seems that with my own homegrown resource I'm a miser. I'm not sure I want to go to my grave—and I do want a grave; I want visitors to leave stones on my marker—not in one piece. I feel loyal to my body. It is, for better and worse, for all its betrayals and my abuses, mine. I imagine a final leave-taking, when death comes, and body and soul part ways: Bye-bye, the soul might say to the body. Bye-bye, the body, shrugged off and discarded now, replies. It's been quite a ride, both agree. They embrace, one last conjoining. Take care. Be well. Have a good flight.

And the soul takes off. And the body is at rest.

The body, of course, is penetrated by sex. There we are, wagging penises, tongues, fingers, fists, dildos. Various objects, human and otherwise, seek and gain entry. My friend Nancy's sister was an STD nurse in California, and reported a whole range of objects she and her medical colleagues had to remove from the orifices of the human body, placed there for some giddy mixture of pleasure, intimacy, experiment, cruelty, humor, and then, when the time came for departure . . . stuck. It seems we have the urge to enter, gain access, grant, and be granted right-of-way.

Recently I spent the afternoon thumbing through an anatomy book. I was looking for a picture that would show everything, the whole works, all the body's parts and interconnections. What I found instead were pictures of systems: the skeletal system, the central nervous system, the circulatory system, the gastrointestinal tract. I found myself growing impatient, each system seeming to bar me from another, a series of looping cul-de-sacs—when all I wanted was access to the whole. Somehow, I'd likened the body to a structure with a shell, and thought that if I cracked the shell open, I would get to the center, the very core.

But, I reminded myself, I'd already been inside. Over 20 years ago, as a graduate student in exercise physiology, I'd taken a human anatomy course where we dissected cadavers. I'd cut open, and cut up, the human body. I'd picked apart those systems, held a coiled small intestine in my hand. There is no center, no core, not anatomically at least, not like I was looking for—a homunculus pulling the strings, an internal puppeteer—but apparently that doesn't obviate the desire to find one. The center? *Is that the soul?* a voice inside of me asks, and that selfsame voice answers, *I don't know.*

History is full of philosophers and theologians, as well as pedestrian fellow travelers like myself, whose quest for the soul—or something like it—has led, among other sites, to the liver, the heart, the brain. I've held those in my hand as well. I've correctly identified them in a final exam. The ancient Babylonians, who considered the liver the seat of the soul, consulted a sheep's liver before going into battle for help divining the course of the future. The Japanese have long located the soul in the lower abdomen. The practice of ritual suicide, *hara kiri*, literally means to cut open the abdomen and release the soul. In my martial arts practice we speak of moving from your *hara*, your center—your little rice cooker as I once heard it called—located several inches below the navel. The French, who have elevated the liver to a place of great importance, if not the site of the soul, refer to an overall feeling of unwellness as "mal de foie."

But the heart and brain remain the two main contenders. Ancient Egyptians weighed a person's heart after death because they believed the weight of the heart equaled the weight of the soul, the two, in their view, being inextricable. Aristotle said the pneuma, or vital spirit, came directly from the heavens and was distributed throughout the body by the heart, the seat of the soul. The heart has a language of its own, suggesting some deep place, some all-encompassing entirety of being: *heartfelt, heartsick, take to heart, learn by heart, eat your heart out.* After my father died, I developed a pain in my chest, a heaviness that felt like a stone, which my doctor, after putting away her stethoscope, suggested might be heartache.

Descartes, notwithstanding his countrymen's affection for the liver, argued that God placed the soul in the brain: *Cogito ergo sum; I think, therefore I am.* Is that why, I wonder, when Americans, American men at least, commit suicide, they often go right to the source, and blow their brains out? Women, in my unscientific observations, prefer methods with less cleanup. My friend Sandi scoffs at this idea—linking the mode of suicide with the location of the soul—maintaining that people blow their brains out because it works.

What does all this prove? That the soul is a wily creature? That it cannot be pinned down? *My father's brain is in a jar.* I think of it sitting there, on a shelf in Evanston Hospital, where, in my imagination at least, I have placed it, and while I'm not so literal as to believe his soul is trapped inside, I can't help feeling that perhaps some essence is squeezed within that clear contoured glass, some vital distillation, something that made him Nathan Shinner, formerly Shinitzky, charming, funny, loyal, my father.

This is the part of the essay I haven't written; I haven't written until now. The results of the autopsy, which I received, over the phone, three weeks after my father's death. Dr. Eller called me back, or perhaps I paged him; I can't remember which. What I do remember is his uneasiness, as if he were as disconcerted relaying the results of an autopsy, on the phone, to the daughter of the deceased, as I was hearing them. The dead are dead and gone, but for a few minutes at least, one of them had risen, and Dr. Eller had to respond. He went through his list. My father had advanced arteriosclerosis, he said, and immediately I felt upset, taken aback, as if my father were alive and, up until now, healthy—and not, in fact, dead from one of the corollaries of this very condition—and we were receiving the diagnosis for the first time, a diagnosis that would, from here on out, forever change his life. There was no sign of the stomach cancer he'd been treated for two years previous, Dr. Eller continued. Distraught at hearing the diagnosis of arteriosclerosis, I was almost blasé to find out he'd had no recurrence of stomach cancer. As if I expected it; of course he didn't have stomach cancer; he'd beaten it. We found a cancerous mass in the bladder, Dr. Eller said. Cancer of the bladder? Something lying in wait to kill my father—another cancer, no less, which seemed unfair, as if a person should not be made to suffer more than one malignancy—if he hadn't been killed by a stroke instead?

But none of this explained my father's death. None of this explained why he died when he died, at 5:00 A.M., on November 25, 1988. Did I want to know what happened so I could have prevented it from happening, as I had tried to stave off all the events of those preceding four weeks, the brain swelling, brain surgery, tracheotomy, pulmonary embolism, as if by will and love and bedside vigilance I, and I alone, could have altered the course of his condition, or was I casting a question, a plea, up to the heavens? Why did he die? *As for the immediate cause of death,* Dr. Eller said, *we're still examining his brain but have found nothing conclusive at this point.*

Examining his brain? My voice cracked with disbelief. My father, according to Jewish tradition, had been buried expeditiously; he died on a Friday and was buried the next Monday, but they, the doctors, were now, three weeks later, examining his brain. Which meant his brain, to put it indelicately—but is there any other way to put it, for it struck me with blunt, brutal force—was not in his head. Of course, you may say—you, who are reading this (already picturing his brain in a jar), you, that other part of myself who has been wrestling with this ever since—but I didn't know that. I didn't know that an autopsy meant removing organs and not putting them back. I pictured it, if I pictured it at all, as a quick little look-see, a tidy examination, peruse the premises, snip a few tissues here and there, samples to put under the microscope, and then zipper him back up again, untampered, unmolested, everything intact. I didn't expect him to be excavated, for his skull to be scooped clean.

It has been 16 years since my father died. It is now, again, the season of his death. Outside my window, the grass is green and yellow and brown, and the trees are almost, but not quite, leafless. A bird with tattered tail feathers has just stopped on the window ledge to rest. Every year I light a candle to commemorate my father's death, a candle that, even though I buy it at the Jewel grocery, in the kosher-style foods section, comes alive for me, and I stupidly sing, to myself or to Ann, *This little light of mine, I'm going to let it shine,* and the candle burns for 24 hours. I have as well, in these 16 years, kept alive my guilt, kept it alive, I realize now, gladly and energetically, with fervor and dedication. I've read some of what Jewish law says about autopsies, and little bits and pieces from other religions too, and I feel vindicated, not when I find opinions in favor of autopsy, but when I find interpretations against it. A leading rabbinic authority writes, "an autopsy is warranted only . . . for purposes of deriving specific information deemed essential for the treatment of another patient already suffering the same illness, [but not] in the *vague* hope [emphasis mine] that medical knowledge may be . . . enriched," and though part of me blanches at the pure miserliness of this statement, at its unforgivably snide tone (the kind of thing, I hear the accumulated history of anti-Semitism saying, that gives Jews a bad name), another part of me latches onto it as confirmation. *See,* I say, turning to those friends who, over the years, have tried to comfort me. *See,* I say to myself. I feel enlivened by my guilt.

My father and I had a ritual. When he wanted to be affectionate, he would take his fist, which always looked enormous to me, and, slowly but firmly, push it into my cheek. I, for my part, would push back. We'd keep pushing until we reached a point of equal tension, fist to cheek. Then, gently, we'd release. We'd do this in the car, stopped at a light, when I was the driver and he was in the passenger seat, so, I suspect, we could avoid eye contact; we could love each other without looking. I kept my eye on traffic; I don't know where he kept his.

I consented to the autopsy because I wanted to know why he died. But I wasn't, as it turned out—as it turned out in the aftermath of the autopsy—asking a medical question, I wasn't looking for scientific causes and effects. My father had a stroke—an intracerebral hemorrhage, a major bleed—on the Dan Ryan expressway, and four weeks later he died. That's the cause, and the effect. I was asking the gods a question, a child's question about her father, one anyone might ask, but in my confusion I went to the wrong source, I went to the gods of medicine when I should have been beseeching the ever-present gods of fate.

Does he blame me? He was, he could be, a vindictive person. He was the kind of guy who held a grudge. He'd been under the knife a number of times in the last years of his life, and I'd put him under again. What would he say to me, if he could say anything? What would he say to me now? Now Ann pushes her fist against my cheek, over the years she's picked this up, but unlike my father and me, we look at each other and smile. Her hand is smaller than his, but no less tender, and I meet it, pushing back. Then I put the car in gear and we drive off.

My father doesn't say anything. He doesn't let me off the hook, and he doesn't point a finger at me either. He is, and has been, forever silent on this point. That leaves it up to me. I'm in limbo, there's no absolution and no blame. The next time I pay him a visit, I'll tear off a few blades of grass and search for some pebbles and scatter it all on his grave. ■

Roundtable: Research in Nonfiction

Panelists: **John Calderazzo, Michael Gorra,
Kristen Iversen**
Moderator: **Robert Root**

Most people consider nonfiction to be a literary form emphasizing actual events and grounded in careful observation, conscientious recall, and/or documented evidence. In general, literary nonfiction doesn't restrict itself to drawing on only one of those resources, but some measure of the range of possibility in nonfiction can be charted by the relative proportions authors allot to observation, recall, or evidence in their work. In reportage and cultural criticism, for example, writers are more likely to draw on primary or secondary research than they are in the lyrical essay or the personal memoir. Although it's true that academic discourse and journalistic discourse both insist on documentation more emphatically than nonfiction (creative or literary nonfiction, that is) does, increasingly in recent years writers of what might be termed "literary reportage," "personal cultural criticism," or "experimental critical writing," have blurred the boundaries of genre by giving freer rein to their literary instincts at the same time that they incorporate scrupulous documentation into their texts.

This roundtable discussion of research and documentation in nonfiction brings together three writers who have each drawn on considerable research to compose books grounded in personal commitment to their subjects. **John Calderazzo**, who had a background in writing for newspapers and magazines before becoming an award-winning writing teacher at Colorado State University, is the author of articles and essays in such magazines and journals as *Audubon*, *Orion*, *The Georgia Review*, and *Witness*; he has also written a book on writing, *Writing from Scratch: Freelancing*; a children's science book, *101 Questions about Volcanoes*; and a book of creative nonfiction, *Rising Fire: Volcanoes and Our Inner Lives*. **Kristen Iversen** not only was a travel writer and an editor but also taught in the MFA Program at Naropa University and at San Jose University before becoming a writing teacher at the University of Memphis. She is the editor of a text anthology, *Shadow Boxing: Art and Craft in Creative Nonfiction*, as well as editor-in-chief of the literary journal, *The Pinch*, previously *River City*. Her book *Molly Brown: Unraveling the Myth* won the Colorado Book Award for Biography and the Barbara Sudler Award for Nonfiction and was the basis of an A&E program on Molly Brown. She is also the author of the forthcoming book, *Full Body Burden: Living and Dying in the Shadow of America's Nuclear Nightmare*. **Michael Gorra** is the Mary Augusta Jordan Professor of English at Smith College. He is the author of two books of literary criticism, *The English Novel at Mid-Century* and *After Empire: Scott, Naipul, Rushdie*, and for his work as a reviewer has received the Nona Balakian Citation of the National Book Critics Circle. His most recent book is *The Bells in Their Silence: Travels Through Germany*, a work that combines travel narrative with historical and critical approaches to travel writing. Moderator **Robert Root** has written essays emphasizing what he refers to as "intersecting histories"—natural, cultural, personal—and his memoir, *Recovering Ruth: A Biographer's Tale*, is built around such histories, as are his works-in-progress on the Hudson and Rhine Rivers and the Front Range of Colorado. His critical study, *E. B. White: The Emergence of an Essayist*, has inspired several essays of place juxtaposing White's response to locale with his own, and he is editor of and contributor to the anthology *Landscapes with Figures: The Nonfiction of Place*.

Root: This roundtable focuses on a research-based cultural-critical-as-well-as-literary form of nonfiction. Perhaps we should start out by letting each of you succinctly say something about how you'd define the book you wrote and what elements of the book lead you to make that kind of definition.

Calderazzo: Let's start with *Rising Fire*'s subtitle. *Volcanoes and Our Inner Lives* suggests those times and places where the natural world bursts right through rocks, soil, and clouds, and floods the human imagination and sometimes profoundly affects culture. This happens more than you may think since about 500 million people, worldwide, live in the shadows of volcanoes. Consider what can happen when the earth erupts in even relatively slow and subtle ways, like Mount Etna going off for, say, the 20th time in three or four centuries. Several summers ago, I hung around a Sicilian village called Zafferana as roaring Etna pushed out huge, sludgy rivers of lava that crunched downhill only 10 or 20 feet per hour. But that had been going on for weeks, and now some flows were threatening to knock down houses that the same families had occupied since 1512, 1667, etc. So of course I wondered about the locals who, unlike almost everyone in Pompeii in A.D. 79, knew very well that they were living on the slopes of an unpredictable volcano. Now, if you stood at the window of the bedroom where your great-great-grandparents slept and you looked up at this black wall of steaming rock about to enter your vineyard—which thrives because of the soil created by previous lava flows—what would you think about the character of your ancestors, about the nature of the unruly earth? Who or what do you pray to? Are there rituals to perform? Ethical ways to divert the lava when you know it might roll over some other town downslope? Do you leave the only house and village you have ever known? What will your children dream about afterwards? All of these things are elements of our "inner lives" and most also make up cultural responses to natural phenomena. That's what the book's about.

Iversen: *Full Body Burden* is essentially a memoir: the story of a place and the story of a life, or part of a life. You could call it an environmental memoir, which is an inadequate term but hints at some of the political tensions in the story. In this book I trace the history and present conditions of Rocky Flats, a nuclear weaponry facility near Denver, Colorado. Rocky Flats secretly produced plutonium pits for nuclear bombs—the heart of the bomb—for over 40 years, and there has been significant, ongoing contamination in the air, water, and soil. It's also a very personal story about the early years of my life. I grew up near Rocky Flats, and my sisters and I rode our horses though the fields surrounding the plant. We swam in the contaminated lake, not knowing we were stirring up plutonium between our toes. I lived through the peace protests at the plant in the 1970s and 1980s. Later, as a single parent, I worked at the plant to put myself through school. I understand the plant from various angles. *Full Body Burden* is also about my family. We didn't know we were "Cold War Warriors." My neighborhood was on the front line, but no one told us. My parents were raising four children in an environment they thought was ideal—a new subdivision, decent schools, an outdoor lifestyle. They were trying to do more for us than what their parents had been able to do for them. They succeeded in some ways and failed in others. In that way it's probably a very typical story of an American middle-class family dealing with post-Vietnam issues, a new consumerism, and a desire to move up in the world, to live a different kind of life than the previous generation had.

It's difficult to define a work of creative nonfiction and put it in a category that is useful in academia or in the publishing market. Bookstores don't have sections called "Creative Nonfiction." Many creative writing programs are still struggling with the idea of where to put creative nonfiction. Does it belong in composition? Journalism? Does it qualify as "art"? My book *Molly Brown: Unraveling the Myth* should—in my estimation—be classified as narrative biography or women's history. One of the major bookstore chains insists on putting it under "Ships," because of the Titanic references. *Full Body Burden* could be considered a memoir or, given the research and engagement with contemporary issues, literary journalism. It reads like a novel and perhaps will be classified as such, which is what happened with Truman Capote's *In Cold Blood*. Perhaps what we're really doing in the field of creative nonfiction now is challenging the idea of prose narrative, of what constitutes a novel.

Gorra: I usually have a couple of different goals or desires or ambitions in play when I start a book, and a lot of the work involves putting those variables into some relation with each other. With *The Bells in Their Silence*, I knew before I went that I wanted to write an account of the year that my wife and I were going to spend in Germany. But I also knew that I wanted to write about the travel book as a literary form—that I wanted to draw on the things my teaching of a class on travel books had taught me. So I wrote about some of the books that had been important to me and, as the project developed, those included not only other travel narratives, from Goethe to Bruce Chatwin, but also some novels as well. It included considering things like the role that figurative language plays in travel writing—that led me to Italo Calvino and *Invisible Cities*—or about the function of fragments and digressions. The final product tries to give equal weight to my hours in the library and the time I spent in the street outside. And near the end of the process I found the perfect epigraph. It's from a nineteenth-century social geographer named Wilhelm Heinrich Riehl: "We ramble about in open country so as to learn how to ramble about in the singularly dusty world of books."

Root: How did you each come to write this particular book? What was its genesis in your life and career?

Calderazzo: My book grew directly out of a children's science book I wrote in 1993, and *that* grew out of my teaching the creative nonfiction workshops I developed at CSU. In the late 1980s I became friends with a student close to my age, Randy Jorgen, an all-around outdoor guy and fine writer who after graduation became a book editor. Randy soon decided to launch a series of nature books for kids aged 8 to 12 called *101 Questions About*—swamps, Southwest deserts, grizzlies, you name it. He thought that the questions should be the kinds that kids really asked and not the ones that adults might think are "good" for them. I agreed. He then sent me a list of topics. "Pick one you love, and that'll be our first book," he said. I chose volcanoes, mostly because I didn't know a thing about them—didn't even know if there were any active ones in Colorado—and I knew that the research would be a great way to learn wondrous, true things. That alone probably drives about half of what I do. But also, as I scanned Randy's list, I noted that "Volcanoes" instantly brought up a moment I'd long forgotten, a time in third or fourth grade when I sat on the linoleum floor of my school library with a picture book in my lap. It showed a Mexican farmer, sombrero flying off, sprinting from a crack in his cornfield where hot rocks and fire were spitting up—the birth of a volcano! I remembered being wowed by this amazing fact. Now, diving into research, I could learn much more about that story and be wowed to my heart's content. That memory also gave me my opening question for the book: *Could a volcano erupt in my back yard?*

Which brings me to one of my core beliefs about nonfiction writing and maybe any creative endeavor. In my pre-CSU, freelance magazine writing days, I had come to understand something that I now tell my students on the first day of class and repeat later. The world is full of awe-inspiring, wonderful (though not always merely "nice") things. They float around us all the time, everywhere. And it's our job, our privilege and sometimes also our burden, to find and flesh out these wonders in our own way, to celebrate the extraordinary inside the ordinary. This is a little like what E. B. White once wrote about feeling charged "with the safekeeping of all items of worldly or unworldly enchantment, as though I might be held personally responsible if even a small one were to be lost." Pretty soon my kids' book research brought me plenty of wonders, and when I finished writing it I realized that I had not only failed to exhaust the topic of volcanoes and culture, but I'd been thinking about it in ways that would take me an adult book to investigate.

Iversen: I grew up with two toxic environments: plutonium and my father's alcoholism. My siblings and I were not allowed to talk about either of these things; we learned to look away and pretend that they didn't exist. Silence is a very powerful thing, and this book has turned out to be about silence or silencing at many levels: family, community, government. I've always wanted to be a writer but it took me awhile to see what I needed to write about. In my 20s I spent several years as a travel writer in Europe, interested in everything and trying different things. It turns out that the big story was literally in my backyard. This book was a turning point for me. I have many books I want and need to write, fiction and creative nonfiction, but I had to write this book before I could move on to anything else. I've carried it in my head and heart for a long time.

Gorra: I'd tried something similar once before, in a 1994 essay in *Transition* that bounced back and forth between Henry James's travel writing, my own trips through Italy and India, and some current scholarship on travel writing as a form. It worked well enough to make me want to try it again, at greater length. And I also wanted to write something that would stretch me as a writer—not another book on novels, but one that would call on as many different parts of me as possible. To write with all my voice, or several of them. Though at the same time I wanted to make the result as seamless as possible. I've always been a bit suspicious of those moments of confessional scholarship in which the writer announces that he or she is going to switch voices or modes, that he or she will now be "personal," or suddenly puts a chapter in italics. I don't think the kind of work we're describing here is all that new, anyway—though it may hark back to some earlier, pre- or non-academic protocols. I mean, what else is *A Room of One's Own*? It too is a personal essay that also required substantial research. At the time I started this project I had just finished a book on postcolonial fiction and was reviewing a lot. In the reviews I was trying to stretch as well, to write a more bristly, full-throated prose. I'd always been interested in travel writing, precisely because of the way in which it seemed able to stretch, to digress, to accommodate all sorts of different kinds of writing, ways of thinking. You've got a narrative frame on which to hang things—anecdote, scholarly aside, a report on your reading—and whatever you think as you walk along can become part of that narrative itself.

Luckily the chance to spend a year abroad coincided with the moment at which I was ready to try a different kind of writing, while the project itself gave me an excuse—or a kind of spur—to wander, to get out onto the streets. Really I got lucky. My wife was asked to run a study-abroad program, and Germany isn't a place about which there are many travel books—lots of journalism, but no travel narratives. Which was freeing in a way that trying to do Italy might not have been, even if writing about the place did impose certain burdens of its own.

Root: What did you know about this subject before you started working on this project? How did you determine what you needed to learn further about the subject? How did you think you would get the expertise sufficient to write on the subject?

Gorra: Not much. A few years before I'd spent a month in Hamburg, where we were based. Then about a year before we went I started to read German history—mostly large narrative things, and mostly about earlier periods. Not just the Nazi stuff anyway, but things like James Sheehan's eighteenth-century history. And I read W. G. Sebald's *The Emigrants* just as it appeared in English. The main preparation was taking first-year German. Once I'd gotten going, I kept on reading on an ad hoc basis, with the reading often determined by the places I found interesting. So histories of Berlin because I knew I wanted to write about it; Goethe because I was going to Weimar, etc. But often enough the reading would lead me to a particular place—Schama's *Landscape and Memory* did that. After a while the entire process became dialectical.

And I always worried about expertise—especially when I found myself playing with very large historical questions. At moments like that, I kept telling myself that the next time I wrote a book it would be about something I was familiar with *before* I began. Some passages I cut out—some whole sections—because I knew they were thin, e.g., a few pages on post–World War II refugees from the Sudetenland. But I always felt I was skating up against the limits of my knowledge, and counted on German colleagues at Smith College to keep me from saying anything egregious.

Calderazzo: My kids' book research helped me build a general understanding of the science behind eruptions, the basic plumbing of the earth, the history of volcanology, and some compelling anthropological facts— like the amazing and profoundly sad discoveries in only the last few years that many of the highest Andean peaks hold the frozen remains of Incan boys and girls who had been marched up there and sacrificed to gods of water and sun and fertility. But I still needed to learn more science. Though I like to think of myself as "good" at this—former math nerd, engineering major as a freshman, etc.—I have to remind myself that my BA

is in English and MFA in fiction writing. So I'm not exactly NASA material, not any more, which means that I need to get as much help as I can,
especially for an area new to me. As it happened, I insisted that my kid's
book have a technical consultant, who could give me some credibility with
librarians. I found one in Robert Tilling, of the USGS, who'd become an
amiable go-to guy on the phone before I realized he was one of the leading volcanologists in the country. In his new capacity, he directed me to
great books and websites and saved me lots of time. Mainly, though, he
saved me from some boneheaded errors and sharpened some of my explanations.

Later in the process than I should have, I found a similar savior for the
adult book. I got to know and admire Tom Simkin, of the Smithsonian
Institution's Global Volcanism Program, while I was lurking "behind the
walls," as they say, of the Institution. Tom was not just one of the grand old
men of the field, he stayed current *and* was avidly interested in the ways
volcanoes affected people's lives. Moreover, he never minced words. My
favorite memo from him began, "Oh, dear John, you are *desperately* wrong
in explaining this process which . . ."

The other thing I knew I needed to learn further was the lay of land on
volcanoes themselves.

Iversen: Rocky Flats held a looming, almost Kafka-esque place in my life.
I knew the rumors, the stories. I knew what it looked like from the outside and eventually I learned what it looked like from the inside (although
I never personally worked in the most notorious buildings). The buildings
themselves, squarish and government-style, expressed a kind of unnamed,
unspecified fear. It was a place of bureaucratic labyrinths, of lies and
death—directly and indirectly—and yet it also represented American pride
and national security.

When I began to work seriously on the book, I knew I had an enormous amount of research to do. I had to understand the story as fully as
possible and go far beyond my own experience and perspective. I began by
reading as much as I could about plutonium and bomb making. I studied
the history of the plant and compiled a huge database of newspaper articles. Many things unexpectedly worked in my favor. I benefited from the
openness of the Clinton administration and Energy Secretary Hazel
O'Leary; previously classified documents were suddenly available for public scrutiny (although this openness has changed in recent years). I was for-
tunate to have the Carnegie Library in Boulder, which holds nearly 100

interviews with Rocky Flats employees, activists, and others. This is a collaborative project between the Maria Rogers Oral History Program and the Rocky Flats Cold War Museum, and it's a very rich, very important resource. I conducted interviews on my own and talked to workers, residents, and activists, as well as some of my old neighbors.

I will never have as much expertise as I would like on this subject. I am not an engineer or chemist or scientist. I worked at Rocky Flats but I never worked on a glovebox; I don't know what it feels like to hold a plutonium disk in my hand. The politics are deeply complex and ongoing. But I am diligent and thorough in my research and I like to think that I bring a strong sense of integrity to the work.

Root: How did primary (on-the-ground, on-site) research figure into the drafting of your book? How did secondary (in-the-library, in-the-archives) research figure into the drafting?

Iversen: Most of my research was primary, simply because the subject is still so new, so raw. People don't know how to talk about it; many people don't want to talk about it at all. Plutonium is not a popular subject. People don't want to think about how the government may have lied to them. I read a great deal about nuclear politics (Helen Caldicott, for example, among others) and related issues. But I think we're still in the very early stages of trying to understand the atomic age and nuclear weaponry and what it means for our culture, what role it plays in our lives. Rocky Flats produced the plutonium pit for essentially every nuclear weapon in the U.S. arsenal. When my family moved to Arvada, Colorado, we unwittingly became a part of the atomic legacy that began with the Manhattan Project and led to the destruction of Hiroshima and Nagasaki. (We unknowingly came very close to destruction ourselves with the 1968 Mother's Day fire at Rocky Flats.) How do you talk about the connection between global death and the pretty, flickering lights you see each night outside your bedroom window? The number of books that deal with American nuclear policy and its consequences for the lives of private citizens are few indeed. I relied mostly on primary sources, with the exception of a few books like Len Ackland's *Making a Real Killing: Rocky Flats and the Nuclear West.*

Calderazzo: I just love to do research, and not only because it's much less painful to me than writing. But as much as I enjoy noodling around old libraries or discovering obscure websites (like the one for Japan's Institute for Singing Sand!), I like talking to people even more. And even that pales compared to strapping on my boots and hiking off through wild nature. As I was happily aware, *Rising Fire* required me to do all of these things, often in gorgeous places.

A good example: in 1998 I used my ten-day Thanksgiving break from school, as well as a modest CSU research grant, to visit the green dot in the Caribbean Sea that is Montserrat. All of 6 miles wide by 11 long, the British protectorate, once a lively tourist destination, had been suffering from a suddenly-awakened and extremely dangerous volcano in its midst, and over the previous two years most of the residents had either fled their lifetime home and flown to London or backed off into unfamiliar and none-too-large coastal "safe zones." The evacuated capital, like the airport, had been overrun by a broiling gas avalanche called a pyroclastic flow, and so almost every aspect of "The Emerald Isle" was in chaos—all of which later figured in my 55-page chapter.

I'd gotten background material from NPR, *National Geographic, Discover* magazine, etc., but on the eve of my trip, I found anything other than technical eruption news hard to get, and I didn't know a soul on the island, which I had never seen. My big victory was finally booking by phone one of the half-dozen or so guest rooms still operating. But then, I knew, a bed and a few meals were all I needed. After I ferried over from Antigua in a rough storm—which later became a "journey" scene—I met my guest-house host, a chatty and smart woman named Shirley Spycala. Within 20 minutes, I realized that I had stumbled onto one of my favorite types of characters, and the gold key to a writer seeking entrée into unfamiliar territory: The Person Who Knows Everyone. While this was great luck, my magazine literary journalism background had taught me that if I simply immersed myself long enough in a place and kept my ears open, one or several people like Shirley would eventually emerge. By the next day I was driving around the island and even sneaking into the "exclusion zone" with people I'd met through Shirley. As I walked or hitchhiked around the island, one relationship built on another, and after five days I had enough material—not counting some follow-up research—for my rather thick chapter.

Gorra: I'm no longer sure I can tell the difference between them—but usually I'd have some basic library or guidebook knowledge of a site, then go, and then find I needed to do some reading to understand the visit I'd just paid. But at times they coincided. I knew, for example, that I needed to read more Theodor Fontane, the nineteenth-century Berlin novelist. Not much of him is translated, but I took a volume that was along to that city, and started reading it there. And that act of reading—of looking up from my book and trying to map the scenes he was describing onto the place where I was walking—that became in itself a major part of my chapter on that city. I kept on reading Fontane after I got back, and the whole book was enriched because of it—he's one of the things I'm most glad to have learned about.

Root: Did either kind of research change the direction or the tenor or the approach you took to the book?

Calderazzo: Yes, both reading and travel widened the scope of my inquiry and made me want to learn more, more, more. In fact, for almost every chapter, I finally had to tell myself to stop researching and start making sentences (which an old journalism teacher of mine liked to call "pushing a noun up against a verb without having an accident"). In the case of Montserrat, a book I read after I got home, written by a man I'd heard about during my visit, opened a whole new dimension to my story. The guy was a Catholic priest who lived on the island in the 1970s but who also did a serious anthropological study on voodoo trance rituals and night monsters. His work made me think back to how many Montserratans had made serious or even joking references to voodoo. After I mulled this over during some of my habitual "thinking walks" in the Rocky Mountain foothills, I did extra library research on the movement of voodoo through the Caribbean. Then I rechecked descriptions in my notebooks and volcano books on phenomena like glowing lava sliding through the countryside at night, and I realized that Montserratan descriptions of night spirits were almost identical! Who says that landscape (especially the moving kind) doesn't have profound influences on the human psyche?

Iversen: When I concluded my interviews, I realized that the entire story had to be character-driven, not just my part of the story. I had to tell the story of the plant through the personal stories of the people who worked there and lived nearby or were involved in some way. In the first draft, I played around with an objective, expository, omniscient point of view interwoven with my own, first-person narrative, but I eventually abandoned that for the most part. The book became less strident as I worked through my research. I understood why a person might choose to work at

Rocky Flats (I chose to work there myself), and why they might stay for 20 or 30 years, even after they realized what was going on out there. Many employees didn't know at first. I think or at least I hope my tone became more compassionate.

Gorra: There are a couple of chapters in the book that are more driven by "secondary" research than the others. Those are the chapters that concentrate on travel writing as a form, and in writing them I did, to some degree, select scenes and moments from a variety of different experiences and different places, stitching them together around the library work. They're the chapters that have the most explicit argument, or at least they lean that way. And they're the hardest ones too, the most allusive. I conceived of my chapter on fragments, for example, in terms of some things I wanted to say about the notebook sections of Chatwin's *Songlines*, and throughout it I found myself using places as a way to explore a set of ideas and texts, rather than the other way around, as I did in writing about Berlin.

Root: How do the research and the drafting relate to one another? To what degree are you able to completely do one before doing another?

Calderazzo: Drafting often shows me what I know and don't know, not in general, but for the purposes of the story unfolding on the page. At the same time, except for the case of some personal memoirs, where I can often root around in my past as I sit at the keyboard, research is essential before or as I write. For me, research and drafting almost always converse. When they don't, I worry about the danger of monologue unchecked by economy and rigor.

Iversen: I like the idea of completing the research before one begins to write, but it doesn't happen that way for me. Writing is an enlivening process. I bring memories to life and they grow and change as soon as I put the words on the page. One fact leads to another, one part of the story connects with another part, and there are all sorts of unexpected synchronicities that occur, things you can't anticipate. The book takes on a life of its own. Each new fact changes things a little. My understanding of the story changed through the writing and the research. Research is writing. Reading is writing. For me it's all inextricably linked.

For this story in particular, it's impossible to say that's it, no more research, I've reached the end. For one thing, the story is ongoing (as I write this, there is a huge class-action lawsuit against Rocky Flats about to go to trial). This story is not going to go away for a long time. Plutonium has a very long half-life. My research will be finished when the book is printed and bound and I can't scribble in the margins anymore. But the story will go on.

Gorra: These questions are running into one another, and I hope what I'm going to say now doesn't contradict what's above. In general, the writing and research were entirely dialectical, or symbiotic. I kept computer notebooks into which I poured narratives of individual trips, notes on my reading, observations from the street, menus, all of it mixed up, and dated as in a diary. That was, in a way, my research, and once I'd shuffled them around the best of those notes moved quite seamlessly into the draft as well. Probably that was made easier by the fact that the book is more a collection of essays than a strict narrative—I'd go through the notebooks, sifting out the material that seemed to belong together, open a new file . . .

Root: Did you find yourself wrestling with the problem of writing a book that drew on other resources at the same time that you wrote a book of intense personal interest to yourself? What are the pitfalls of writing nonfiction heavily reliant on primary or secondary research?

Calderazzo: Going into this project I didn't have a particularly long-standing obsession about volcanoes themselves. But for years I'd been deeply curious about ways in which people, culture, and nature interact—ways that I think we often overlook. I appear to have the wrong upbringing for this. I grew up in Brooklyn and then in a Long Island suburb where the chances of seeing even a deer were nil. I also had ardently indoor parents; my dad's reply when I begged him to take me camping was, "I did that already. It was called World War II." But I had a bike and their permission to ride it all day. Then I became a Boy Scout, my ticket to wild nature beyond the range of my peddling. Finally, when I got my own car, I began to seriously wander—into Florida swamps, the Rockies, Death Valley, the Big Bend country of Texas—and I never really quit.

So by the time I got to this book there were lots of personal experiences and ideas I wanted to explore *in light of* what I was discovering about other people and the science of volcanoes. This is why, early on, I decided to use first person liberally. It was a technique I had used in some of my literary journalism for magazines like *Audubon* and *Ohio*. I'd also taken careful note of how Joan Didion achieved this even in a big issues book like *Salvador*, and what guys like Richard Rhodes and Ron Rosenbaum did in their magazine pieces. I noticed that they never threw themselves into a narrative just because they felt like it—only if their presence could illuminate the effect of large forces on an individual. In extremely serious sections of my book dealing with major destruction, or the deaths of people like the French volcanologist couple Maurice and Katia Krafft, I tended to stay the hell out.

Iversen: I had to be very hard on myself. I had to constantly question the lens through which I was seeing and interpreting people, events, facts, even memories. The net a writer casts has to be very wide. You have to accept and examine conflicting information. You have to doubt your own perceptions and beliefs. At the same time you have to stay in touch with the passion that brought you to the subject in the first place.

Sometimes people say they don't write creative nonfiction because they don't like to feel constricted by fact. I don't buy that argument. The factual aspect of a story is a rough scaffolding at best. It provides a form or tentative framework, but just as in fiction, the story is not so much who and where but why. And how. It's what happens between the lines.

Gorra: No. I certainly didn't worry about the legitimacy of it, or anything like that. There were some worries on the level of the page or the paragraph—hitting the right balance, i.e., in whether I was doing it all well enough. The big worry was in finding a publisher—at times I thought I'd impaled myself on a fence post, and that the result wasn't going to be personal enough to interest some publishers, nor scholarly enough for others. That's probably the biggest difficulty with this kind of hybrid, or crossover, or even self-reflexive work.

Root: How would you compare what you're doing with a strictly academic form of writing? To what extent would you say what you've written *is* an academic text on a par with similar academic texts on the same subject?

Calderazzo: "Strictly academic" may be an endangered term. I think some but certainly not all of the best scholarship has often been very creative and frequently well written. Plus it seems that more "academics" are using storytelling techniques to make their work more compelling. I'm thinking of very learned folks like biologist E. O. Wilson, historian Stephen Greenblatt, and especially philosopher Susan Griffin, whose *Women and*

Nature: The Roaring Inside Her used all kinds of voice techniques to underscore her points. In fact, the world of nature scholarship is just loaded with this. On the other hand, no, I don't think what I do is academic, even though I sometimes have to commit serious scholarship to tell my stories.

Iversen: In strictly academic writing, the writer is generally invisible and the tone is objective and analytical. This has changed somewhat in recent years, but there is a linguistic style and method of argument that is recognized and expected in academic discourse. Creative nonfiction can be objective in tone and analytical in its approach, but there is a personal, reflective element that generally doesn't exist in academic writing. The audience is different. Most academic writing is directed toward a particular readership, a specialized audience. Creative nonfiction, like other forms of creative writing, reaches for a larger and more diverse audience. In creative nonfiction, there is a more obvious connection to the real world, the lived world. People want to read about experience—experience distilled through an analytical lens—from a voice that's more intimate and reflective than what they get in the newspapers or on television.

The aim is different. Academic discourse seeks to take things apart and put them back together in ways that reveal deeper layers of meaning in a text. Creative nonfiction essentially does the same thing, but the subject of the analysis is the lived life, the personal experience of contemporary life and culture. Picasso said art is a lie that makes us realize a truth. One way of thinking about creative nonfiction is to say that creative nonfiction is a partial truth that makes us realize a greater truth.

Gorra: I'm neither a Germanist nor an historian, so right away the book found itself up against two disciplines in which I am best an amateur. The moments in *The Bells* that draw most heavily on those fields are also the ones closest to good journalism, e.g., an account of a visit to Buchenwald, or a description of Berlin's reconstruction. At those moments it felt as though I were channeling something like the *New Yorker* writer Jane Kramer, or trying to; Jane Kramer on an off day, perhaps. Anyway, I found her *Politics of Memory: Looking for Germany in the New Germany* an absolutely essential source, and at times a model of how to combine hard reporting with bits of personal anecdote.

I do think I managed to say some things about travel narratives as a form that hadn't been said before, or that at least hadn't been tested in this way—about their generic borders and formal properties. So insofar as I talk about travel writing as such, the book can stand as an "academic text." At other moments I found myself writing about fiction—Fontane, Mann—in a rather different way than I usually do. Chattier, with a bit more plot summary/commentary, cutting quickly from text to text, and with enthusiasm worn on my sleeve. Less a critical argument than a portrait. I'd like to do more with that, and suspect that will spill over into whatever I do next.

Root: How is the author of one of your texts different from or identical to the author of another one of your texts? Do you see yourself as presenting the same persona in all your books? And, if not, which text does the best job of presenting the persona you think best "persona-fies" you?

Calderazzo: Actually, yes, I think I have pretty much presented the same persona in the great majority of my *literary* nonfiction, short and long, over the years. Now, some of my earlier, quickie commercial magazine stuff replaced the longer rhythms and reflective tone of my then-serious work with a more wisecracking and up-tempo voice, but I don't do that kind of pay-the-rent writing anymore. Recently, possibly as a reaction to all the hard work that went into my volcano book, I have found myself writing poems like mad. I'm serious about these, too, but God, you get done with them fast and can then forget 'em! Recently I compared some of them with poems I wrote in my angry or at least intense young-man days, and I see little resemblance. I'm still intense, but really, I'm a very different guy, and so are my poems.

Iversen: In *Molly Brown: Unraveling the Myth*, I was clearly the author, the biographer, and thus responsible for remaining invisible and objective with all the problems and contradictions that the word "objective" implies. In *Full Body Burden*, I am a character in the story and thus responsible for creating myself on the page. The story is deeply and intensely personal, and yet it takes an objective, interpretive act to create myself as a character on the page. I am and I am not the Kristen Iversen in that particular story.

As people, we respond to circumstances differently. I am a slightly different person as a teacher in the classroom compared to when I'm sitting down with a friend and having a cup of coffee. In the same way, my position as author and/or character changes slightly with each manuscript or story. It's something I'm very conscious of. When I'm writing fiction, it's comforting to have that mask between writer and reader. Regardless of how "true" the story is, the veil of genre distinction—false or problematic as that can be—

allows a degree of license, poetic and psychological. The writer says, this is fiction, so it's not fair to question certain things. In creative nonfiction, you take away that veil, that mask. In most forms of creative nonfiction you present yourself as yourself, even though you know it is, to a certain extent, a linguistic gesture, a constructed identity or personality.

Each story changes in the retelling. We can never simply recreate the person or the event about which we are writing, even if we're writing about ourselves. There is always a process of selection and interpretation. And our audience changes as well. Whether we like it or not, as authors we are keenly aware of the eyes following our words on the page and we anticipate what the reader may think or feel in response to the narrative.

Gorra: This book draws on a fuller range of my experience, including childhood and family background. It's the voice, the persona, I would like my work to have, or to have more often than it does. In some ways, both it and my reviews are much closer together than either of them is to the voice of my last "straight" academic book. Which I guess means that I tried to write as well in the book, and with as much attention to an audience, as I do in reviewing new fiction—to be as alive and interesting over a 10,000-word chapter as I can be over 1,500 on Sunday morning.

Root: Did you have any problem shifting from a narrator's voice to an expositor's voice, that is, from the voice of a person living through an experience to the voice of a scholar-critic-researcher?

Gorra: My first impulse is to say no, not really. But again, there were passages I cut in which I was writing *only* as an expositor; and others where the first-person impressions seemed unbuttressed by any more substantial knowledge. Neither fit with the kind of rhetorical back-and-forth, slipping and sliding, that I'd developed in the first pages I wrote. So I'd have to say that in most of the book I'm trying to do both at once, and that the parts that work best are precisely the ones where it works.

Calderazzo: I have problems with everything that writing requires of me, it seems. But this kind of shifting can really be tricky, especially if you have to bring the reader up to speed on not-always-common knowledge, like geology or the way GPS satellites can help somebody's grandparents to decide whether to flee their home. My best solution for this tone problem is to revise, revise, revise.

Iversen: I don't experience this as a struggle. There are various ways to approach it. I like to think in terms of scenes, and I tend to use white space to clarify transitions in voice, style, or "plot." Tone is more problematic than structure; you have to maintain a compelling tone regardless of changes in voice or point of view. The important thing is to constantly and subtly cue the reader about where the story is going and how you're putting it together, and hold the reader's trust and interest.

Root: What models, if any, did you have in mind for the book you eventually wrote?

Gorra: Inspirations more than models. Sebald, clearly, though I'd gotten the basic idea in my head before I read him—he showed me how to execute it. The "Fantasy and Ruins" chapter in V. S. Naipaul's *Area of Darkness*; that whole book in fact. Jane Kramer, Patrick Leigh Fermor's *A Time of Gifts* for its zest and its balance of innocence and experience; Rebecca West's *Black Lamb and Grey Falcon*, for the way in which she presents a historical narrative and makes you believe it matters to her personally, that her reporting can save her. Eleanor Clark's *Rome and a Villa*. These are the great travel books I had in mind. On a different level I learned a lot from David Denby's *Great Books* about how to make a kind of drama out of plot summary, though that's something any reviewer works on anyway. I also got a few tricks from Joan Didion's book on Miami, ones I used consciously, and then through osmosis I suspect a lot more from reading Ian Buruma's *The Wages of Guilt* and Timothy Garton Ash's *The File* about the integration of personal materials and historical narrative. Academic models—not so much, except as things I wanted to resist. We tend to be too self-conscious when we try to step outside the usual categories—a self-awareness that just serves to underline them. I prefer to ignore them, or at least to try.

Iversen: I've been deeply influenced by Christa Wolf, a German writer, and her book *Accident: A Day's News*, which details the effects of Chernobyl in a haunting monologue that could almost be read as poetry. *Refuge: An Unnatural History of Family and Place*, by Terry Tempest Williams, is a powerful book that is lyrical and yet efficient in structure and tone. This book may ultimately have as much impact as Rachel Carson's *Silent Spring*. I've enjoyed the poems of Debora Gregor, who also writes about nuclear issues. These are the books I had in mind as I was writing *Full Body Burden*.

Calderazzo: Aside from the ones I mentioned earlier, Jon Krakauer's *Into the Wild*, which combines elements of the mystery thriller, personal essay, history book, investigative report, nature mediation, you name it. It's deeply personal, heartwrenching, *and* expository in a very research-based way. A great achievement! Other good models for me for this book were Barry Lopez's *Of Wolves and Men*, John McPhee's *The Control of Nature*, Barbara Ehrenreich's *Nickel & Dimed: On (Not) Getting By in America*, and Ted Conover's *Coyotes: A Journey Through the Secret World of America's Illegal Aliens*. And flat out the best collection of literary journalism I've ever read is *The Literary Journalists*, edited by Norman Sims.

Root: Marianna Torgovnick, introducing the collection *Eloquent Obsessions: Writing Cultural Criticism*, asserts that "[w]riting about culture is personal," by which she means, "Writers find their material in experience as well as in books." She argues for writers having the freedom "to explore the autobiographical motivation" behind their work "for often this motivation is precisely what generates writers' interests in their topics." She also claims that "[w]riting about culture is informed" (that is, usually draws on considerable research) and "Writing about culture is text or phenomenon based" (that is, has a cultural subject and a more transactional aim than solely expressive or poetic aim). Given those parameters, do you think your work qualifies as cultural criticism?

Gorra: Sure. But I'm skeptical of such programmatic definitions. A few weeks ago I came across an interesting distinction—I think it was in the *Chronicle of Higher Education*, and if I'm remembering correctly, in an interview with Leo Carey, the *New Yorker*'s book review editor. What readers want, he said, is for a writer to tell them *what* he knows. Academic writing tends instead to tell a reader *that* the writer knows. Of course the border is blurry, and I can imagine cases where *that* is indistinguishable from *what*. Still, it's a useful distinction. I like a lot of Torgovnick's work, but attending to the statements above could lead to one's straying over that line more often than one wants. Or than I want, anyway—I'm sure there are spots in *The Bells* that have too much *that*, and I promise to do better next time.

Calderazzo: Absolutely, I think *Rising Fire* and a lot of my nonfiction qualifies as cultural criticism, though maybe I wouldn't call my stuff cultural criticism only. My favorite phrase is pretty simple: *storytelling*. Storytelling that's verifiably true. I mean, the book has some pretty personal

sections about ways in which the transitory and regenerative nature of even
our rock-hard world helped me deal with some important things in my life,
now or in hindsight. For instance, a spooky bout with malignant melanoma
when I was still in my 30s. The premature death of my dad. My wife
SueEllen's views of my volcano risk-taking. My Italian grandmother's
childhood stories and how those might have been influenced by volcanoes
that, I know now, she undoubtedly saw erupting. My camping trip through
northern California right after college and how that paralleled, or didn't,
the serious or more often loony spiritual odysseys of the New Agers I
recently met while hiking on and near Mount Shasta—the people I come
to call Shastafarians. How I have learned to find solace from environmental destruction, or eco-grief, in the liquid nature of rock, in the imperma-
nent nature of everything. And lots more. In other words, significant
chunks of the book explore how volcanoes and my journeys to them have
profoundly affected *my* inner life.

Iversen: *Full Body Burden* falls under the umbrella of cultural criticism for
all those reasons and more. There is a cultural subject and a transactional
aim, but it goes beyond that. I want the reader to think, to see something
in a new light, and possibly take action in some way. There is a political
aim. Creative nonfiction can enact change; it can be a voice for change.
Unlike fiction, creative nonfiction can respond in a more personal and
more immediate way to events that affect readers' lives through a voice in
some ways more intimate than fiction or poetry—that is, no obvious mask.
Through a voice that is reliably real, personal, and reflective—unlike objective journalism or cloaked fiction—it can affect the way people think about
culture and history. It's based in an urge to change something in the culture. At the same time, creative nonfiction engages literary style and technique and the work must stand on its own aesthetic and artistic merit, just
like fiction and poetry. It is a very rigorous genre. ■

Photo Essay

Luke Swank: A Life and Legacy Rediscovered

Howard Bossen

The light was flashing on my answering machine. "Hello, my name is Grace Swank Davis. I'm Luke Swank's granddaughter and I'd like to talk to you." An adrenaline rush of excitement left me stunned and speechless. I had been searching for more than a year for Harry Swank, Luke's son, or one of Swank's heirs. To know that a grandchild had somehow found me was exciting and humbling. Maybe I could now fit more pieces of the Luke Swank puzzle together.

It had started with a simple proposition to the curators at the Carnegie Museum of Art (CMA) in Pittsburgh. "If you allow me access to the photography collection," rich in photographs that relate to the industrial heritage of western Pennsylvania, "I'll identify a project of mutual benefit." It was January 2002 and I had just begun my semester-long visiting appointment at Carnegie Mellon University. Little did I know where that request would lead; it started me on a journey that revised the history of photography and changed my life. Eventually, my book *Luke Swank: Modernist Photographer* enabled me to reinsert a magnificent photographer into the discussion of 1930s photographic modernism and give a granddaughter back her grandfather's legacy that had been lost to time.

On my fourth or fifth visit to the photography collection at CMA, one of the two-handled, nondescript metal storage cabinets was opened. A black portfolio case was removed and placed on the large, plain worktable. The curator opened the portfolio and began to show the 20 or so matted, vintage prints of 1930s America. I was struck by the first print's beautiful tonal properties and luminescent light. It was a large print for the 1930s, approximately 11 x 14 inches without the mat. It was urban. I assumed made in Pittsburgh. I was shown a second and a third print. Each one was more impressive than the previous one. By the fifth print I knew I was

"Man Crossing City Street," c. 1935
9 x 7 inches; mount 18 x 14 inches; signed
Carnegie Museum of Art; Gift of Edith Swank Long by transfer from the
Pennsylvania Department, Carnegie Library of Pittsburgh, 83.40.93

viewing something extraordinary, yet the full name of the photographer hadn't even registered. "Luke who?" I asked. "Luke Swank," she repeated. As someone who had spent most of his life immersed in the history of photography, *how could I never have heard of him? Why had he been lost to history?* My task, I came to realize, was to give Luke back his voice, to return his photographs to public consciousness and place his art within the context of the history of photography and American culture.

There was no real order to these photographs as they emerged from the case. The work represented several themes: working-class Pittsburgh; western Pennsylvania rural scenes combining landscape and architecture; portraits of circus clowns; and striking modernist abstractions of steel mills. The images flashed one after another, all astonishingly strong. They connected in a way that I could at that moment sense but not yet fully understand. My excitement swelled as I looked at each image.

I asked the curator how many Luke Swank photographs were in the collection. She told me there were more than 360, plenty to select from for a one-person exhibition and possibly a large enough body of work for a book. Then she let the bomb drop. A sister institution, the Carnegie Library of Pittsburgh, she told me, owned more than 2,000 additional prints and all of Swank's known negatives. As we continued to look at Swank's photographs and she began to tell me what little was known about Swank, I realized I was looking at the work of an artist who had vanished, lost to the shadows of time.

The Carnegie Library collection of Swank's work, consisting of boxes of contact prints, loose prints, mounted prints, glass-plate stereographs, and color transparencies, presented me with a wealth of images and an almost complete lack of any documentation and personal history. In order to mount a major exhibition and write a book, images alone weren't sufficient. I needed to be able to reconstruct Swank's life and place his work into the context of his era. I needed to find out who Luke Swank was and what he thought.

I knew that Swank had come from a prominent merchant family in Johnstown, Pennsylvania. I soon discovered that he was well educated, had a degree in horticulture, trained German Shepherds [dogs] before World War I, was an avid gardener, and became a cook of such quality that in the late 1930s the *Pittsburgh Sun Telegraph* raved about his culinary abilities. During the First World War, he served as a research chemist at a facility in Washington. He was injured in a chemical accident that seemed to have affected his health the rest of his life. His only child, Harry, was born in 1918.

Swank had worked for the Western Pennsylvania Architectural Survey in the 1930s and did most of the photography for the book *The Early Architecture of Western Pennsylvania*, a classic on pre–Civil War architecture. I discovered he worked as a commercial photographer for H. J. Heinz Company in the 1930s and 1940s. The collection of his work at the Carnegie Library includes the index card records of his commercial projects. It shows that he began to photograph food products for Heinz in 1936 and made more than 5,000 negatives for Heinz by the time the last record was made in late 1943, several months before Swank's death.

I had access to a few snippets of newspaper and magazine reviews and a copy of a mid-1970s letter gifting Swank's work to the Carnegie Library. This letter proved to be one of the keys to solving many mysteries about his life and work. Although the letter was almost 28 years old, a query was sent to the listed address. I got lucky. It turned out that while the executor of Swank's wife's estate had died in the 1990s, the property was still in the family. A man called who identified himself as John, the husband of Luke Swank's niece, Claudia. He indicated that not only would he and his wife be happy to help with the project, they had material I would want to see.

A few weeks later I met them at their home. I learned from Swank's niece that her parents had kept letters, photographs, and memorabilia that Aunt Edith, Luke's second wife, had sent to or left in the care of her brother and sister-in-law. As I sat in Claudia and John's living room, I was presented with letters by Edward Weston, Willard Van Dyke, and Frank Lloyd Wright.

By the mid-1930s, I soon learned, Swank was a close friend of Edgar Kaufmann, the Pittsburgh department store magnate who commissioned Frank Lloyd Wright to build the architectural masterpiece Fallingwater at Bear Run, Pennsylvania. Swank photographed Fallingwater during the construction process and for years afterward. Several of his photographs appeared in the Museum of Modern Art exhibition and catalog "A New House by Frank Lloyd Wright on Bear Run, Pennsylvania." Edith's letters describe visits by her and Luke to Fallingwater and include observations about the personalities of both Edgar and his wife, Lillian. Her letters also describe their February 1940 honeymoon at Fallingwater. Several nude studies Swank made of Edith at Fallingwater were included in Claudia's papers.

From letters Edith had sent to her family describing her life with Luke, I discovered that Edith had been a professional writer. These letters weren't the garden variety. They were lengthy, often typed single-spaced, and some ran six, eight, ten, even a dozen pages in length. As I read these letters, I realized that not only had I begun to gain an invaluable understanding of the last seven years of Swank's life, I was also in the presence of a gifted writer.

The project would take two more years to complete. It was after the first year that Grace left her extraordinary message on my answering machine. I immediately contacted her. Grace knew almost nothing about her grandfather. He died in 1944, three years before she was born. She had never seen any pictures by him. Despite the fact that she had nothing that belonged to Luke and knew little about his life, her bits and pieces of stored family history helped connect many dots in her grandfather's emerging biography. Although Grace didn't know much about her grandfather and nothing of her grandmother, she did know a great deal about the circus, one of Luke's major subjects. Her father, Harry, went to work for the circus at 16 despite his affluent background. He spent the years before World War II working in the circus and helping at his father's studio. After the war, he spent the rest of his life associated with the circus. Grace, whose mother was a circus performer, grew up in the back lots of circuses.

   In addition to these personal connections I made with his family, letters and other materials found in archives provided more insight into Swank's life and work. From the archives of the seminal New York art dealer Julien Levy to the Museum of Modern Art and the Center for Creative Photography came fascinating details. Swank first contacted Levy, I learned from a letter written in late December 1931, after seeing a short article about the just opened gallery in the *New Yorker*. Levy invited Swank to contribute to the Museum of Modern Art's "Murals by American Painters and Photographers" landmark 1932 exhibition, the first one at MoMA to include photographs, and Levy gave Swank a solo show, "Photographs of the American Scene," in 1933. In other letters, Swank describes how he learned photography by emulating the work of photographers he admired and when he decided to leave the family businesses to devote his life fully to image making. In a historian's dream letter, I found out what Alfred Stieglitz, one of the most important figures in American art and photography in the first half of the twentieth century, thought of Swank's work in the 1941 "Sixty Photographs" exhibition. This was the first exhibition organized by the newly formed Department of Photography at the Museum of Modern Art. The letter was written by Beaumont Newhall, destined to

become one of the twentieth century's most respected historians of pho-
tography, to Ansel Adams, his co-curator of "Sixty Photographs." In 1941
Adams was well known, but certainly not the towering figure he became
in later decades. Newhall discussed Stieglitz's observations at length, calling
Swank's work "especially fine," even going so far as to report to Adams on
Stieglitz's thoughts on how the photographs were hung and sequenced.

One of the most unusual documents I found was in the papers of the
American photographer Margaret Bourke-White, who visited with Swank
and son Harry in Swank's downtown Pittsburgh studio and home in
November 1937. Among Bourke-White's papers at Syracuse University, I
ran across a one-act play written by Swank in homage to Bourke-White.
In that play, Swank talks about light as a photographer would, linking the
quality of light and the working conditions found in a steel mill. Swank
wrote, in part, "From a small barred window high on the wall comes light
faint and cold as winter moonlight on the slabs in a country graveyard. The
darkness consumes the light before it can touch anything. All is as quiet as
dim deep dungeons in a ruined castle. The light fades from the window.
Then a glow yellow and sulfurous as hellfire in a midnight fog flickers and
fades. Again all is dark. But into the darkness writhe and crawl creatures vis-
ible only by the light they give off—a light soft and phosphorescent as from
corpses rotting in tropical jungles."

As a photographer, Swank uses light to direct the viewer and to create
spaces of shadow with subtle detail and highlight that retains tone. He
focuses on the little moments of life that reveal rhythms of 1930s American
culture. His poetic realism is evident in most of his work. Nowhere is it
more apparent than in his study of urban life, his largest and most profound
set of images, as exemplified by the photograph on the cover of this issue
of *Fourth Genre*. "Man Crossing City Street" (circa 1935) was shot from
above, looking down on the street. This photograph represents a formalist
approach to an unfolding moment. The frame is carefully composed; a tri-
angular shaft of light guides the eye across the street, leading the viewer past
the "Do not park here" sign to the man leaning against the building. The
tiny spot of light on the brim of the man's hat combined with his casual
body stance pointing to the right pulls the eye to the right where it is swept
back around in a curve to the man with the umbrella in hand. The man
with the umbrella has been stopped in mid-step, his left foot slightly
blurred. The leg is bent at a similar angle to that of the man in the background. In the foreground, the man with the umbrella is pointed to the

right, just slightly, but enough for the eye to sweep through the curve of tones in the street and back to the man leaning against the building, creating a self-reinforcing visual rhythm. Anchoring the left side of the image with interesting detail is the back half of the taxi.

Like many of Swank's photographs, "Man Crossing City Street" records a tiny slice of the world in front of his lens that is cinematic in quality. It has the appearance of a frame pulled from an unfolding event and frozen for study and contemplation. Its mixture of documentary description, formalist sophistication, and mastery of light combined with an intuitive understanding of the precise moment to click the shutter, that moment when all elements within the frame come together, the moment the French photographer Henri Cartier-Bresson would define in the 1950s as the "decisive moment," results in visual poetry.

After almost two years spent tracking down documents, conducting interviews, and studying and cataloging Swank's photographs, I was finally ready to begin writing the book. Between writing, editing, and all the things that need to be done to create a major retrospective exhibition, more than another year would pass.

When the Swank exhibition finally opened at the Carnegie Museum of Art in November 2005, Grace still had never seen an original Luke Swank photograph. The front of CMA was decked out with a huge banner showcasing Swank's lyrically sculptural modernist steel image "Skip Bridge" (circa 1931–32). Entering the museum the visitor could look from the ground level up the long, wide staircase to the second-floor entrance area of the Heinz Galleries, which was hung with a floor-to-ceiling, wall-to-wall portrait of Luke with his ever-present pipe. Before men in black ties and elegantly gowned women, who assembled for the opening, were allowed to enter, my wife and I escorted Grace into two huge galleries. In front of her were more than 140 original photographs—her first look at a photographer's legacy . . . and for a grandfather she was coming to know intimately for the very first time. ◼

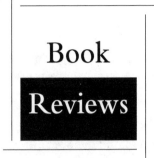

Book Reviews

Full-Length Reviews

The World Before Mirrors
By Joan Connor
University of Nebraska Press, 2006
148 pages, paper, $14.95

The essay has been called an intimate form, intimacy being a hallmark of the confession. By confession, I don't mean necessarily the Catholic ritual of naming acts (in a dark booth on Saturday mornings, as I recall from childhood), but rather a revelation of thoughts. More so than any genre, the reader of essays enters the mind of the writer, and sees there the architecture of thought itself. In an essay collection, it follows, the reader enters not just the mind of the essayist, but the many-roomed mansion that is the heart and soul of the writer, the very world as seen through the writer's lens. You'd better be sure it's a place you want to be. Joan Connor's collection of essays, *The World Before Mirrors*, which won the *River Teeth* 2005 Literary Nonfiction Prize, was a place I wanted to be, almost like home.

Perhaps because her life story is/has been similar to mine (a woman alone in the world, an easterner stuck in Ohio—a scathing argument against Ohio pops up in many of Connor's essays, so piercing and artful that one begins to pity the state), Connor's literary terrain feels familiar, but her appeal is more universal. Throughout the collection she wrestles with the loftiest themes, love and desire, place and displacement, memory and loss, the very meaning of life itself. Her voice is astonishing; she is witty and elegiac both, erudite and silly, eloquent and plain speaking. As a writer she has enormous range, intellectually and artistically, and she allows herself the freedom to cavort wildly in her field of inquiry. One essay is called "Flying Rabbits and Disappearing Playground," which sounds like the title to an abstract painting, appropriate for the form of this piece, which affects the reader like a mood (if this essay were a color, it would be indigo). This essay takes an almost exaggerated license to travel; an essay is *supposed* to meander, to wander about, but this piece is an *uber*-form: it circumnavigates. Connor ambles from two boys she recalls from childhood, the proverbial good and bad brothers (two sides of herself), to rabbits, hobos and their esoteric pictograms, the sexual molestation Connor suffered as a child, loneliness, turning 50, email spam, a back road in Vermont, seahorses (death and cruelty), Edith Metzger (the girl who died in Jackson Pollock's car, the friend of his lover), the etymology of the word *boudoir*, menopause, a cow and a moose in love, and finally, the act of writing, a reason for living, a mark we make upon the world. It may strain credulity after the list above to say that the essay coheres, but it does. The piece is ultimately about love.

Love, in fact, is the theme that tethers the essays to each other and unifies this collection. "Do not ask me what love is," Connor writes, though she will answer the question through a variety of metaphors and musings. "Riding a horse is like loving someone. Illusions of control. Delusions of control. You sit on the back of an animal who could kill you on a whim, who outweighs you, outruns you, who, truth to tell, is only humoring you and only for the while. Rein right, rein left, indeed. Gee. Haw. Golly gee and haw, haw. You're on your back and staring at the stars, you ass. Hee haw, haw, haw."

The narrative is rendered taut by the powerful undercurrent of longing. "I worry that love's unattainability may be what makes it love," she writes. At times, Connor is petitioning: "Is that life, finally, tiptoeing through some desolate room waiting for a stranger to speak? Where are you? I've been waiting. Speak to me now. I am in the ballroom in my prettiest dress and waiting to hear your voice. Let's leave something of ourselves, our love behind in this aging world. Speak to me. Now." Yet at other moments, she renounces: "I no longer believe in love. Love schmove."

Throughout the book, several chronological strands intertwine. Connor's only child, her son Norman, grows from adolescence to 18, ready to leave for college, as she turns 50. Connor reunites with a lover from young adulthood, and past confronts present. These progressions form a suboceanic river that provides occasion for and pulls along the philosophical and spiritual and psychological musings that eddy throughout the essays, a Gulf Stream of warm prose that softens the sometimes chilling moments of despair: "Particularly on Sunday afternoons in February, I feel as if I have outlived my time. In two years my son will be in college, and I suspect that I will be ready to check out of Hotel Joan." Connor's despair does not overwhelm the reader, though, balanced as it is by her libidinous lust for life: "I sit at a huge banquet table, offering so many groaning pleasures. I want to taste them all. I want to eat it all. I have had difficulty with monogamy because alternate lives have always seemed possible to me."

Stylistically, Connor's writing moves frenetically. The essays are characterized by wordplay, a kind of literary echolalia. Some passages feel like small storms of the brain (microbursts, meteorologically speaking), petit mal seizures of creative connection, which are sometimes amazing, funny, and/or poetic, and occasionally (only occasionally) overdone and annoying. Here's an example that seems superfluous, the mind at unrest: "On a card, I hand-wrote—'I am typing on Thurber's Underwood,' then typed,— 'See?' and sent the card to my former lover. But he didn't see. I, however, did. I saw. Seesaw. *My love is like a see-saw*, so Aretha sings. I came. I saw. I left. Veni. Vidi. And wee wee wee all the way home."

In the example that follows, the repetition and reverberation seem to serve a larger meaning and form: "Places that have outlived their usefulness observe time's poetry, the forward march of iambic feet. Spanning time, they scan it. I similarly scan for meaning, survey these places. Iamb. A heartbeat. It's over in a heartbeat. I am. Still I am. I am still." Connor's stylistic tic, in those few instances when it doesn't work, is a mere peccadillo compared to her mostly gorgeous prose and clear ringing truths such as, "We do not, I suspect, know the moment of our happiness as we live it," or "We need love for this: to mark each other's passing."

Because very little of the collection is concrete (unlike a memoir, which typically has a clear story line or dramatic arc), we reside in the realm of thought and meditation. These essays are philosophical ponderings, and they can be slippery. I found myself having to reread them, though this turned out to be a good thing as I discovered more richness each time I revisited a piece. There is something new in them every time, like a magic trick we are trying to figure out: how does she do that?

Connor's is a quiet book that I deeply admire, for her essays have that great and rare quality, to cause the reader to examine her own thoughts, and life, and choices. By entering Connor's peripatetic mind, we enter—perhaps anew—our own. By bearing her heart so openly on the page, we must face our own, too. "The essay is a recalcitrant form," Connor writes, "a flexible form, a resistant form. It is a way to transmute self-loathing into something of beauty." In *The World Before Mirrors*, this transmutation has been accomplished.

Reviewed by Maureen Stanton

Strange Piece of Paradise: A Return to the American West to Investigate My
Attempted Murder—and Solve the Riddle of Myself
By Terri Jentz
Farrar, Straus and Giroux, 2006
535 pages, cloth, $27

On June 22, 1977, the summer after their freshman year at Yale, Terri Jentz
and a roommate began riding the "BikeCentennial," a cross-country bicycle route. On the seventh day of the trip, they parted company with a couple they'd met along the way and ridden with for a time, set up camp in a
day-use-only park, ate simple food heated on a tiny camp stove, crawled
into mummy bags in their small tent, and fell asleep. That was the end of
the first part of Jentz's life. She awoke to the sound of squealing tires.
Suddenly a truck was on her shoulder and chest, and while she gasped for
shallow breaths, she heard her roommate's screams and the dull thud of axe
striking flesh. Then the truck moved, and this is what she saw: "the headless torso of a fit, meticulous young cowboy suspending an axe over my
heart."

In the lengthy subtitle to her harrowing memoir, *Strange Piece of Paradise:*
A Return to the American West to Investigate My Attempted Murder—and Solve
the Riddle of Myself, Jentz gives away the bare-bone plot of the book. She
almost died out West, and the person who nearly murdered her sent her
reeling into a haunted future, a riddle to herself. But Jentz understands that
the facts don't make a story, and it is that knowledge, combined with her
powerful writing, that makes this memoir so successful. The heart of the
book is Jentz's threefold search: to make meaning out of the apparently random attack; to find herself; and to identify, long after the police have
dropped the case, the man who almost killed her and derailed her life.

It took Jentz 15 years to realize that the crime had damaged not just her
arm and shoulder, but also her psyche. Until that time, she used the facts
of the story—and her scars—sometimes as a kind of wry anecdote, other
times as a way of taking the measure of potential friends. During those
years, Jentz felt haunted by a scarecrowlike self, a product of that night, a
ghoulish underbelly of a self that scrawled notes about violent crimes and
saved artifacts from that night. Sometimes she felt suddenly empty, inspiring a colleague to quip that the puppeteer had gone home. Images from the
night crept into her waking life: the smell of blood ("copper pennies held
in a damp palm"), the feel of her fingertips on her friend's exposed brain.
Horrific nightmares ruined her sleep. Axes cropped up everywhere: the

word on her own license plate; in the hands of the statue on the Oregon state capitol building's dome; license plates of cars cutting her off. The headless cowboy revisited too, in the memory of a childhood toy, a 3-D Viewmaster disk of just such a cowboy pointing a gun at the viewer. And for a while, she obsessively collected axes and hatchets from flea markets and hardware stores.

In 1992, driven in part by a desire to confront writer's block, but also to heal the mystery of herself, to find the part of her she believed remained in Oregon ("our blood soaked the earth that night, and surely it hadn't left"), and to solve the case, Jentz returned to the scene of the crime. There, she drove the route she'd biked, right into the park, and lay in the spot seared into memory, the precise location of the attack. It is the first time readers see the night through her eyes, not as a summary, not as a clipped story told to friends, not as a newspaper record, not as a police report. Of the attacker slicing her repeatedly with the axe, she writes: "A starburst explodes in my head. Then another. . . . I forget my eyes; my fingers are alert, grabbing the end of what is striking me. . . . A brilliant show of light. . . . Consciousness darkens, ebbs away. Yet a flicker remains alive to take note: this is what dying is."

Only the briefest portrait of her old self—childhood, time at Yale, family members—introduces readers to the person she was before. Even fewer details characterize her current life as a screenwriter in California. But Jentz makes those smaller portraits work. Those glimpses of the past self are only a starting point. For Jentz, the story lies in the journey and discovery.

As she returns to Oregon again and again, Jentz reintroduces herself to people from that grisly past: the couple who rescued her; nurses who worked on her; local people who may or may not know or be related to the attacker; and men who may or may not be that cowboy torso himself. (But not her traveling companion, who wanted no part of the reexamination of their past, and who ended the friendship shortly after the attack.)

The memoir follows Jentz's efforts to examine the crime from multiple angles. She creates portraits of townspeople who helped or turned away. She examines the sociology of violent crime; images of American masculinity; feminist views of women's bodies; gender roles; small-town dynamics; and class. She considers the cultural moment of 1977, the dreams and discontents of that era. She provides a kaleidoscopic view of the night she was attacked: "As the earth slowly turned in the dark, Americans in one time zone after the next settled in front of their TVs, safe in their living rooms [watching] the CBS Wednesday-night movie, the world television premier of a dark and unsettling Western, one of those edgy films . . . that reflected the mood of national cynicism."

Read this book and you will undergo a journey not only into the way a violent attack shapes one woman's life and body and mind, but also into the dark underbelly of American culture in 1977, and its lingering effects through the next two decades.

Reviewed by Jocelyn Bartkevicius

Perishable
By Dirk Jamison
Chicago Review Press, 2006
212 pages, cloth, $22.95

The publisher's pitch on the cover of Dirk Jamison's *Perishable* makes the Jamison family sound like a good candidate for the Jerry Springer Show: "Hilarious, horrifying, and ultimately heartbreaking, *Perishable* is a childhood memoir that chronicles seven years in the life of an almost ordinary American family—that ate garbage." Such a description is unfortunate because Dirk Jamison has written a wry chronicle that people amused by Springer's wacky, psychosocial dysfunctionaries would likely find completely disappointing. However, devotees of National Public Radio's *This American Life* will admire Jamison's intelligent and entertaining presentation of his peculiar family.

Dirk's father, in his quest to be an unencumbered ski bum, successfully gets fired from his construction job, goes on unemployment, and with almost religious zeal provides free food to the family from grocery store dumpsters: damaged boxes of cereal, pastries past their "use-by" dates, and dented cans of fruit, vegetables, and soup. Dirk's mother (described as huge) is a secret consumer of buckets of fried chicken, when she isn't busy making meals, sewing clothes, and decorating birthday cakes. His older sister is a bully who routinely kicks, hits, punches, and chokes Dirk. These attacks are frequent and one supposes their mother, who is usually nearby, at the sewing machine, or in the kitchen decorating a cake, or on the telephone with one of her many sisters complaining about their father, should notice and do something. With two such distracted and self-absorbed parents, Dirk and his siblings rarely seem to get enough attention, except when it serves as ammunition in the ongoing battle over religion (Mom is a Mormon, Dad is a free spirit), food, and, ultimately, custody of the children.

Jamison presents his chronicle in three chapters, each with several brief scenes; reading the book is like watching a well-edited montage of a family's Super-8 movies. Jamison rarely interposes a personal insight or reveals his reactions; there are no voice-overs to explain how young Dirk feels when his father takes their dying dog to a truck stop where he leaves it with a bag of kibble, or when Dirk barely escapes sexual abuse by the Boy Scout troop leader. He doesn't comment when his mother sews a hideous yellow outfit for his first day at school. He simply presents the facts. It is up to the reader to understand the pain of being abandoned by his father, ignored by his mother, and continually tortured by his sister; it is up to the reader to make assumptions about the effects on young Dirk, and to watch and take note as his parents, seemingly, did not.

Several lines of white space, a small black mark, and more white space set off each scene. In these intervals the reader is left alone—given a moment to worry about young Dirk. It's a clever technique that evokes the reader's own memories and emotions. Many scenes end with a lasting image of young Dirk in trouble. One occurs on his first day at school. His mother doesn't put zippers in his clothes, making it necessary for Dirk to drop his pants to use the urinal. Three older kids "taught me about zippers by pinning me in it [the urinal] and counting out twenty-five flushes."

On the next page a school bully attacks Dirk. The scene ends with Dirk on the ground thinking, "My sister had taught me enough about kicking to know that it was rarely happenstance."

The reader is told about the father's ultimate plan to abandon the family via his *Enemies* list: "Written by Dad during a night panic, then hidden in plain sight on the bedside dresser. The list was long, and Mother is working on forgetting about it. But she is having trouble forgetting the first two items on the list:

1. Wife
2. Kids"

The scenes pile up, one painful event following another: the church fellowship dance where he doesn't get to be with the girl who relieves the boys' erections is juxtaposed to the father's failed attempt to stop a frantic young goat, held down by Dirk, from bleeding to death. The torments are sometimes presented one on top of another to the extent that the reader may suffer sympathetic exhaustion. It's important to note that young Dirk is ostensibly unaffected by these very same events.

Seven years in Jamison's early life have been acidulously edited down to a few dozen carefully chosen, carefully cropped scenes in which the reader does not see young Dirk complain or get frustrated, sullen, or angry. Emotional reactions are the prerogative of the reader, not Jamison. Perhaps it should not be surprising that Jamison, who rarely caught the full attention of his parents, has found a way to thoroughly engage the reader's attention and at the same time appear to be unconcerned with it.

Reviewed by Priscilla Hodgkins

■

Birdsong: A Natural History
By Don Stap
Scribner, 2005
261 pages, cloth, $24.00; paper, $15.95

As the literature of the past few thousand years makes plain, humans from various cultures have maintained a consistent fascination with—and admiration for—the songs of birds. And if poets have sometimes doubted their ability to adequately describe birdsong, it appears that scientists have not been much more successful. Despite having one of the most compelling subjects in the biological world, scientists who study "avian bioacoustics" continue to be troubled by a number of fascinating questions. Some of these questions involve complex evolutionary issues. For example, what is the role of song dialects within bird communities, and what effect does dialect range have on avian genetic fitness and speciation? But many of the questions that remain will strike readers as surprisingly basic. How do birds learn their songs? What is the window of opportunity for that learning? Why do certain individuals customize their expression of a shared song? Is bird singing strictly related to mating and territorial behavior, or is it possible that birds actually sing for the sheer pleasure of it? Why *do* birds sing? Don Stap's *Birdsong: A Natural History* reminds us from the outset that we do not yet know the answer to this fascinating question.

Among the pleasures of *Birdsong* is Stap's effective use of what scientists already know about birdsong to help revivify our admiration for all that chirping and warbling that we hear around our homes. For example, a singing bird uses almost 100 percent of the air passing across its vocal cords to make sound; compare that to the 2 percent or so used by the bird's human neighbor who is singing in the backyard. Or, consider that the average brown thrasher knows more than 2,000 songs. How many of us could say the same? And many bird species have, over millennia, shaped form to function by developing anatomical adaptations that allow for amazingly complex vocalizations. Many birds, for example, have evolved a syrinx with dual bronchial tubes that can be used to produce sounds of completely different frequencies—a neat trick that allows the bird to simultaneously project two sounds that are not harmonically related and thus, in effect, "[sing] a duet with itself."

Though it is not his main subject, Stap is also interested in human conceptions of birdsong, and some of the book's most illuminating moments examine this cultural link between people and birds. "Frogs croak, crickets chirp, wolves howl, and lions roar," he writes, "but birds sing." Do birds communicate in a way that is fundamentally different from other animals, many of which also use vocalizations in complex ways? Or is it the case that the beauty of the warble is in the ear of the beholder? Does our use of the word "song" to describe avian vocalization reflect something fundamental to the sound itself, or do we call bird vocalizations "song" simply as a way of expressing a human aesthetic preference for the sound of the house finch over that of the bullfrog? In discussing this issue of what we might call "acoustic aesthetics," Stap tells fascinating stories of interactions between human and bird "music"—as in the case of Beethoven, Mozart, and Bartók, all of whom incorporated avian melodies into their compositions. (Next time you hear Beethoven's Sixth, listen for cuckoo, nightingale, and quail song!)

Birdsong incorporates and describes biological science, but is not itself a scientific book. Instead, Don Stap's primary technique—one that has been used by many environmental writers and documentarians—is to follow scientists around in the field, describing their work and translating their hypotheses and findings into language that nonspecialist readers can understand and appreciate. To this end Stap has made a sort of literary character of his main figure, renowned avian bioacoustics specialist Don Kroodsma. Kroodsma tramps around the world, hauling piles of field equipment and recording gear, and showing infinite patience as he waits for the right moment to funnel a rare song into the cone of his parabolic microphone.

While a great deal of science these days occurs only in labs, in Stap's account Kroodsma becomes the romantic field naturalist of old: driven by genuine curiosity, a desire to be in the field, and a lifelong admiration for birds, he is a man who loves the questions more than the answers. Although it is sometimes difficult to tell where the real biologist ends and the literary hero begins, Stap's Kroodsma is nonetheless an effective center to a book that is not only about birds, but also about the equally curious human animals that seek to understand them. Readers who find Kroodsma especially interesting will want to examine his own *The Singing Life of Birds* (Houghton Mifflin, 2005), a recently published and surprisingly accessible book that documents many of his experiments in avian bioacoustics from a first-person point of view. Readers interested in approaching the subject of birdsong from a more philosophical angle will want to read another fine new book, *Why Birds Sing* (Basic Books, 2005), by environmental musician and philosopher David Rothenberg.

The strength of Stap's approach is his keen ability to be an observer of the observer, and not only an observer of the observed. He is careful to keep Kroodsma at the core of his narrative—even when he is relating his own field experiences or educating us about birds—which gives *Birdsong* a coherent feel and also provides a human interest story for readers who might find the detailed discussions of avian evolutionary biology slow going. This approach falters only toward the end of the book, where Stap has chosen to commit the final one-third of *Birdsong* to the single subject of Kroodsma's study of the three-wattled bellbird in Costa Rica. Here the narrative lingers too long on a single subject that, though interesting, would have been more effective had it been presented in a more dynamic and less protracted way.

On the whole, however, *Birdsong* combines personal narrative, science writing, and travel writing in very effective ways. This book will be especially welcome to those who find the subject fascinating but the science behind it daunting. In his role as a cultural translator who makes the intricacies of field biology accessible to general readers, Stap has done a real service—a service that is the more valuable because it reminds us not only of the answers science has provided, but also of the questions science must still ask. Living as we do in an age in which the human genome has already been mapped, it may be comforting to know that birdsong is a gift that remains beyond the reach of both poets and scientists.

Reviewed by Michael Branch

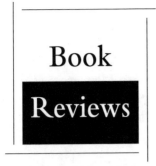

Book Reviews

Reader-to-Reader: Capsule Reviews

This column invites readers to share their favorite nonfiction books in print. Memoirs, travel writing, nature writing, essay collections, biography, and true adventure are all welcome in these capsule reviews—both of new books and of old favorites still available. Our aim is to keep the best nonfiction alive in a reader-to-reader kind of way. If you have books that you'd like to recommend in this column, contact Mimi Schwartz at mimi.schwartz@worldnet.att.net.

PATRICK MADDEN

Brian Doyle has a storyteller's blood, which came to him from his Irish forebears, so he calls himself a storyteller, which is true, since he tells stories, and most of them true, so you can call him a nonfiction storyteller. But he doesn't stop at the stories. He allows himself the meditative space to think on the stories he tells, whether they happened to him or to interesting others, and that makes him an essayist after the order of Montaigne, who once prescribed a formula for writing thusly:

> These are my . . . true stories, which I find as entertaining and as tragic as those that we make up at will in order to give pleasure. . . . And if anyone should wish to build up an entire and connected body of them, he would need to furnish only the connecting links, . . . and by this means he could amass a great many true events of all sorts, arranging and diversifying them as the beauty of the work should require.
>
> — "Of Three Good Women"

That's what Brian Doyle does, amasses a great many true events, arranges them, makes them beautiful on their own and in harmony with the others. For his efforts, he's been chosen four times for the *Best American Essays* (1998, 1999, 2003, 2005) and four times for the *Best [American] Spiritual Writing* (1999, 2001, 2002, 2005). He's published seven books of nonfiction, four of them in the past three years, all strikingly good, wonderful, fantastic, inspirational. Here are three:

Leaping: Revelations and Epiphanies, by Brian Doyle. Loyola Press, 2003. 194 pages, paper, $13.95.

This is Brian Doyle's best book; so if you buy only one, buy this one. (But go ahead and read about the other two, too, since they're still excellent.) *Leaping* is a greatest hits collection, divided into six sections of grouped essays that vary in length from 2 to 20 pages. Their subjects range from visiting with the Dalai Lama to action figures' lost limbs to crushing a car to the Catholic Mass to teaching Sunday School to migrating geese to Jesus to the secret sensory organs of anchovies. This collection contains three *Best American Essays:* "Altar Boy," "The Meteorites," and "Yes," and three from the *Best Spiritual Writing* (which added "American" in 2004): "Eating Dirt," "Grace Notes," and "Leap," all of which have repeatedly knocked my socks off. This last, "Leap," surmounts the insurmountable task of writing deeply and unmaudlinly about the September 11th attacks. After initially refusing the request, feeling himself unable or unworthy, Doyle produced the most moving essay on that subject I have yet read. It begins—

> A couple leaped from the south tower, hand in hand. They reached for each other and their hands met and they jumped.
> Jennifer Brickhouse saw them falling, hand in hand.

—and continues with its matter-of-fact, reportorial, repeatorial tone, a litany of simple sentences with subjects before verbs and objects trailing, revealing a mind numbed by reality, seemingly unable to do more than retell, from multiple perspectives, the happening. But he does snap out of it, through some lines from the *Apocalypsis*, to a sort of understanding:

> Their hands reaching and joining is the most powerful prayer I can imagine, the most eloquent, the most graceful. It is everything that we are capable of against horror and loss and death.

Leaping: Revelations and Epiphanies is full of such gems; it is rife with the essays I turn to again and again for teaching and inspiration.

Spirited Men: Story, Soul, and Substance, by Brian Doyle. Cowley Publications, 2004. 148 pages, paper, $14.95.

This is a weirder book, a collection of biographical essays about 11 mostly dead white men. There is William Blake, Plutarch, Robert Louis Stevenson, Graham Greene, James Joyce, and (not dead) Van Morrison, along with others whom I didn't know before reading about them. Doyle is less present in this book, focusing more on his subjects, but he lends his rhythmic ear to the prose he employs to recount these men's lives. For instance, Plutarch. Who reads or writes about Plutarch anymore? And what does anyone know beyond the bare skeleton of his biography? Yet Doyle sets out to "enflesh him, bring back something of the personality and character of the man, in the way he saved so many notable men of his time from desiccated hagiography" and succeeds in weaving pathos (in the death of a daughter) into the stuffy statistical or summarized stuff. Doyle also weaves in some literary criticism, kind of, tackling the task, say, of reviving Robert Louis Stephenson's status:

> Considering that the man threw fastballs in most every literary genre there is, and considering that none of the many writers of genius we know threw such high heat in so many ballparks, it seems to me we might account the grinning Scotsman with the tubercular cough and cigarette and stories always on his lips to be maybe the best writer our language has known; or at least the most comprehensively accomplished.

Throughout the book, Doyle vivifies, interrogates, and praises his men, seeking out their quirks and sparks, injecting his enthusiasm into his retellings of their lives.

The Wet Engine: Exploring the Mad Wild Miracle of the Heart, by Brian Doyle. Paraclete Press, 2005. 160 pages, cloth, $17.95.

This is a book-length essay about hearts. When was the last time you read a book-length essay? It's great that such a thing still exists, and Doyle's example is primo. Among its pages, *The Wet Engine* contains "Joyas Voladoras," which made *both* the *Best American Essays* and *Best American Spiritual Writing* anthologies in 2005. But it's a lot more than that. The plot is that Doyle's son Liam was born with only three chambers in his heart, thus he needed emergency surgery and another operation 18 months later; he is now ten and in good health, although he will eventually need a heart transplant. This harrowing experience led Doyle down the twisting and bifurcating associative pathways that he explores lyrically and meditatively in this book: from the myriad ways a heart can malfunction to the earliest experimental heart surgeries to the growing-up years and courtship and marriage of his son's surgeon to that surgeon's mother's years in a Japanese internment camp in Utah to the pope keeping certain cardinals' names secret for their protection to the metaphorical possibilities of the heart to the hummingbird's and the blue whale's hearts to when pediatric heart patients die to medical relief work in Armenia to genocides to miscarriages to prayers to God to Thomas Hardy's heart eaten by the mortician's cat (and more!). Underpinning it all, Doyle reveals his occasion, his reason:

> When my son was little, and all this was happening to him, all this editing and twisting and icing and stitching and worrying and weeping and beeping and not sleeping, I used to lie awake thinking about what I would tell him about this time. Someday, if he lived, he would ask me what happened then, and I would have to answer him with all the honesty and eloquence demanded of love. (151)

I am glad for a man like Brian Doyle, who gives that answer not only to his son, but to us, a man who will chase his interests as wide and as far as they stretch, and who has the time and the skill to craft them into a coherent, tender whole for us to read.

■

MIMI SCHWARTZ

One pleasure of creative nonfiction is the way it lets me enter new worlds: those I've missed and those I hope to visit. Guidebooks and history books give me the facts of place, but it's creative nonfiction—be it memoir, literary journalism, or personal essay—that lets me feel as if I'm there. What follows are three favorite armchair trips: one, to war-torn Hungary during World War II; one, to rural Haiti where an amazing man is creating a global health revolution; and one, to Japan, as told by over 40 writers capturing their special moments in a culture where ancient ritual seeks its place in modernity.

Castles Burning: A Child's Life in War, by Magda Denes. Touchstone Books, Simon and Schuster, 1997. 384 pages, paper, $8.95.

While writing about my family's leaving Hitler's Europe, I read many books about those years. *Castles Burning*, a memoir that reads like a novel, is one of the most vivid, making me able to picture myself in that place at that time. "I begged, and often my brother obliged. In the dark when I couldn't sleep, Ivan told me fairy tales in a whisper." So begins Magda Denes's story as a Jewish child trapped in Hungary during the Second World War. She was five when her father left for America, leaving Denes, her mother, and her brother, Ivan, to fend for themselves. By seeing Budapest through her young eyes, we experience normalcy trying to stay afloat in an increasingly brutal world. Humor merges with great sorrow, small insults with great sacrifice, as the quotidian turns into increasingly dangerous turf that the family must negotiate to stay alive. They have help: from Christian friends, from decent strangers, from the Jewish underground—and later, after the DP camps, from an agency that helps them get to America. The book is a page-turner, full of scenes and dialogue recreated by a sassy child with savvy instincts. We feel the adult reality hovering, but it's the child's country we travel through, her voice guiding us with the spunk, anger, jokes, toughness, and loyalty needed to make it out of one world and into another.

Mountains Beyond Mountains: The Quest of Dr. Paul Farmer, a Man Who Would Cure the World, by Tracy Kidder. Random House, 2003. 317 pages, paper, $10.50.

I never planned to go to Haiti, but thanks to Tracy Kidder's literary journalism—and Dr. Paul Farmer, his subject—I feel as if we all should go to help, and soon. With these two as guides, we come to understand the headlines made by desperate people whose land was decimated, whose family life and traditional healthcare, destroyed. This is the country that Paul Farmer, as a medical school student at Harvard, comes to, bringing a vision of curing infectious diseases through modern clinics for the poor. Within a few years, "on a treeless baked brown landscape" a three-hour drive from Port-au-Prince, there's a sign on a collection of concrete buildings that make "a dramatic appearance, like a fortress on its mountainside," and it reads ZANMI LASANTE (Partners in Health). It is the first of many clinics that Dr. Paul Farmer makes happen—in Haiti, Peru, Cuba, and Russia—to combat TB and AIDS among the world's poor. Kidder, who accompanies Farmer on and off, over many years, comes to understand a man who is a hero, but not a saint. Farmer is brilliant, quirky, charming, unbelievably energetic, irritating, and a master at combining idealism with its implementation. Kidder discovers this, not only in boardrooms of the powerful, but on narrow mountain trails, climbing with him for hours so that Farmer can visit a patient too sick to come to the clinic. Doctor Farmer continues to do this even after he is famous enough to meet with Bill Gates and talk before the United Nations—and that's his secret. "If you focus on individual patients," says his colleague, "you can't get sloppy." The book's title comes from a Haitian proverb—"Beyond mountains, there are mountains"—and through Kidder's inspiring book, we discover how one great man handles that.

JAPAN: True Stories, Travelers Tales, edited by Donald W. George and Amy G. Carlson. Travelers Tales, 2005. 400 pages, paper, $18.50.

What is it like to stay in a *ryokan* inn that's "the best hotel in the world," teach English, harvest rice, miss the last train to Takeatsuki, go to the Toyko Fish Market, and clean toilets for a Zen experience? These wonderful essays—almost 50 of them—put you in one person's shoes and let you walk around Japan for a while. You learn, with Cathy Davidson, how Japanese friends willingly violate their own mores in order to help her and her husband through terrible misfortune in "Grief." You meet memorable characters, like the old woman and her grandson, visiting a shrine in Donald Richie's "The Magic of Miyajima." And you come to understand, in Pico Iyer's "An Alchemy of Absences," the Japanese aesthetics of "the way the maple leaves were scattered across the garden, the reflection of a candle off the polished wood, the whisper of stockinged feet on bamboo mats." And also the challenge to ancient rituals in modern Japan where "in the past decade alone, 40,000 *machiya*, or traditional wooden houses, have been razed to the ground."

Travelers' Tales, fortunately, are now available for 27 places, including Paris, the Grand Canyon, Turkey, Cuba, Ireland, Italy, and Tibet. The full list is in the back of their books and more books are planned. So if you like good travel memoir—to read it and possibly to write it—here's a venue worth exploring. ■

190

About the

Contributors

Eve Abrams is a freelance writer, radio producer, and educator living in Brooklyn, New York. She thinks constantly about moving to New Orleans.

Jocelyn Bartkevicius is the book review editor of *Fourth Genre*. Her work has appeared in such journals as the *Hudson Review,* the *Missouri Review,* the *Bellingham Review,* and *Gulf Coast,* and has been awarded the *Missouri Review* Award in the Essay and the Annie Dillard Award. She is completing a memoir, *The Emerald Room.*

Howard Bossen is on the faculty of Michigan State University, where he is a professor in the School of Journalism and an adjunct curator at the Kresge Art Museum. *Luke Swank: Modernist Photographer* was published by the University of Pittsburgh Press (2005) in conjunction with the Carnegie Museum of Art and Kresge Art Museum retrospective exhibition by the same name.

Michael Branch is Professor of Literature and Environment at the University of Nevada, Reno, where he serves as director of graduate studies in the English Department. He is book review editor of the journal *ISLE: Interdisciplinary Studies in Literature and Environment* and coeditor of the University of Virginia Press book series *Under the Sign of Nature: Explorations in Ecocriticism.* He has published numerous essays, articles, and reviews on environmental subjects. His most recent book is *Reading the Roots: American Nature Writing before Walden* (University of Georgia Press, 2004).

Rebecca J. Butorac is enrolled in the Nonfiction Writing Program at the University of Iowa.

John Calderazzo teaches nonfiction writing workshops and literature classes at Colorado State University, where he has won the Best Teacher Award. He is the author of a textbook, *Writing From Scratch: Freelancing*; a children's science book, *101 Questions About Volcanoes*; and the creative nonfiction book, *Rising Fire: Volcanoes and Our Inner Lives*. His essays and fiction have been cited in *Best American Stories* and *Best American Essays* and published in *Georgia Review, Audubon, Orion, Witness*, and many other magazines.

Brad Comann teaches English and Religious Studies at Penn State-Erie. His literary nonfiction has appeared in *Cream City Review* and *Raritan Review*.

Casey Fleming was born and raised in Texas, where she is now finishing her MFA in creative writing at the University of Houston. She has a BA from Smith College and an MA in Spanish from American University. In 2003 she was a finalist for the Willis Barnstone Translating Poetry Contest, and she was recently nominated for *Best New American Voices*. She currently serves as fiction editor for *Gulf Coast*.

Michael Gorra is the Mary Augusta Jordan Professor of English and the chair of the English Language and Literature Department at Smith College, where he teaches courses in fiction in the English language and the literature of travel. He is the author of *The English Novel at Mid-Century*, *After Empire: Scott, Naipaul, Rushdie*, and *The Bells in Their Silence: Travels Through Germany*, and editor of the *Portable Conrad*. His teaching interests include the literature of travel and fiction in English from Jane Austen to last week. His book reviews appear in British and American newspapers.

Priscilla Hodgkins's fiction and nonfiction have appeared in *Agni, Creative Nonfiction*, the *Milwaukee Sentinel*, and *Confrontation*. Her essay "Einstein Didn't Dream of My Mother" was recognized in *Best American Essays* and her story "Bread and War" was nominated for a Pushcart Prize. She is associate director of the Bennington Writing Seminars, a graduate program in writing at Bennington College.

Kristen Iversen is the author of the award-winning biography *Molly Brown: Unraveling the Myth* and the textbook *Shadow Boxing: Art and Craft in Creative Nonfiction*. She is completing *Full Body Burden: Living and Dying in the Shadow of America's Nuclear Nightmare*. Formerly a travel writer in

Europe, she teaches creative writing and fiction at the University of Memphis and is Faculty Editor of the literary journal, *The Pinch*, formerly *River City*, of the University of Memphis.

Richard Katrovas is the author of ten books, most recently *The Years of Smashing Bricks,* a memoir. He teaches at Western Michigan University and is the founding director of the Prague Summer Program. "The Lear Years" is from *Raising Girls in Bohemia: Meditations of an American Father,* a work in progress.

Nancy Lord is the author of three books of creative nonfiction: *Fishcamp, Green Alaska,* and *Beluga Days.* She lives in Alaska and in 2005 received a nature writing fellowship for a residency at the Writers Colony at Dairy Hollow in Eureka Springs, Arkansas, where she wrote this essay. This is her second appearance in *Fourth Genre.*

Patrick Madden is an assistant professor of English at Brigham Young University. His essays have recently been published in *Portland Magazine, River Teeth,* and *Northwest Review.*

P. M. Marxsen's stories, essays, interviews, and reviews (art and books) have appeared in over 40 publications. Her particular interest is travel literature that explores the roles of power, personality, and culture in shaping concepts of place. She is currently working on a collection of essays on islands with French connections.

Desirae Matherly earned her PhD in creative nonfiction from Ohio University in 2004. Currently she is a Collegiate Assistant Professor in the Humanities and a Harper Fellow at the University of Chicago.

Susan Messer has fiction and nonfiction published in *Glimmer Train Stories, North American Review, Colorado Review, Creative Nonfiction, Another Chicago Magazine, killingthebuddha.com,* and others. Awards include an Illinois Arts Council Fellowship in prose, an Illinois Arts Council literary award for creative nonfiction, and prizes in *Moment* magazine's short fiction competition, Chicago Public Radio's Stories on Stage competition, and the Jewish Cultural Writing Competition of the Center for Yiddish Culture. She has also been a finalist in the *Chicago Tribune*'s Nelson Algren competition, the

Writers@Work fellowship competition, and Chicago's Guild Complex nonfiction competition.

Nedra Rogers is pursuing an MFA in creative writing at the University of Kansas. Her award-winning poetry has appeared in *Marlboro Review, Potpourri, Lullwater Review,* and other journals.

Robert Root is the Interviews/Roundtable editor of *Fourth Genre,* author of *Recovering Ruth: A Biographer's Tale,* and coeditor of *The Fourth Genre: Contemporary Writers of/on Creative Nonfiction,* now in its fourth edition. He is also the editor of and contributor to *Landscapes With Figures: The Nonfiction of Place.*

Mimi Schwartz's recent books are *Thoughts from a Queen-Sized Bed* (2002) and *Writing True, the Art and Craft of Creative Nonfiction* (with Sondra Perl, 2006). Her latest book, *Good Neighbors, Bad Times, Echoes of My Father's German Village,* is forthcoming from the University of Nebraska Press.

Peggy Shinner's work has appeared or will appear in *Alaska Quarterly Review, Bloom, Daedalus,* the *Gettysburg Review, TriQuarterly, Western Humanities Review,* and other publications. Currently, she's at work on a book of essays about the body.

Jan Shoemaker is a middle-aged English teacher with a formidable bun. Her writing has appeared in a variety of publications, among them *The Sun, Progressive Christian, The Other Side, Redwood Coast Review, Magical Blend,* and *Karamu.*

Maureen Stanton's works have appeared in many literary journals and anthologies, including *Creative Nonfiction, Iowa Review, River Teeth, Fourth Genre,* and *The Sun.* She teaches creative nonfiction writing at the University of Missouri in Columbia.

Nicole Walker recently began teaching creative writing as an assistant professor at Grand Valley State University in Michigan. Her work has appeared in *Ploughshares, Black Warrior Review, New American Writing, Fence, Seneca Review,* and *Iowa Review,* among other journals.

DoubleTake

M A G A Z I N E
Spring/Summer 2007

Editors' Story

We live in a world today wherein refugees from Africa's Sudan come to live in America's Nebraska, as Mary Pipher urges us to remember; meanwhile others in these pages, with her, also ask us to consider the working life of children, and on a continent to the south a Brazilian city's passing life. In America, for instance, we are asked to connect, in the act of imagination, with Native Americans of Arizona; with the Wall Street world of high (sometimes cunning, sometimes shaky) finance; with those newcomers who yearn to arrive and stay in our American Southwest; with vulnerable young girls in our poor neighborhoods, who teach their teacher a thing or two; with a short story's teen-age loner who seeks so earnestly, relentlessly some place (and people) she can trust; with a hurricane's devastation—once more we witness and get to comprehend, as we did in our previous issue, how nature's fiercely insistent assertion can shape our lives (in this instance, three sisters and two dogs offer a Chekovian drama of loss and recovery); and not least, the tale—again, Chekovian—of an American minister who reaches across the seas to the Ukraine's street children (the world afar, more of God's chosen terrain).

Goril Trondsen Booth

Alexandre Orion

Robert Gamble

Subscribe online: www.doubletakemagazine.net
Or phone The Johns Hopkins University Press 800-548-1784

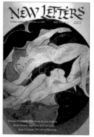

Library Recommendation Form
For

Fourth Genre: *Explorations in Nonfiction*
ISSN 1522-3868

I'd like to recommend the acquisition of *Fourth Genre* (ISSN: 1522-3868), published two (2) times a year by Michigan State University Press. Subscription prices for U.S. institutions: $50 for 1 year, $95 for 2 years, $120 for 3 years. Prices for international institutions: $68 for 1 year, $128 for 2 years, $162 for 3 years. Add $16 per year for air mail delivery.

Thank you for your consideration of this request.

Print
Name:_____

Signature:_____

Institution: _____

Department:_____

To subscribe, send purchase order or payment to:

Michigan State University Press
Journals Division
1405 S. Harrison Rd., Ste. 25
East Lansing, MI 48823-5245
Phone: (517) 355-9543 x 130
Fax: (517) 432-2611
Email: journals@msu.edu

—Print, complete, and forward this form to your library—

Fourth Genre

Explorations in Nonfiction

2006–2007 SUBSCRIPTION RATES

	1 Year	2 Years 5%	3 Years 20%
Buy 2–3 years at a Savings of:			
U.S. Individual	$35	$67	$84
U.S. Institution	$50	$95	$120
International Individual	$47	$90	$113
International Institution	$68	$128	$162
Student Rate	$26	$50	$63

Single copy: $20

Air Mail: Add $16 per year

Print and electronic subscriptions available online at
www.msupress.msu.edu/journals/fg. Save 30% when you order both!

❏ Yes! I would like to subscribe to *Fourth Genre*.
❏ Please renew my subscription.

Name _____

Address_____

City _____State ____ Zip _____

Phone _____Fax _____

E-mail Address _____

❏ Payment enclosed, check made payable to *Michigan State University Press*
Please charge my: ❏ Visa   ❏ MasterCard

Acct #_____ Exp. Date _____

Signature _____ Date _____

Mail completed form to:
Michigan State University Press
Journals Division
1405 S. Harrison Rd., STE. 25
East Lansing, MI 48823-5245
Tel: (517) 355-9543, X 130 Fax: (517) 432-2611
E-mail: journals@msu.edu
Website: *www.msupress.msu.edu/journals/fg.*